2ᵉ COLLECTION FELIX POTIN

JEAN LORRAIN
HOMME DE LETTRES

COLLECTION FÉLIX POTIN

SARAH - BERNHARDT

COLLECTION FELIX POTIN

EDMOND DE GONCOURT

3ᵉ COLLECTION FELIX POTIN

COMTESSE DE NOAILLES
FEMME DE LETTRES

2ᵉ COLLECTION FELIX POTIN

KIPLING
HOMME DE LETTRES

COLLECTION FÉLIX POTIN

GUY DE MAUPASSANT

COLLECTION FELIX POTIN

GYP

THE MAN IN THE RED COAT

THE MAN IN THE RED COAT

Julian Barnes

ALFRED A. KNOPF · NEW YORK · 2020

THIS IS A BORZOI BOOK
PUBLISHED BY ALFRED A. KNOPF

www.aaknopf.com

Knopf, Borzoi Books, and the colophon are registered trademarks of Penguin Random House LLC.

Library of Congress Cataloging-in-Publication Data

Names: Barnes, Julian, author.
Title: The man in the red coat / Julian Barnes.
Description: First edition. | New York : Alfred A. Knopf, 2020. |
Identifiers: LCCN 2019028764 (print) | LCCN 2019028765 (ebook) |
ISBN 9780525658771 (hardcover) | ISBN 9780525658788 (ebook)
Subjects: LCSH: Pozzi, Samuel, 1846–1918. | Gynecologists—France—Biography.
Classification: LCC RG76.P69 B37 2020 (print) |
LCC RG76.P69 (ebook) | DDC 618.10092 [B]—dc23
LC record available at https://lccn.loc.gov/2019028764
LC ebook record available at https://lccn.loc.gov/2019028765

Jacket image: *Dr. Pozzi at Home* (1881), by John Singer Sargent (detail). Armand Hammer Foundation, USA/Bridgeman Images
Jacket design by John Gall

Manufactured in Germany
First United States Edition

TO RACHEL

THE MAN IN THE RED COAT

In June 1885, three Frenchmen arrived in London. One was a Prince, one was a Count, and the third was a commoner with an Italian surname. The Count subsequently described their purpose as "intellectual and decorative shopping."

Or we might begin in Paris the previous summer, with Oscar and Constance Wilde on their honeymoon. Oscar is reading a recently published French novel and, despite the occasion, happily giving interviews to the press.

Or we could begin with a bullet, and the gun which fired it. That usually works: a sturdy rule of theatre declares that if you show a gun in the first act, it will assuredly be fired in the last. But which gun, and which bullet? There were so many of them around at the time.

We might even begin across the Atlantic, in Kentucky, back in 1809, when Ephraim McDowell, the son of Scottish and Irish immigrants, operated on Jane Crawford to remove an ovarian cyst containing fifteen litres of liquid. This strand of the story, at least, has a happy ending.

—

Then there is the man lying on his bed in Boulogne-sur-Mer—perhaps with a wife beside him, perhaps alone—wondering what to do. No, that's not quite right: he knew what to do, he just didn't know when or whether he would be able to do what he wanted to do.

Or we might begin, prosaically, with the coat. Unless it is better described as a dressing gown. Red—or, more exactly, scarlet—full length, from neck to ankle, allowing the sight of some ruched white linen at the wrists and throat. Beneath, a single brocade slipper allows tiny dashes of yellow and blue into the composition.

Is it unfair to begin with the coat, rather than the man inside it? But the coat, or rather its depiction, is how we remember him today, if we remember him at all. How would he have felt about that? Relieved, amused, a trifle insulted? That depends on how, at this distance, we read his character.

But his coat reminds us of another coat, painted by the same artist. It is wrapped around a handsome young man of good—or at least prominent—family. Yet despite standing for the most famous portrait painter of the day, the young man is not happy. The weather is mild, but the coat he is being asked to wear is of heavy tweed, intended for an altogether different season. He complains to the painter about its choice. The painter replies—and we only have his words, so cannot tell the tone on a scale from gently teasing to professionally commanding to magisterially contemptuous—the painter replies: "It's not about *you*, it's about the coat." And it's true that, as with the red dressing gown, the coat is now remembered more than its young inhabitant. Art outlasts individual whim, family pride, society's orthodoxy; art always has time on its side.

—

So let's continue with the tangible, the particular, the everyday: with the red coat. Because that's how I first encountered the picture and the man: in 2015, hanging in the National Portrait Gallery in London, on loan from America. I called it a dressing gown just now; but that's not quite right either. He hardly has pyjamas underneath—unless those lacy cuffs and collar were part of a nightshirt, which seems unlikely. Do we call it a day coat, perhaps? Its owner has hardly just fallen out of bed. We know that the picture was painted in the late mornings, after which artist and subject had lunch together; we also know that the subject's wife was astonished at the painter's large appetite. We know that the subject is at home, because the picture's title tells us so. That "home" is expressed by a deeper hue of red: a burgundy background setting off the central scarlet figure. There are heavy curtains tied back by a loop; and a further, different swathe of fabric, all of which melts into a floor of the same burgundy colour without any obvious dividing line. It is all highly theatrical: there is swagger not just in the pose but also in the pictorial style.

It was painted four years before that trip to London. Its subject—the commoner with the Italian name—is thirty-five, handsome, bearded, gazing confidently over our right shoulder. He is virile, yet slender, and gradually, after the picture's first impact, when we might well think that "it's all about the coat," we realise that it isn't. It's more about the hands. The left hand is on the hip; the right hand is on the chest. The fingers are the most expressive part of the portrait. Each is articulated differently: fully extended, half-bent, fully bent. If asked to guess the man's profession blind, we might think him a virtuoso pianist.

Right hand on chest, left hand on hip. Or maybe something more suggestive than this: right hand on heart, left hand on loins. Was that part of the artist's intention? Three years later, he painted a portrait of a society woman that had a scandalous effect at the Salon. (Could the Paris of the Belle Epoque be shocked? Certainly; and it could be just as hypocritical as London.) The right hand plays with what looks to be a toggle fastening. The left hand is hooked into one of the coat's twin waist cords, which echo the curtain loops in the background. The eye follows them along to a complicated knot, from which dangle a pair of feathery, furry tassels, one on top of the other. They hang just below groin level, like a scarlet tassel. (Where is its partner? It seems to be grasped in that right hand, the one against the heart.) This tassel hangs just below groin level, like a scarlet bull's pizzle. Did the painter intend this? Who can tell? He left no account of the picture. But he was a sly as well as a magnificent painter; also, a painter of magnificence, not afraid of controversy, indeed perhaps drawn towards it.

The pose is noble, heroic, but the hands make it subtler and more complicated. Not the hands of a concert pianist, as it turns out, but of a doctor, a surgeon, a gynaecologist.

And the scarlet pizzle? All in good time.

So yes, let's begin with that visit to London in the summer of 1885.

The Prince was Edmond de Polignac.

The Count was Robert de Montesquiou-Fezensac.

The commoner with the Italian name was Dr. Samuel Jean Pozzi.

Their first item of intellectual shopping was the Handel Festival at Crystal Palace, where they heard *Israel in Egypt* to celebrate the bicentenary of the composer's birth. Polignac noted that "the performance made a gigantic effect. The 4,000 executants royally fêted *le grand Haendel* [sic]."

The three shoppers also came bearing a letter of introduction from John Singer Sargent, the painter of *Dr. Pozzi at Home*. It was addressed to Henry James, who had seen the picture at the Royal Academy in

Dr. Pozzi at Home, John Singer Sargent (1881)

1882, and whom Sargent was to paint in full mastery years later, in 1913, when James was seventy. The letter began:

> Dear James,
>
> I remember that you once said that an occasional Frenchman was not an unpleasant diversion to you in London, and I have been so bold as to give a card of introduction to you to two friends of mine. One is Dr. S. Pozzi, the man in the red gown (not always), a very brilliant creature, and the other is the unique extra-human Montesquiou.

Strangely, this is the only letter from Sargent to James which survives. The painter seems unaware that Polignac was also to be of the party, an addition which would surely have pleased and interested Henry James. Or perhaps not. Proust used to say that the Prince was like "a disused dungeon converted into a library."

Pozzi was then thirty-eight, Montesquiou thirty, James forty-two and Polignac fifty-one.

James had been renting a cottage on Hampstead Heath for the previous two months and was about to return to Bournemouth, but put off his departure. He devoted two days, 2 and 3 July 1885, to entertaining these three Frenchmen who, the novelist subsequently wrote, had been "yearning to see London aestheticism."

James's biographer Leon Edel describes Pozzi as "a society doctor, a book-collector, and a generally cultivated conversationalist." The conversation went unrecorded, the book collection is long dispersed, leaving only the society doctor. In that red gown (not always).

The Count and the Prince came from old aristocratic lines. The Count claimed descendence from D'Artagnan the Musketeer, and his grandfather had been an aide-de-camp to Napoleon. The Prince's grandmother had been a close friend of Marie Antoinette; his father was Minister of State in Charles X's government and the author of the July Ordinances, whose absolutism set off the 1830 Revolution. Under the new government, the Prince's father was sentenced to "civil death," so that legally he did not exist. Frenchly, however, the non-existent man was permitted conjugal visits during his imprisonment, one of which resulted in Edmond. On his birth certificate, in the space for "Father," the civilly dead aristocrat was listed as "the Prince called Marquis de Chalançon, currently travelling."

The Pozzis were Italian Protestants from the Valtellina in northern Lombardy. In the religious wars of the early seventeenth century, a Pozzi was among many burnt to death for their faith in the Protestant temple of Teglio in 1620. Shortly afterwards, the family moved to Switzerland. Samuel Pozzi's grandfather Dominique was the first to arrive in France, crossing the country in slow stages and finally setting up as a patissier in Agen; he Frenchified the family name to Pozzy. The last of his eleven children—inevitably called Benjamin—became a Protestant minister in Bergerac. The pastor's family was pious and republican, devoted to God and conscious of its social and moral duties. Samuel's mother, Inès Escot-Meslon, from the Périgord gentry, brought into the marriage the charming eighteenth-century manor house of La Graulet, a few kilometres outside Bergerac, which Pozzi was to cherish and expand all his life. Always frail, and worn out by child-bearing, she died when he was ten; the pastor swiftly remarried a "young and robust" Englishwoman, Marie-Anne Kempe. Samuel grew up speaking both French and English. He also, in 1873, restored the family name to Pozzi.

"What a strange trio," muses Pozzi's biographer Claude Vanderpooten of that London trip. Partly he means the disparity of rank; but also, perhaps, the presence of a famously heterosexual commoner along-side two aristocrats of "Hellenic tendencies." (And if they sound like characters out of Proust, that is because they are all—partially, refractedly—related to characters in Proust.) There were two immediate destinations for Parisian aesthetes visiting London at that time: Liberty & Co., opened in Regent Street in 1875, and the Grosvenor Gallery. Montesquiou had admired Burne-Jones's *The Beguiling of Merlin* at the 1875 Paris Salon. Now they met the painter himself, who took them to the "Abbey-Phalanstery" of William Morris, where the Count selected some fabrics, and to the studio of William De Morgan. They also met Lawrence Alma-Tadema. They went to Bond Street for tweeds and suitings, hats and coats and shirts and ties and scents; to Chelsea to seek out Carlyle's house; and to bookshops.

James hosted them assiduously. He reported finding Montesquiou "curious but slight," and Pozzi "charming" (again, Polignac seems to have passed unnoticed). He had them to dinner at the Reform Club, where he introduced them to Whistler, to whom Montesquiou became powerfully devoted. James also arranged for them to visit Whistler's Peacock Room at the house of the shipping magnate F. R. Leyland. But by then Pozzi had been called back to Paris by a telegram from the wife of one of his celebrity clients, Alexandre Dumas *fils*.

From Paris, on 5 July, Pozzi wrote asking the Count to return to Liberty's and add to the order he had already placed there. He wanted "thirty rolls of the seaweed-coloured curtain material of which I enclose a sample. Please pay on my behalf. I shall owe you thirty schillings [sic] and much gratitude." He signs himself "The devoted friend of your Preraphaelitehood."

When that "strange trio" arrived in London, none of them was much known outside their immediate circles. Prince Edmond de Polignac had unrealised musical ambitions, and had spent many years, at the insistence of his family, touring Europe in a genial, halfhearted, theoretical search for a wife; somehow, he—more than she—always evaded capture. Pozzi was a decade into his career as a doctor, surgeon and socialite, working in a public hospital while building up a fashionable private clientele. Each would attain a certain level of fame and satisfaction in future years. And this fame, such as it was, had the advantage of being based—as far as it ever is—on a public knowledge of more or less exactly who they were.

Montesquiou's case was more complicated. He was the best-known of the three in the world they mostly shared: a society figure, dandy, aesthete, connoisseur, quick wit and arbiter of fashion. He also had literary ambitions, writing Parnassian poetry in strict metre and squibbish *vers de société*. As a young man about town, he had once been introduced to Flaubert at the Hotel Meurice. He was so overcome that he found himself speechless (a very rare occurrence), but consoled himself that "I had at least touched his hand and so received from him, if not a torch, at least a single flame." However, a rare and unenviable fate was already beginning to close in on the Count: that of being confused in the public mind—or at least the readerly mind—with an alter ego. His life, and afterlife, were to be dogged by shadow versions of himself.

Montesquiou was thirty when he arrived in London in June 1885. Exactly a year earlier, in June 1884, Joris-Karl Huysmans had published his sixth novel, *A Rebours*—translated as *Against the Grain* or *Against Nature*—featuring a twenty-nine-year-old aristocrat, Duc Jean Floressas des Esseintes. Huysmans' five previous novels had been exercises in Zolaesque realism; now he threw all that aside. *A Rebours* is a dreamily meditative bible of decadence. Des Esseintes is a dandy and aesthete, sickly from too much inbreeding, the last of his line, with strange and corrupting tastes, a love of apparel, jewellery, scents, rare books and fine bindings. Huysmans, a minor civil servant who knew Montesquiou only by repute, had obtained a background briefing about the Count's house from his friend the poet Mallarmé. The Count had fresh and idiosyncratic theories of home decoration: he displayed a sledge on a polar bearskin, items of church furniture, an array of silk socks in a glass case, and a live, gilded tortoise. That such details were authentic was vexing to Montesquiou, because some readers would hear the clicking latch of a *roman à clef* and assume that everything else in the novel was true too. The story goes that Montesquiou once ordered some rare volumes from a bookseller who happened to be one of Huysmans' friends; when he went to collect them, the bookseller, failing to recognise the Count, commented annoyingly, "Why, Monsieur, these are books fit for Des Esseintes." (Or perhaps he *had* recognised him.)

And here is another parallel. The year before Montesquiou made his first trip to London, his shadowy fictional counterpart had set out with exactly the same intention, and this "journey" forms one of the novel's most celebrated chapters. Des Esseintes is living in spiritual if suburban isolation at Fontenay; one morning, he asks his manservant to lay out a suit ordered from London, where all well-dressed Parisians obtained their clothes. He takes the train to Paris, arriving at the Gare de Sceaux. The weather is filthy. He hires a cab, which he rents by the hour. It takes him first to Galignani's bookshop in the rue de Rivoli, where he examines guides to London. Browsing in Baedeker, he finds a list of London art galleries, which sets him dreaming about modern British art, and especially Millais and G. F. Watts: the latter's pictures seem to him as if "sketched by an ailing Gustave Moreau." The weather outside continues to be atrocious—"an instalment of English life paid to him on account here in Paris." The cabbie drives him to the Bodega, which, despite its name, is a haunt of the English; here both expatriates and tourists find the fortified wines they prefer. He sees "a line of tables loaded with baskets of Palmer's biscuits, and stale, salty cakes, and plates heaped with mince pies and sandwiches whose tasteless exteriors contained burning mustard-plasters." He drinks a glass of port, then one of amontillado sherry. He is surrounded by English people, and finds them mutating into characters from Dickens. "He settled down comfortably in this London of the imagination."

Hunger announces itself: he is driven to a tavern in the rue d'Amsterdam opposite the Gare Saint-Lazare, from where the boat train will depart. This is recognisably Austin's Bar, otherwise the English Tavern, later the Bar Britannia (and still extant as the Hotel Britannia). His dinner consists of greasy oxtail soup, smoked haddock, roast beef and potatoes, Stilton cheese and rhubarb pie; he drinks two pints of ale, a glass of porter, coffee laced with gin, then a brandy; between the porter and the coffee he smokes a cigarette.

At the Tavern, as at the Bodega, he is surrounded by "a crowd of islanders with china-blue eyes, crimson complexions, and earnest or arrogant expressions, skimming through foreign newspapers; but here there were a few women dining in pairs without male escorts, robust Englishwomen with boyish faces, teeth as big as palette-knives, cheeks as red as apples, long hands and long feet. They were enthusiastically attacking helpings of rump-steak pie."

(This thing about Englishwomen. They are the subject of generic mockery in France at this time, seen as large, ruddy, awkward out-doorswomen, manifestly inferior to Frenchwomen, and especially Parisiennes, who are the perfection of the species. Englishwomen are often described as being oddly unawakened in their sexual presence, which in turn could only be the fault of Englishmen, unable to ignite their wives—or even their mistresses—into sexual beings. This conviction that the British and sex are a matter for concerned pity is a persistent dogma. I remember being in Paris shortly after the news broke of Prince Charles's continuing relationship with Camilla Parker-Bowles throughout his marriage to "LaddyDi," as the French pronounced her. "How extraordinary," more than one delighted Parisian murmur informed me, "to choose a mistress who is plainer than one's wife!" Really, these Anglo-Saxons, *ils sont incorrigibles.*)

Des Esseintes still has time to catch his train, but finds himself reflecting that when he had previously travelled abroad—to Holland—his expectation that Dutch life would be similar to Dutch art had been rudely unfulfilled. What if London life similarly fell short of his Dickensian preconceptions? "What was the point of moving," he asks himself, "when a fellow could travel magnificently just by sitting in a chair? Wasn't he already in London?" Why risk reality when the imagination can be equally, if not more, compelling? And so the faithful but expensive cabbie takes his fare back to the Gare de Sceaux, from where he returns home.

Montesquiou caught the train, Des Esseintes missed it; Montesquiou is social, Des Esseintes a recluse; Montesquiou gave little thought to religion (except for its artefacts), Des Esseintes, like his creator, was heading tormentedly back to Rome. And so on. But still Des Esseintes "was" Montesquiou: the world knew. And I knew too, because when I bought my Penguin edition of *Against Nature* in 1967, the cover was a headshot from Boldini's portrait of *Le comte Robert de Montesquiou.*

Des Esseintes never got to London, nor did Huysmans; while *A Rebours* was not translated into English until 1922, fifteen years after

Count Robert de Montesquiou, Giovanni Boldini (1897)

its author's death, and a year after that of Robert de Montesquiou. But in another way the book did cross the Channel, arriving in London very precisely on the afternoon of 3 April 1895. It—or at least its title and contents—was produced in evidence by Edward Carson QC, MP, at the Old Bailey during the second of Oscar Wilde's three trials. The barrister, acting for Lord Queensberry, is asking about a scene in Wilde's novel *The Picture of Dorian Gray*. It concerns Lord Henry Wotton's gift to Gray of a French novel—in itself a sinister matter, as any patriotic British jury might be tempted to conclude. Wilde at first half-denies, but then admits, that the book in question is indeed *A Rebours*. At the same time, Wilde tries to distance himself from Huysmans' novel, saying, "I do not admire it very much myself," and, "I consider it a badly written book."

Wilde must have been hoping that the other side didn't subscribe to a press-cuttings service. Because while on honeymoon a decade previously, he had given an interview to the *Morning News* (20 June 1884) in which he stated: "This last book of Huysmans' is one of the best I have ever seen." But then Wilde lied a lot during his trials. He is nowadays viewed as a gay saint, a martyr to English puritanism and heteronormality. He was all this, but not just this. It was, after all, Wilde who brought the criminal action against Lord Queensberry in the first place. If he was brave, he was also foolish, and dangerously vain. To read the transcript of that second trial is to witness a man weirdly confident that the repartee which delighted the West End would work equally well in a high court of justice. He parades his wit; he patronises Carson by explaining to him what art and morality are; and he never scruples to lie on the central issue—that he has committed homosexual acts. By the law of the land he was, at the end of the third trial, correctly convicted.

He also discovers that—despite a historical overlap between lawyers and dramatists—the courtroom is only partly theatre. So as he cracks jokes and seeks to torment Carson with sophistication, he forgets two things: first, that a jury is not a dressed-up theatre audience—six of the twelve came from Clapton in East London, and there was a bootmaker, a butcher and a bank messenger among them; and secondly, that a QC likes nothing better than an overconfident witness who thinks himself a star, and consequently overreaches.

In *The Picture of Dorian Gray* Wilde gives a lyrical summary of *A Rebours*, which Carson reads out to the jury:

> It was the strangest book he [Gray] had ever read. It seemed to him that in exquisite raiment, and to the delicate sound of flutes, the sins of the world were passing in dumb show before him. Things he had dimly dreamed of were made suddenly real to him. Things of which he had never dreamed were gradually revealed . . . The life of the senses was described in terms of mystical philosophy. One hardly knew at times whether one was reading the spiritual ecstasies of some medieval saint or the morbid confessions of a modern sinner. It was a poisonous book. The heavy odour of incense seemed to cling about its pages and to trouble the brain.

Carson asks if *A Rebours* is an immoral book. He knows how Wilde will answer, because they have been there before. "Not very well written," Wilde answers, "but I would not call it an immoral book. It is not well written." Carson has previously established that in Wilde's view there is no such thing as a moral or immoral book, only books that are well written or badly written. Carson plays the plodder: "May I take it that no matter how immoral a book was, if it was well written it would be a good book?" Wilde explains that a well-written book produces a sense of beauty, and an ill-written one a sense of disgust.

> Carson: A well-written book putting forth sodomitical views might be a good book?
> Wilde: No work of art ever puts forward views of any kind.
> Carson: What?

Like any effective lawyer, Carson repeats the phrase he wants the jury to remember. "Was *A Rebours* a sodomitical book?" "Was it a book, sir, dealing with undisguised sodomy?" At one point, Wilde offers the literary (and convoluted) defence that while his description of "the strangest book [Dorian Gray] ever read" was remarkably close to *A Rebours*, when, later on, he actually quotes from this French novel, the passages were not citations from *A Rebours* itself, but ones invented by him. Carson is unmoved: "My Lord, I asked him the question as to whether the book *A Rebours* was a book depicting sodomy." And so on. The jury has surely got the point.

It is the strangest English trial of a French book. Not of some imported piece of pornography, but the trial of an untranslated French novel's influence on an English novel, and whether in consequence it might be correct to assume that the author of the English novel was a "posing somdomite," in Queensberry's famous misspelling. There is, alas, no evidence that Huysmans either knew at the time or later discovered that his novel had been put on such a quasi-trial at the Old Bailey in London.

The fact that France was generally a source of Filth was common English knowledge by the time of the Wilde trials. Only seven years previously, following a campaign by the National Vigilance Association,

Edward Vizetelly, the publisher of (already somewhat bowdlerised) translations of Zola's novels, was prosecuted for his firm's edition of *La Terre*. At the Central Criminal Court the solicitor general, Mr. Poland, declared that the novel was "filthy from beginning to end," and that while a routinely filthy book might contain one, two or even three filthy passages, *The Earth* contained no fewer than twenty-one, each of which he intended to read to the jury. The recorder agreed that though they were "all revolting to a degree . . . they are charged in the indictment, and must be proved." One juryman, quailing at the burden of his duty, nervously asked, "But is it necessary to read them all?" Mr. Poland reminded the jury that it was going to be just as unpleasant for him to have to read the extracts out as for them to have to listen, but proposed this solution: "If you think, subject to what may be said by my learned friend on the part of the defence, that these passages are obscene, I will stop reading them at once."

At which point Mr. Williams, counsel for Vizetelly, wisely changed his client's plea to guilty, thus sparing the jury public embarrassment. There then followed one of those comic exchanges which decorate any obscenity trial:

> Mr. Williams: I would remind your Lordship that these works were works of a great French author.
> The solicitor general: A voluminous French author.
> The recorder: A popular French author.
> Mr. Williams: An author who ranks high among the literary men of France.

Whichever it was, Vizetelly was fined £100 and bound over to keep the peace for twelve months.

The British press responded to the Vizetelly case with a mixture of applause, moral indignation, patriotism, and a certain suspicion: not about the filthiness, but rather the identity of the Filth-locator. National Vigilance was, after all, one of the cherished functions of the press, rather than of some other, equally self-appointed censor. A more thoughtful point was made by the *Liverpool Mercury*:

> Where we find an inconsistency is the impunity enjoyed by those who retail the same works when clothed in the original French. If the English versions are offensive to the law, it is hard to understand why the far more revolting French versions are allowed to circulate. The effect must be as grave upon the more educated as upon the less educated. A man is not a superior person morally because he can read French, and there is no logical reason why he should be privileged on this account to touch and look on rank fruits which are wisely forbidden to the exclusively English reader.

This was perceptive: four years previously, Oscar Wilde, despite being on his honeymoon, was eager and able to read a corrupting novel in the original French, with all too predictable and public consequences.

Montesquiou and Polignac had met in Cannes in 1875, at the villa of Polignac's niece the Duchesse de Luynes. Montesquiou was not yet twenty, but fully formed in taste and vanity. The two men took walks together between Cannes and Menton; over glasses of sherry they read one another their favourite passages of literature. Polignac introduced Montesquiou to music he was unfamiliar with; the Count returned the favour with prose and poetry. Though there was twenty years between them, they shared an equality of artistic understanding, with the Count's self-assurance set against the Prince's doubts. Polignac, as a closeted homosexual, certainly responded to Montesquiou's confidence around such matters; though the Count was not so much out of the closet, more one who decorated its door with flowers and verses and surprising colours, as if this were normal. The Count had known Pozzi only a year or two at the time of their excursion to London. What might account for the addition of his presence? True, he spoke excellent English, but then so did Edmond de Polignac, having been brought up trilingually (French, English, German). A more likely explanation might lie in the nature of shopping. All shoppers—from the High Street to the "intellectual and decorative" end of the spectrum—love and need other shoppers, especially those, like Pozzi, who go about it in a zealous, companionable, tasteful (and equally well-funded) manner.

But there is another possible explanation: gratitude. In late June 1884, a year before the London trip, Pozzi received a present from Montesquiou: a luxurious Morocco-leather travelling bag from Asprey's in Mayfair, stamped on its top side with a gilt coronet and the letter *R*. When he opened it, he discovered a series of envelopes of diminishing size, one enclosing the next. At the centre, in the smallest envelope, was a poem by the Count, written in scarlet and violet inks, thanking Pozzi for having treated what is referred to as "my dead-leaf vitality." Pozzi's surgeon-biographer, Claude Vanderpooten, interprets the phrase and the poem as depicting sexual failure—either impotence or perhaps premature ejaculation. He further speculates that Pozzi treated the condition by means of "empirical, fraternal, friendly psychotherapy," and that the "infirmity" became "definitive." A poetic, if not necessarily fictional, diagnosis a century after the facts. Whatever they were, the invitation to Pozzi could have been a thank-you for his treatment— and also an occasion for him to use his travelling bag.

But if the biographer is right, here is another curious parallel. In the prologue to *A Rebours*, we are told that Des Esseintes, as a young man about Paris, had greatly indulged his sexual appetite. First with singers and actresses, then with mistresses "already famed for their depravity," and finally with prostitutes, until satiety, self-disgust and doctors' warnings about syphilis make him give up sex. But only for a while. After this break, his imagination is fired again, this time by his own kind, by "unnatural love-affairs and perverse pleasures." Again, there is satiety, nervous strain and a collapse into lethargy. Furthermore, "impotence was not far off." (Huysmans himself, if less extravagantly debauched than his creation, had also suffered from impotence.)

Des Esseintes, however, being both a dandy and a contrarian, does not despair at this turn of events; rather, he rejoices in it. Impotence is, after all, one way of leaving the world, and withdrawing from it in a larger way is exactly what he is planning to do. If he is to become a successful modern hermit, then loss of sexual appetite will obviously help. So in the novel's first chapter, Des Esseintes celebrates this development with a "black" dinner. Invitations are sent out in the style of funeral notices; the decor, flowers and tablecloths are all black; so is the food and wine; so are the waitresses; while in the background a hidden orchestra plays funeral marches. It is a camp and cheerful farewell to the annoying press of potency.

Quite what Montesquiou made of these four paragraphs is unknown. They must have struck him as a coincidence rather than a giveaway. Though in any case, the dandy-aesthete in general loves to flutter the norms; and sex, even in its more variant manifestations, can become normative, and therefore bourgeois. Sex also leads to marriage and family, and responsibility, and a career, and a seat on the board, friendship with the local bishop, and so on. Impotence might be playfully parlayed into a statement of revolt against the despised bourgeoisie, and further evidence of the aesthete's superiority.

—

The first bullet in this story is historical and very literary. Count Robert de Montesquiou had a cabinet of curiosities—indeed, his whole house amounted to one, the outward display of his inner aestheticism and connoisseurship. Léon Daudet, elder son of the novelist Alphonse Daudet, recalled in one of his many volumes of memoir being given a curated tour by the Count of especially prized items. One was "the bullet that killed Pushkin." The poet had been killed in a duel in 1837 with Georges-Charles de Heeckeren d'Anthès, a French officer in the Russian Chevalier Guard Regiment. The manner of his death was one Pozzi would become all too familiar with, and would try in his lifetime to mitigate or circumvent. The bullet had entered Pushkin's body at the hip and proceeded on into the abdomen. No surgery was possible at that time, and after two days agonising, the poet died. Eighteen years later, Montesquiou was born. How the bullet came to be in the Count's collection is not recorded.

Pozzi came from the provincial bourgeoisie, whom Montesquiou would instinctively look down on. The Count delighted in displaying "the aristocratic pleasure of displeasing" (the phrase is from Baudelaire). But Pozzi escaped his censure and, most of the time, his snobbery. He had what might be called "the bourgeois pleasure of pleasing," and was from the start an adroit social tactician.

When he arrived in Paris to study medicine in 1864, he was not entirely without connections. He had friends from the Protestant southwest among his fellow students; and already in place was a Pozzi cousin, Alexandre Laboulbène, twenty years his senior, a well-known society doctor, whose patients included the ruling family of Napoleon III. Pozzi was charming and ambitious; mainly, though, he was a star student. In 1872 he won the gold medal for best intern of the year. He specialised in the abdomen. In 1873 he gained his doctorate on fistulas of the upper rectum. His thesis was entitled "The Value of Hysterectomy in Treating Fibroid Tumours of the Uterus." And he found a key patron in Paul Broca (another Protestant from the southwest), a famous surgeon at the Lourcine-Pascal Hospital; also, the founder of the Anthropological Society, which Pozzi joined. Broca put Pozzi's name forward to co-translate Darwin's *The Expression of the Emotions in Man and Animals*, published in France in 1874. When Broca died suddenly in 1880 at the age of fifty-six, his autopsy was divided between four of his colleagues: Pozzi was awarded the skull and the brains. Years later, the Lourcine-Pascal was renamed the Broca Hospital; and for thirty years, Pozzi was its skull and brains.

COLLECTION FELIX POTIN

BROCA

COLLECTION FELIX POTIN

LECONTE DE LISLE

His other patron in those early days was the Parnassian poet Leconte de Lisle. They appear to have met around 1870, when the poet and his wife took Pozzi under their wing. Leconte, the son of a military surgeon, was a great believer in the reunification of science and poetry, so long divorced from one another. He was also a freethinker, and helped extinguish any lingering religious faith Pozzi might have brought from

Bergerac. He took him into literary circles, and introduced him to Victor Hugo; he listened to Pozzi's not very good verses, and encouraged him to learn German. When Leconte died in 1894, he made Pozzi his literary executor, and left him his library and papers.

Leconte was a key if unwitting contact in promoting Pozzi's early—indeed, precocious—affair with Sarah Bernhardt. He was a medical student in his mid-twenties; she was two years older and already a rising star: an actress with a new kind of naturalness (though, naturally, a naturalness that was entirely controlled), and of a different physical type—slenderer and more petite—than the average leading lady. A fellow medical student later recalled how he and Pozzi had invited Bernhardt to supper to meet the poet. He came, she recited from memory what sounds like half his oeuvre, the poet wept and kissed her hands; the evening was a great success. Soon Pozzi would be having supper chez Bernhardt—with her and her small son, the boy's tutor, and a niece given into her care. They would dine *en famille*, the children would be sent to bed, and the two young adults left alone. Quite what started when, we cannot know, nor how long it went on; but the affair matured into a friendship lasting half a century. Each of them wore a godlike tag: he was always "Docteur Dieu" to her, while she was "the Divine Sarah" to (almost) everyone. He also had a more terrestrial nickname, bestowed by the society hostess Mme Aubernon: "*L'Amour médecin*." This is the title of a Molière play, "Love Is the Best Medicine," though more usually rendered in Pozzi's case as "Dr. Love."

They were well matched in temperament: passionate, but with a low degree of possessiveness—or a high degree of restlessness. Bernhardt knew how to flatter the male ego while defusing buckish rivalry; also, how to keep things light when necessary. They were each greedy for lovers. Pozzi's biographer gives a Leporello-like list of the physical types Pozzi was attracted to (i.e., every type), and then adds, with an odd

Sarah Bernhardt by Nadar (*c.* 1864)

primness (or naivety), "He is sincere, every time." Also, "One thing is certain, all these women remained his friends." This does sound much too good to be true.

The details, even many of the names, are guesswork. Pozzi was highly discreet, and seems not to have gossiped; or if he did, the gossip was not written down. His letters to Bernhardt do not survive; some of hers to him do. They deal in heartfelt expressions, and immediate needs; but it's hard to sense the texture, or even the frequency, of the relationship in these early years. In one letter, she writes to him: "I lied to you, it's true, but I never deceived you." This sounds a very French piece of sophistry, but it makes a certain sense: I always told you I would sleep with others, and if it was necessary to tell you a lie to do so, then the larger truth holds even if the lesser one is broken.

One key to their relationship, according to Pozzi's biographer, was "the known affinity between Protestant and Jew." (Was this more than a necessary solidarity between two historically excluded minorities within Catholic France?) But the matter goes deeper, according to Vanderpooten: Pozzi, in his view, had "a Jewish sensibility." He also had "many Jewish friends"; indeed, "He ought to have married a Jewess."

But not Sarah Bernhardt. She knew she was not for marrying: her one attempt—the wedding took place in London in 1882—was a disaster. Instead, Pozzi went to see her on stage, welcomed her to his salon, became her doctor and surgeon whenever required—even, when necessary, by transatlantic cablegram—and lent her money. Sarah Bernhardt's life of sexual freedom was a scandal to many, but the kind of scandal correct French society had come to expect from actresses over long centuries; indeed, the repetition of such scandals merely reconfirmed society in the correctness of its morals.

With Broca and Leconte as his patrons, and Sarah Bernhardt

sometimes in his (or her) bed, could any young medical student in Paris be better launched?

Merrie England, the Golden Age, la Belle Epoque: such shiny brand names are always coined retrospectively. No one in Paris ever said to one another, in 1895 or 1900, "We're living in the Belle Epoque, better make the most of it." The phrase describing that time of peace between the catastrophic French defeat of 1870–71 and the catastrophic French victory of 1914–18 didn't come into the language until 1940–41, after another French defeat. It was the title of a radio programme which morphed into a live musical-theatre show: a feel-good coinage and a feel-good distraction which also played up to certain German pre-conceptions about oh-la-la, can-can France. The Belle Epoque: locus classicus of peace and pleasure, glamour with more than a brush of decadence, a last flowering of the arts, and last flowering of a settled high society before, belatedly, this soft fantasy was blown away by the metallic, unfoolable twentieth century, which ripped those elegant, witty Toulouse-Lautrec posters from the leprous wall and rank *vespasienne*. Well, it might have been like that for some, and Parisians more than most. But then as Douglas Johnson, wise historian of France, once wrote, "Paris is only the outskirts of France."

At the time, however, the Beautiful Era was—and felt—an age of neurotic, even hysterical national anxiety, filled with political instability, crises and scandals. In such hyperventilating times, prejudice could swiftly metastasise into paranoia. So that "known affinity" between the historically persecuted Protestant and Jew could be turned by some minds into vivid threat. In 1899, a certain Ernest Renauld published *Le Péril protestant*, whose purpose, he explained, was "to unmask the enemy, the Protestant, allied with the Jew and the Freemason against the Catholic."

Nobody knew what would happen, because what "should" have happened rarely did. The Prussian demand for reparations in 1871, which should have crippled the country for decades, was quickly paid off, and cost France much less than the phylloxera epidemic which had devastated the French vineyards from 1863 onwards. Enormous constitutional changes which should have come about were averted at the last minute for seemingly trivial reasons. After the defeat by Prussia, the monarchy was all set to return until the Pretender, the Comte de Chambord, jibbed at having the *tricolore* as the national flag. He insisted on the white fleur-de-lys or nothing; he got nothing. In the late 1880s General Boulanger—Catholic, royalist, populist, Revengist—was expected to win power in the 1889 election. (One of his more unlikely candidates was Prince Edmond de Polignac, chosen to stand in Nancy, but who found the campaign trail all too fatiguing and withdrew.) After this democratic bid failed, a coup d'état seemed certain; except that Boulanger too baulked at the last minute, seemingly on the advice of his exquisitely named mistress, Mme de Bonnemains. One major constitutional change which did happen was the separation of church and state; the law of 1905 remains the basis of the French secular state to this day.

The cure for—or at least distraction from—domestic political confusion is often the same: foreign adventure. The French believed at this time, as did the British, that they had a unique *mission civilisatrice* in the world; and each, predictably, thought their own civilising mission more civilised than the other's. Although to the actual civilisees, it felt different—more like conquest. Thus, in the spring of 1881 the French invaded Tunisia, and in the autumn of that year they put down a rebellion. In between, they signed a "treaty of protection" with the country's previous rulers. The phrase is telling. Those who offer protection have their hands out for protection money: this was the era of gangster imperialism. Meanwhile, between 1870 and 1900, the British Empire expanded to cover 4 million square miles.

Political corruption in France was endemic: it was said that "each banker has his personal senator and his deputies." The press was violent in its language; libel laws slack; fake news prevalent; and killing never far away. In 1881 the International Anarchist Congress gave approval to "propaganda by the deed" (the very phrase was French), and the high life of which the Belle Epoque boasted—the world of opera houses and fashionable restaurants—was targeted. When the Anarchist Ravachol was tried and guillotined in 1892, the response was a nail bomb thrown into the Chambre des Députés which injured fifty. There were high-level assassinations: of the President of the Republic, Sadi Carnot, in 1894; of the Socialist anti-war leader, Jean Jaurès, in 1914.

There was also a rise of blood-and-soil nativism, which urged a "reawakening" of Old Gaul; a fierce desire, articulated by Boulanger, for revenge against Prussia; and convulsive, nationwide eruptions of anti-Semitism. All three strands were plaited into the Dreyfus case, the overriding political event of the period, one which, beyond the "simple" matter of justice, concentrated the past and shaped the future. Everyone was involved, in one way or another. At Dreyfus's "degradation" in 1895, Sarah Bernhardt sat in the front row. At his second trial, at Rennes in 1899, Pozzi was there (Pozzi was everywhere).

And yet—and in keeping with the historical illogic of the period—the Dreyfus case had an effect out of all proportion to its content. Its victim confirmed the rule that the martyr often fails to live up to the mystique of his own martyrdom. "We were prepared to die for Dreyfus," commented the poet Charles Péguy, "but Dreyfus wasn't." As for the gravity of the actual spying, "There was nothing in it," concluded Douglas Johnson. The case was far more important for what others made of it than for what it contained in itself. Indeed, if you were looking for an example of high corruption liable to promote anti-Semitic feeling, then the Panama Scandal of 1892–93—in which three Jewish financiers bribed several cabinet ministers, 150 deputies, and virtually every major newspaper—ought to have been far more significant. But there is often little "ought" in history.

Political memory runs long in France. In 1965, the novelist François Mauriac, then eighty, wrote: "I was a child at the time of the Dreyfus Affair, but it has filled my life." That same year I was teaching in France, and discovering French (and Francophone) singer-songwriters. My favourite was Jacques Brel, who twelve years later—and sixty-three years after the event—was to record his lyrical lament "Jaurès," with the refrain, "*Pourquoi ont-ils tué Jaurès?*"

And then there was a quirky, minor, amusing business thousands of miles away, which nicely demonstrates the historical law of unintended consequence. In 1896, during the Scramble for Africa, an expeditionary force of eight French and 120 Senegalese soldiers crossed the continent from west to east: their target was a ruined fort on the Sudanese Upper Nile. Frenchly, they set off with 1,300 litres of claret, fifty bottles of Pernod, and a mechanical piano. The journey took them two years; they arrived in July 1898, two months after Zola published *J'Accuse*. They raised the *tricolore* at the ruined fort of Fashoda, and seemed to have no more geopolitical purpose than to annoy the British. This they did, just a little, until Kitchener, then in charge of the Egyptian Army (and, contrary to his reputation, a Francophile who spoke fluent French), turned up and advised them to hop it. He also gave them copies of recent French newspapers, in which they read of the Dreyfus Affair and wept. The two sides fraternised, and the British band played "La Marseillaise" as the French withdrew. No one was hurt or abused, let alone killed.

How could this not have been a trifling comic sideshow amid the

broader imperial rivalry? The British have long forgotten Fashoda (but then it was they who forced the tiny withdrawal). In French eyes, however, it was a key moment of national humiliation and dishonour, one that made a profound impact on a certain eight-year-old French boy, who in later years remembered it as a "childhood tragedy." How was Kitchener to know, as he was drinking warm champagne with eight Frenchmen at that distant fort, and noting how its brief occupants had even planted a garden—"Flowers at Fashoda! Oh these Frenchmen!"—that these events would play out, decades later, in Charles de Gaulle's obstreperous and infuriating (translate into French as "determined and patriotic") behaviour during his London wartime exile, then later in his stubbornly vindictive ("principled and statesmanlike") triple refusal to allow Britain to join ("disrupt") the European Common Market?

It might seem obvious now—obvious, because it is true—that the Belle Epoque was a time of great triumph for French art. A year after the trauma of 1870–71, Monet painted *Impression, Sunrise*. By the time the period ended, in 1914, Braque and Picasso had laid the foundations, and painted the purest forms, of Cubism. In between: Manet, Pissarro, Cézanne, Renoir, Redon, Lautrec, Seurat, Matisse, Vuillard, Bonnard and the greatest of them all, Degas. Or: Impressionism, neo-Impressionism, Symbolism, Fauvism, Cubism. What did Britain have to put up against this? The continuing saga of Pre-Raphaelitism, the lingering morbidity of high Victorian art, the stately strangeness of Watts, the Frenchified Sickert, the Scottish Impressionists. A sickly moralising hung over much British art; as Wilde, in *The Picture of Dorian Gray*, put it of the painter Basil Hallward: "His work was that curious mixture of bad painting and good intentions that always entitles a man to be called a representative British artist." (Wilde was half-parroting Flaubert: "You don't make art out of good intentions.") For all the fresh colours and fresh attitudes of the Pre-Raphaelites, theirs had been a backward-looking, historical, storytelling art, about which the British have felt alternately proud and leery over the subsequent century and a half. Whereas the new French art was indomitably modern, in subject matter and technique. Which of course made it offensive to many in France.

So the Parisian aesthete often turned to England, not just for painting, but for the decorative and applied arts. Also for theory: rare for the British to be ahead in this regard. There was Ruskin, whom Montesquiou read and Proust translated; also Walter Pater, the timid Oxford don who urged all to "burn with a hard, gem-like flame" and praised an art "of strange thoughts and fantastic reveries and exquisite passions." The first piece of art nouveau furniture was shown at the 1876 Great Exhibition. In his dream of London, Des Esseintes namechecks Millais' *The Eve of St. Agnes*. Galignani's in the rue de Rivoli sold picture books by Kate Greenaway and Walter Crane.

Strange thoughts and exquisite passions: the English were also more

Montesquiou as the head of John the Baptist

Wilde as a Greek

dangerous in their application. In 1868 Swinburne shared a house in Normandy with his friend George Powell; above the entrance was the inscription "La Chaumière de Dolmancé" (Dolmancé's Cottage), named for the homosexual corrupter in Sade's *La Philosophie dans le boudoir*. Maupassant visited the place twice, and left accounts of a house of decadence staffed by fresh-faced lads, and full of weird knickknacks like a parricide's flayed hand. There was a monkey on the loose, and hard liquor served at lunchtime, after which the two Englishmen pulled out gigantic folios of pornographic photographs, taken in Germany, all of male subjects. "I remember one of an English soldier masturbating on a pane of glass," recalled Maupassant, whose interests lay elsewhere.

And then there was Oscar Wilde—whom the French assumed to be English. He also went too far, though some were unconvinced by the authenticity of his behaviour. When the twenty-eight-year-old Oscar visited Degas' studio in Paris, the painter reported that "he behaves as if he's playing Lord Byron in some provincial theatre." The diarist and novelist Edmond de Goncourt called him "*un puffiste*" (a braggart, a blagger), and theorised that Wilde's homosexuality wasn't original to himself, but imitative, if not plagiaristic—copied from Verlaine, also from Swinburne. Aesthetes loved dressing up. Wilde appears in photographs as Prince Rupert for a costume ball; also in Greek national costume when travelling there in 1877. Robert de Montesquiou outdid him in this regard: he could be spotted in Renaissance costume, as Louis XIV, in Turkish attire and Japanese costume; even as an Englishman. He once staged a tableau for the camera in which his own head stood in for that of John the Baptist on its ceremonial charger. But the two aesthetes also shared the daily pleasure of dressing in their favourite role—as themselves.

—

"Flowers at Fashoda!" Queen Victoria thought the French "incurable as a nation though so charming as individuals." Part of their incurability, to an English eye, lay in their political instability. Every century or so, a new wave of exiles would arrive at the Channel ports: Huguenots, fugitives from the Revolution, Communards, Anarchists. Four successive heads of state (Louis XVIII, Charles X, Louis Philippe and Napoleon III) found safety in Britain; so too did Voltaire, Prévost, Chateaubriand, Guizot and Victor Hugo. Monet, Pissarro, Rimbaud, Verlaine and Zola all headed for England when suspicion (of different sorts) fell upon them. The political traffic in the opposite direction was far more meagre: after the Stuarts, the only significant exiles leaving for France were John Wilkes and Tom Paine. Such an imbalance naturally fed British complacency about their historical and political freedoms. The main reason Britons sought exile in France was to escape scandal (and be able to carry on in their scandalous ways): it was the place to go for the upper-class bankrupt, bigamist, cardsharp and homosexual. They sent us their ousted leaders and dangerous revolutionaries; we sent them our posh riffraff. Another reason

2ᵉ COLLECTION FELIX POTIN

KIPLING
HOMME DE LETTRES

for continental exile was expressed by the painter Walter Sickert in a letter from Dieppe in 1900: "It is bloody healthy here & fucking cheap ('Fucking' used here as an adverb, not a substantival gerund)."

Kipling, in his poem "France," wrote that the French are "First to face the Truth and last to leave old Truths behind." Old fantasies too. When, in the middle of the eighteenth century, the British first gained the upper geopolitical hand over the French, the French prime minister, the Duc de Choiseul, expressed himself "completely astounded." He went on (this is 1767): "One might reply that it is a fact; I must concur; but as it is impossible, I shall continue to hope that what is incomprehensible will not be eternal." This kind of thinking—a magical, free-floating logic, yet one blithely aware of its own contradictions—is something that would never waft through in the mind of a British politician. Shuttle forward nearly two centuries, and here it is again, with De Gaulle declaring that "France must continue to behave as a great power precisely because she no longer is one." Mistakenly believing that your country is more powerful than it actually is—that it is "punching above its weight," let alone "the leader of the Anglosphere"—is a common delusion of British politicians as well; yet the delusion would never be expressed with such a lucid, almost aesthetic, flourish.

Books change over time; at least, the way we read them does. Collectors of first editions sometimes like to imagine themselves back to the day when the book in their hand was freshly printed, smelling of ink and binding glue, before anyone had published any opinions about it, and there were not yet any *idées reçues* out there to impede the innocent reader's untainted response to its contents.

When *A Rebours* came out in 1884, Mallarmé wrote to Huysmans on 18 May to praise "this fine book (the inner room of your mind)," calling it "an extraordinary manual . . . What a surprise for the simple novelists and how wide they're going to have to open their eyes!" He calls Des Esseintes "this poignant and artificial man," for whose "misfortune" one fears "that one won't find sufficient pity." That he admires the novel—which just happens to contain three pages of unshadowed praise for Mallarmé's own poetry, praise which helped launch the poet on the wider world—is no surprise. But to those of us later readers who view the novel as a bible of French Decadence, a strange, dark fantasy, some literary equivalent of the wild imaginings of Gustave Moreau or Odilon Redon, Mallarmé offers us the chastening view of a primal reader:

> It's an absolute vision of the paradise of pure sensation which is revealed to an individual when placed before pleasure, whether barbarous or modern. What is admirable in all this, and what gives your book its strength (which will be decreed as mad imagination, etc) is that there is not an atom of fantasy in it. In this refined tasting of all the essences, you have shown yourself to be more strictly documentary than anyone else.

One of the originalities of *A Rebours* is how it frequently breaks off from its already slender narrative and diverts into essayistic mode. There are reflections on contemporary literature, on art and music; and a long disquisition on late or Decadent Latin literature, which was much acclaimed until, years later, Huysmans admitted that he had largely nicked it from Adolf Ebert's three-volume history of medieval literature. There is also an extensive section on Catholic apologists, among whom is Léon Bloy, Huysmans' almost exact contemporary. Huysmans (1848–1907) describes Bloy as "a savage pamphleteer who wrote in a style at once precious and furious, naive and terrifying." Bloy (1846–1917) returned the compliment, describing Huysmans' style in a way that makes us realise how difficult the book is to translate: "[His style] is continually dragging Mother Image by the hair or the feet down the wormeaten staircase of terrified Syntax."

As for the novel itself, Bloy had a different take on it from Mallarmé:

> In this kaleidoscopic review of all that can possibly interest the modern mind, there is nothing that is not flouted, stigmatised,

vilified and anathematised by this misanthrope who refuses to regard the ignoble creatures of our time as the fulfilment of human destiny, and who clamours distractedly for a God. With the exception of Pascal, no one has ever uttered such penetrating lamentations.

Everyone knows—or rather, "everyone knows"—that Count Robert de Montesquiou owned a pet tortoise, whose shell was painted gold and studded with precious stones. We know this because Huysmans spends four pages of *A Rebours* describing Des Esseintes' acquisition of the beast—"decorative shopping" indeed—and its transformation. The design is given long contemplation, and then discussed with a jeweller: the stones are to trace in outline a Japanese drawing of a heavily flower-laden twig. When the gilding and studding are complete, the ambulant treasure chest is to be placed on a fine Turkey carpet, thus cleverly interacting with its hues and its weft. All this is triumphantly achieved; but a few pages later the poor tortoise keels over and expires because of—and here comes the moral—"the dazzling luxury imposed upon it." The British equivalent of this Gothic-literary death is more humble, imaginatively: that of Jill Masterson in Ian Fleming's *Goldfinger*, despatched by Auric Goldfinger's goons who cover her in lethal gold paint.

The bedizened tortoise was supposedly part of the information pack about Montesquiou which Mallarmé passed to Huysmans, along with the sledge on the polar-bear rug, the church furniture and the silk socks in a glass display cabinet. Those last three items turn up untransmuted in *A Rebours*; but the tortoise is different. Robert Baldick, the novel's British translator and also Huysmans' biographer, says that all Mallarmé saw on his evening visit to "Ali Baba's Cave" was "the remains of an unfortunate tortoise whose shell had been coated with gold paint." So: no jewels, and no actual live tortoise. Which leaves us with the question: whether the Count picked up this piece of aesthetic bric-a-brac ready-made in an antique shop, or whether he bought a bare shell and then whimsically, dandiacally, had it gilded.

On the other hand, according to Philippe Jullian, Montesquiou's biographer, the whole idea of the tortoise—dead or alive, decorated or plain—was "an invention of [the poet] Judith Gautier." Still, in one way this is not a disappointment. Part of the novelist's job is to turn a slight, even false rumour into a glitteringly certain reality; and it's often the case that the less you have, the easier it is to make something from it.

Even allowing for an invitation based on gratitude as well as recent friendship, how did a Paris surgeon, even a successful one, afford the company of a Prince and a Count, plus all the related shopping? Her name was Thérèse Loth-Cazalis, from Lyon, "young, very rich, and beautiful" (strange how that third adjective always adheres logically to the first two). The family was Catholic and monarchist, their money recent, from investment in the railway boom. But the family also had artistic connections. One of Thérèse's cousins, Henri Cazalis, who brokered the marriage, was a friend of Mallarmé; another was Frédéric Bazille, one of the great hopes of Impressionism until he was killed in the war of 1870.

Pozzi is thirty-three and smitten; Thérèse is twenty-three and not worldly; the wooing is swift. He writes that he loves her "with the abandonment of a child, the passion of a young man, and the tenderness of an adult, all at the same time." The dowry is legally decided: what she will bring to the marriage, and what she will keep for herself. Pozzi agrees that their children will be brought up as Catholics. They marry civilly on 9 November 1879 at the mairie of the 8th arrondissement, and religiously on 17 November 1879 at the Parisian chapel of the Dominican order. One of Pozzi's witnesses is his cousin Alexandre Laboulbène, now professor at the Paris faculty of medicine and officer of the Légion d'honneur. Pozzi's pastor father declines to attend. The honeymoon is spent in Spain. In the summer of 1880, the couple move into grand quarters in the place Vendôme, where Pozzi will have his

Comte Henry and Comtesse Elisabeth de Greffulhe

private consulting rooms. Fifteen years after arriving in Paris, Pozzi is launched, once again.

Montesquiou had many women friends. Probably the closest was Elisabeth Caraman-Chimay. She was five years his junior, and called him "Uncle," though he was in fact her mother's first cousin. He chose her clothes and escorted her to concerts. Having "no dowry other than her beauty," she married Count Greffulhe: Belgian, brutish and red-bearded, he was said to resemble the King in a pack of playing cards. He was also staggeringly rich. Montesquiou's (French) biographer tells us that Greffulhe organised "superb parties which the husband gave for a wife of whom he was so proud and whom he yet deceived so publicly."

That biographer's sentence is worth considering. The easy response—the middle-class, English, puritanical response—would be to dismiss the Count's behaviour as purely, Frenchly (and Belgianly) hypocritical. But at the time, at that level of society, it was hardly unusual. This is the world often described by Edith Wharton, where the requirements of money, class, family and sex collide. And sex is often the one that yields—normally at the demand of the husband. I remember an American friend who had married into the upper echelon of Parisian society in the 1950s. Her husband slept with her until she had produced the children that family and tradition demanded, and then went elsewhere for his pleasure. She described how it had come as a great shock, to have the rules of upper-bourgeois French marriage explained to her so late in the day. She took lovers herself, but implied that this was not an ideal, or even an equal, solution.

The British are thought to be pragmatic, the French emotional. Yet in matters of the heart, this order was often reversed. The British believed in love and marriage—that love led to and survived marriage, that sentimentality was an expression of true feeling, and that Queen Victoria's loving marriage and loyal widowhood were a national example. The French had the more pragmatic approach: you married for social position, for money or property, for the perpetuation of family, but not for love. Love rarely survived marriage, and it was a foolish hypocrisy to pretend that it might. Marriage was merely a base camp from which the adventurous heart sallied forth.

These rules, of course, were laid down by men, and did not find expression in the marriage contract.

Edmond de Goncourt had a female cousin called Fedora, who in August 1888 was lamenting how poor one branch of her family had become. "Just imagine," she told him. "They are people who for five generations have married for love!"

It was said that when in town, Count Greffulhe bedded his mistresses on a strict daily rota, to which he stuck so rigidly that his carriage horses knew to stop outside each day's different address without the need for any prompting from the driver.

A question for Montesquiou's (now dead) biographer: If Count Greffulhe "deceived [his wife] so publicly," how was that deceit?

On 8 December 1881 Guy de Maupassant, his judgement clearly uncorrupted by his visits to Swinburne's Sadean cottage, wrote in the literary periodical *Gil Blas*:

The English are a great nation, a true nation, balanced about life, firmly planted in reality. They are a nation of gentlemen, of commercially irreproachable merchants, a healthy, strong and honourable nation. They are in addition nowadays, a nation of philosophers; the greatest thinkers of the century live amongst them; they are a nation devoted to progress and to hard work.

But the English gentleman does not fight; that's to say, he doesn't fight duels, and regards this activity with the greatest of disdain. He judges life to be worthy of respect; also of value to his country . . . He understands courage differently from us. He only allows courage that is useful—to his country, and to his fellow citizens. He possesses an eminently practical turn of mind.

This praise from one who has not yet inspected the English in situ comes from an essay on the absurdity and futility of duelling, and the false sense of honour a fight's participants claim. "Honour! Oh, you poor old word from another time, what a clown they have turned you into!" Duelling, Maupassant goes on, "is the safeguard of the suspect: the dubious, the shady and the compromised attempt by means of it to buy themselves a cut-price new virginity." In France, "There exists a mad mental condition—quarrelsome, flippant, whirling and emptily sonorous—which circulates from the Madeleine to the Bastille, and which could be called The Mentality of the Boulevards. And it has spread from there throughout the whole of France. It is to reason and true thought what phylloxera is to the vine."

Teasingly, Maupassant continues:

There is one kind of duel which I can accept, and that is the industrial duel, the duel for publicity, the duel between journalists. When a newspaper's circulation begins to dip, one of the editors gets to work and writes a scathing article in which he insults one or other of his colleagues. The other answers back. The public's attention is caught; they watch as if they're in a wrestling booth at a fair. And a duel takes place, which is talked about in fashionable society.

This procedure has one excellent thing in its favour: it will dispense with the requirement that editors should know how to write French. All they will need is to be good at duelling . . .

Maupassant wasn't quite as aloof as he sounds. Only the previous month he had served as second to the journalist René Maizeroy in a duel with the editor of a rival newspaper in the Bois du Vésinet.

COLLECTION FELIX POTIN

GUY DE MAUPASSANT

Five years later, Maupassant paid his first visit to England. Naturally, he carried a letter of introduction to Henry James, who seemed to get an annual Parisian visitor to squire around. In 1884, Sargent had sent him the novelist Paul Bourget, an excellent choice, since the Frenchman's Anglo-snobbery matched James's Franco-snobbery. In 1885, Sargent sent the "strange trio." And now, in 1886, Bourget despatched Maupassant, inevitably suggesting that James take him to see Burne-Jones. The novelist also showed him the Earl's Court Exhibition, and introduced him over dinner to George du Maurier and Edmund Gosse. Next, Maupassant stayed at Waddesdon as the guest of Ferdinand de Rothschild, then visited Oxford, and returned to London, where he was taken to Madame Tussaud's and a Gilbert and Sullivan operetta at the Savoy Theatre.

At which point he ran away. He pronounced himself charmed and grateful, but left the next morning with the excuse: "I am too cold; the city is too cold; I am leaving for Paris. Au revoir!" Naturally, it had rained a lot. And naturally, being a Frenchman, he found that "the women here haven't the charm of ours—I mean, the women of France. People claim that only their appearance is severe, but when one confines oneself to appearances—and such has been my case—one has the right to ask that they be a little less forbidding."

He never returned.

Maupassant's response to London is typical of the period. The French are fascinated and appalled and depressed by the city. And whether characters in a novel, or real people, they wonder if this is the inevitable future for them as well.

Here is Des Esseintes, sitting in his Parisian cab, while the rain buckets Englishly down outside, anticipating what awaits him. He

> conjured up a picture of London as an immense, sprawling, rain-drenched metropolis, stinking of soot and hot iron, and wrapped in a perpetual mantle of smoke and fog . . . Along every street, big or small, in an eternal twilight relieved only by the glaring infamies of modern advertising, there flowed an endless stream of traffic between two columns of earnest, silent Londoners, marching along with eyes fixed ahead and elbows glued to their sides.

Des Esseintes imagines himself "lost in this terrifying world of commerce . . . caught up in this ruthless machine which ground to powder millions of poor wretches."

Purposeful chaos, noise, filth, devotion to Mammon . . . When Rimbaud and Verlaine arrived a dozen years before "the strange trio," they discovered a pandemonium of "carriages, cabs, buses (filthy), trams, incessant railways on splendid cast-iron bridges, grand and lumbering; unbelievably brutal, loud-mouthed people in the streets." London's racial diversity also came as a shock. As they set off up Regent

Street, they were astonished to see so many black people: "It seems to have been snowing negroes," Rimbaud observed. But the weather pleased them: "Imagine a setting sun seen through grey crêpe." The attraction for Monet, who first visited in 1870–71, is evident.

Nor was it just the French who had this reaction. Wagner, sailing up the Thames with his wife Cosima in 1877, said to her: "This is Alberich's dream come true—Nibelheim, world domination, activity, work, everywhere the oppressive feeling of steam and fog."

It might be hell, but it was also modern hell: Rimbaud admired the docks at Woolwich as being suitable for his "increasingly *modernistic* poetics." Huysmans, much as he deplored modernity, accurately identified one of its key factors: that "nature has had its day." The distinctive mark of human genius had always been artifice: now the artificial was replacing the natural (this a century before the Situationists made the same discovery). For Des Esseintes, mechanical creations are now superior to human creations: "Does there exist, anywhere on earth, a being conceived in the joys of fornication and born in the throes of motherhood who is more dazzlingly, more outstandingly beautiful than the two locomotives recently put into service on the Northern Railway?"

But not all French visitors saw London as a filthy and soulless Mammon, because not all were poetic modernists. Some viewed it more benignly and romantically:

> Within a milky, smoky crystal, the shapes and colours dissolve; passing uniforms blaze up in a brief splash of red which is quickly extinguished. The hansom cabs glide along like harnessed gondolas, each roof surmounted by a gondolier-coachman whose oar is a whip. Through the narrow window, sights crowd in on one another: flocks of peacocks perch in the trees of the great parks, with soot-coloured sheep beneath them; while music radiates from unseen barrel-organs. In the windows of Pre-Raphaelite shopkeepers one sees women dressed in olive-green, dying of love for sunflowers.

The author of this atypical portrait of London was Robert, Comte de Montesquiou.

It's hard to imagine Oscar Wilde fighting a duel: he would doubtless have judged it "vulgar." Or Swinburne; or Thomas Hardy; or even the campaigning journalist W. T. Stead. Duelling had fallen out of fashion in England back in the 1830s. Not so—despite Maupassant's scorn—in France. Whether you were a writer of genial stories or decadent poems, you never seemed to believe that words were enough; that they could, indeed should, settle things. If—as Whistler proclaimed—a friendship was only a stage on the way to a quarrel, then a catty newspaper paragraph might be a stage on the way to an out-of-town encounter with a quartet of seconds, a doctor standing by, and a priest hiding underneath a bridge in case the worst happened. If there was any sense in the business, it was perhaps this: that a duel was both quicker and cheaper than a lawsuit for libel or slander.

Between 1895 and 1905, at one very conservative estimate—and merely in the area of politics, journalism and literature—there were at least 150 duels in Paris. And if some involved firing in the air, or stopping as the first drops of blood were spilt, others were more violent and more crazed. Names recur frequently in the list of combatants: Georges Clemenceau, campaigning journalist and war leader (also doctor and friend of Pozzi), who fought twenty-two duels in total; the poet and inveterate hothead Catulle Mendès; the poet Jean Moréas; the political journalists Henri de Rochefort and Edouard Drumont; the novelist and politician Maurice Barrès. Those on the right were more often in a foaming rage than those on the left: for instance, the journalist and novelist (and royalist and anti-Semite) Jean Lorrain; or Léon Daudet, royalist, nationalist, virulent anti-Semite, Germanophobe and hater of democracy. He was always boiling over about something, and expert at crafting an insult. But it wasn't until his middle years that words became insufficient and blood was called for. Daudet fought his first duel, against a socialist journalist, in 1902 at the age of thirty-five; then two more in 1910, three in 1911, and the last, at the age of forty-seven, in 1914.

Statistical spikes in the number of duels can be directly matched to the politics of the time. One such spike had occurred during the eruption of Boulangism. When the Dreyfus Affair blew up, the writer-duellist Eugène Rouzier-Dorcières, a famous director of combat—who had himself fought twenty times and was to direct 192 duels—expressed delight at the prospect of new business. The manageress of the restaurant at the Tour de Villebon, a popular site for duels, concurred: "Yes indeed, sir, we'll be going back to the good old days of Boulangism, when we often had three duels here in a single morning!"

Maupassant's "Mentality of the Boulevards" is well exemplified by a duel in 1901 between the endlessly combative Catulle Mendès and a certain Georges Vanor, who had never been beaten in a fight. Mendès was now nearing sixty, his opponent much younger; the two of them fought violently, with blood spilt on both sides; the bout ended when Mendès was struck in the abdomen. After a quick examination, the doctor present assured the poet's seconds that the wound was superficial, and departed the scene. As it happened, Vanor's blade had penetrated the peritoneum to a depth of seven centimetres, and Mendès lay close to death for three weeks, but survived. And the cause of it all? The two men had fallen out backstage at the theatre about exactly how thin Sarah Bernhardt had been when she played the role of Hamlet.

Still, the most poignant cases involve young writers who hoped to make their name through words, but instead left it attached to a needless death while fulfilling an outdated social rite. In 1886 Robert Caze, a novelist and journalist who had already been taken up by Edmond de Goncourt, fought the journalist Charles Vignier. The cause was contorted. A third journalist, Félicien Champsaur, had made an allusion in an article to a certain young writer taking his mistress by special train to Lourdes. Caze believed that the insinuation was aimed at him. He had an altercation in a café with Champsaur, but declined the latter's suggestion of a duel: wisely, modernly, he instigated legal proceedings. Whereupon Vignier (who already had an animus against Caze) joined in, accusing Caze in *La Revue Moderniste* of having allowed himself to be given a good thrashing by Champsaur.

This time, there was (seemingly) no escape. Caze and Vignier fought on 15 February in the Bois de Meudon; Caze died five weeks later, leaving a widow, two children and the meagre royalties from his first, just-published novel. But he died with a true writer's words on his lips. Huysmans and Goncourt went to visit him on his final, fatal day. Huysmans was allowed a few seconds with the young novelist, who just had enough strength to ask him, "Have you read my book?"

Nine years later, the journalist Jules-Hippolyte Percher, who wrote under the name of Harry Alis, succumbed to the writer's least acceptable professional hazard: that of being killed by one of his own readers. Alis was thirty-seven at the time, a friend of Maupassant, and an Africanist. In the *Journal des Débats* on 24 February 1895 he argued the case for French colonial expansion in the Congo. A certain Captain Le Chatelier, who ran the Société des études du Congo français, wrote a letter of correction. Alis added his own commentary at the foot of the published letter, and wrote privately to Le Chatelier. The exchanges grew harsher in tone—Le Chatelier accused Alis of "having sold his pen to the Belgians"—until each was accusing the other of financial malpractice. In their terms, a duel was inevitable.

Alis, not wishing to alarm his wife and children, took them for a picnic at La Grande Jatte (which Seurat had painted ten years previously). He installed them at an open-air café, and excused himself, saying he was going to meet a friend. He walked to the nearby restaurant Le Moulin Rouge. The duel took place in the establishment's dance hall. The next time Alis's family saw him, he was dead.

And Pozzi? Where was Pozzi among all these furious scufflings induced by that clown, honour? We might imagine him present in a medical capacity, ready to staunch a burst of virtuous blood. He was indeed there in support when even the cool and aloof Count Robert de Montesquiou was provoked to fight. And we might imagine him a scientific observer of these supposedly romantic exchanges of bullets and swordpoints. But Pozzi was everywhere, so Pozzi was here too, at the centre of the action. In late 1899, by which time he had been elected senator for the Dordogne, the Chamber was sitting as a High Court of Justice enquiring into the seditious activities of a group of blood-and-soil nativists and royalists. Chosen by lot, Pozzi was among the investigating senators who voted to put the conspirators on trial. One of them was Paul Déroulède, who had tried to persuade a general to lead his troops against the presidential palace, and had also demanded to be arrested for treason; in spite of this, he was acquitted. The following June, at the Medical Club in the avenue de l'Opéra, Pozzi encountered Dr. Paul Devillers, a friend of Déroulède's.

After an exchange of words, Devillers flung his glove in Pozzi's face. Pozzi sent his seconds round—rationally, sensibly—to explain that he had not even taken part in the final senate vote, having been ill at the time. But Devillers, far from withdrawing his accusation, chose to stand by it in the light of "Dr. Pozzi's general attitude in the senate." This made a duel inevitable. Since Devillers was known as a fine shot,

Pozzi—then fifty-four—chose swords. The two doctors fought near Louveciennes, with the *chef de clinique* of the Broca present on Pozzi's side. Pozzi swiftly received a wound to the hand—one of his operating hands, a lover's hand, a hand painted pianistically by Sargent. Honour and stupidity were satisfied.

The second bullet—closer to our story—was fired in May 1871, as government troops were crushing the Commune. Dr. Adrien Proust, twelve years older than Pozzi (soon to be his friend and colleague), was walking to work at the Hôpital de la Charité when he was brushed by a stray bullet. His pregnant wife was so overcome by shock at the news that the family moved to Auteuil on the outskirts of the city for the duration of the fighting. Two months later, Marcel Proust was born.

If Samuel Pozzi were to be considered for a new dictionary of quotations, it should be for this line, from the introduction to his treatise on gynaecology: "Chauvinism is one of the forms of ignorance." He was patriotic, serving as a medical officer in the Franco-Prussian War—receiving an unheroic wound when a horse-drawn ambulance ran over his ankle—and later in the First World War. But he was never chauvinistic. If the professional truth lay abroad, then he would seek it there. The argument that doctors did something a certain way because they were French, and the French had always done it that way, did not convince. Surgery was a conservative practice, and often chauvinistic by default. Certainly the flow of information across borders was slow. Florence Nightingale had demonstrated the effect of basic hygiene and sanitation on survival rates during the Crimean War of 1853–56. But the squalid old habits continued in the American Civil War of 1861–65 and the Franco-Prussian War of 1870–71. Pozzi saw how injured soldiers were much more likely to die from infection and septi-caemia than from the initial wound: surgeons operated in filthy, cross-contaminating conditions, and the wounded were often transported from the front lying on the shit-ridden straw of carriages previously occupied by horses. Even in peacetime surgery, basic hygiene was fre-quently neglected. The American surgeon Charles Meigs (1792–1869) had been famously outraged when it was suggested that he and his colleagues should wash their hands before operating. "Doctors are gentlemen," he had insisted, "and gentlemen's hands are clean."

To begin with, Pozzi was an Anglophile—and not just in the matter of buying curtain material from Liberty's. His widowed father had married an Englishwoman, and his half brother Paul was to marry another, Miriam Ashcroft, in Liverpool in 1876. That was also the year Pozzi made his first trip to Britain, to attend the British Medical Association conference in Edinburgh. There he met Joseph Lister, as he had hoped, and learned the principles of Listerism, as he had planned.

It was, he discovered, a thoroughgoing process, and no step could be omitted. There was carbolic acid to prevent wounds from becoming infected, a weak solution of phenol for handwashing, a fine phenol spray in the room during the operation; stitching was done not, as in France, with silver wire (often extremely painful and a cause of infection) but with catgut, which dissolved after a few days. Instead of leaving wounds relatively uncovered, Lister used sterilised dressings soaked in phenol, and rubber drainage tubes beneath the wound. Did "the Scottish rite," as Pozzi termed it, work? The answer lay in simple statistics: Lister found that with amputations, if all the stages of his procedure were followed, the death rate fell from 50 to 15 percent.

On his return to Paris, Pozzi wrote up his findings, and started implementing Listerism. Unable to find either catgut or an apparatus to produce a phenol spray in France, he imported them from England at his own expense. His meeting with Lister was the start of a lifelong series of exchanges with European and American colleagues.

Pozzi was a highly intelligent, swiftly decisive, scientific rationalist—which meant that life was comprehensible, and the best course of action obvious to him, in all areas except those of love and marriage and parenthood. Otherwise Pozzi was, as we now like to say, "on the right side of history." He was also a member of a generation inevitably in conflict with its predecessor: not about clothes or hair length or idleness or sexual morals, but about the entire history and origin of the world.

In 1874 Reinwald published Samuel Pozzi and René Benoît's translation of Charles Darwin's *The Expression of the Emotions in Man and Animals*. Almost simultaneously, Hachette published *The Earth and the Biblical Story of Its Creation* by Benjamin Pozzy—still with the family *y*—"member of the Anthropological Society of Paris" (as was his son). The pastor's work is a refutation of Darwinist transformationism and a restatement of the Bible's unchanging truth. The son's book covers 404 pages, the father's 578. The luxuriously bound copy the father gave the son has a pencil dedication on the title page: "To my dear son Samuel, B. Pozzy." His work is full of scholarly references, from French, German, Swiss and British sources. One name that fails to feature is that of Charles Darwin.

The tectonic plates were shifting and an inevitable and irreparable split occurred, as father held to fixed gospel truth and son to mobile scientific truth. The British equivalents were Philip and Edmund Gosse, whose conflict is described in *Father and Son* (1907) by Edmund, born three years after Samuel Pozzi. Like Benjamin Pozzy, Philip Gosse held "steadily to the law of the fixity of species," and

Pozzi: "disgustingly handsome," according to Alice, Princesse de Monaco

believed in the "catastrophic act of creation" by God, in which "the world presented, instantly, the structural appearance of a planet on which life had long existed." He attempted to square the Bible with recent geological evidence in a book called *Omphalos*, which attracted much ridicule. Benjamin Pozzy was not mocked, but he was politely ignored.

Pozzi was always well dressed, and his "English frock coats" were commented upon; he was described as "almost a dandy." He was one in the loose, vernacular sense; but he could never be one in the fullest meaning of the term. The dandy was an Anglo-French phenomenon, crisscrossing the Channel throughout the nineteenth century. Beau Brummell was the exemplar of the perfectly dressed, witty, spendthrift member of high society. Class was essential: you could hardly be a middle-class, let alone working-class, dandy in England. In France, you were allowed to be a dandy in artistic, bohemian circles. Brummell's French biography was written by Barbey d'Aurevilly, a late-Romantic dandified Catholic novelist who hinted at aristocratic lineage while coming from the provincial bourgeoisie. The French dandy was more of a writer than the English version: Baudelaire was the poet-dandy's poet-dandy. The fictional dandy Des Esseintes commissions a "magnificent triptych" of quasi-medieval tapestry to stand in the centre of a chimneypiece. The words, in "exquisite missal lettering," are decorated with magnificent illumination. The three sacred texts are all from Baudelaire: sonnets to the left and right, and in the middle the prose-poem with the (English) title "Any where [sic] out of the world."

Montesquiou was the exemplar of the aristocrat-poet-dandy, thereby giving himself three separate reasons to feel superior to others. His grandfather had white peacocks roosting in a catalpa tree. The grandson sought out grey flowers to decorate his grey room. He went to

fancy-dress balls as both Louis XIV and Louis XV. He served tea
à l'anglaise—that's to say, he poured it himself. He was one of the first
Frenchmen to wear a dinner jacket in the evening—made of velvet,
either scarab-green or burgundy. His biographer described him as "a
shining, buzzing, virulent scarab." Léon Daudet, in his memoirs, wrote
that the Count was "varnished for eternity." The dandy is an aesthete,
one for whom "thought is of less value than vision." Fine bindings
delight him as much as the words inside.

For twenty years (1885–1905) Montesquiou shared his life with the
younger Gabriel Yturri, the Argentinian secretary whom he poached
from under the nose of the famously debauched Baron Doäzan. He
had been "brought up by English priests in Lisbon in order that he
might be removed from the temptations to which, in the hotter climate
of his native land, his good looks might have exposed him." Clearly,
the plan did not wholly work. Yturri had been a tie salesman in the
rue de la Madeleine when he was first spotted by the competing Baron
and Count. Some saw him as an adventurer, others as Montesquiou's
soulmate (the two are not incompatible); also, his gofer and fixer.
They liked dressing up in matching costumes, on one occasion as
"Englishmen." Alas, there seems no photographic record of this poignant moment: "frock coat by Poole, with a large buttonhole of Parma
violets such as the English are accustomed to wear on Sundays when
they go to church." Shortly after meeting the Count, Yturri wrote
to him: "I should like to put under your dear tired steps a carpet of
thornless roses." This is both camp and touching. Perhaps camp is
like sentimentality, of which Alain-Fournier wrote: "It's sentimentality
when it doesn't come off; it's art, sorrow and life when it does."

In the 1880s Montesquiou had a dalliance—of taste and
temperament—with Whistler, the Anglo-Americano-French dandy.

Montesquiou and Yturri in oriental costume

Who in turn had an avuncular, jousting relationship with Oscar Wilde, twenty years his junior. As these examples suggest, the dandy is excited by his own self-creation and self-celebration (and it is always "his own," female dandies being held not to exist). The dandy is excited to be wittier and better-dressed, and to have better taste, than the rest of humanity. Whistler dedicated his *Gentle Art of Making Enemies* to "The rare few, who, early in Life, have rid Themselves of the Friendship of the Many." (Those first three words are French-influenced, derived from Stendhal's dedication "to the happy few.") Wilde liked to refer to "the elect," whose task was to guide the multitudinous non-elect in matters of taste and beauty. Though of course, if too many were to copy him, the dandy would have to move on, and make himself special again. The dandy is a decorator, a decorator of houses and apartments, a linguistic decorator. The dandy is an arbiter and exemplar of taste. Not of art, of taste.

Degas said: "Art is killed by taste."

Baudelaire described dandyism as "an ill-defined institution, as strange as the duel." It absorbs time and money in large quantities. It "arises especially in transitional epochs, when democracy is not yet all-powerful, and the aristocracy only partially shaken and debased." (The dandy is largely apolitical, though, given that his vocation requires a lot of money and he generally doesn't do a job, he inevitably leans more to the right than the left.) In Barbey d'Aurevilly's analysis, English Puritanism—the mortal enemy of dandyism—had returned in full force across the Channel with Victoria's reign. "England, the victim of its own history, having taken a step towards the future, has now gone back to squatting in its past . . . indestructible, immortal *cant* has won another victory."

Baudelaire views dandyism as "the last outburst of heroism in decadent times"; it is "the setting sun, that star, which when it falls is magnificent, yet without heat, and full of sadness." This notion of costly display combined with inner coldness is central to most explanations of dandyism. Baudelaire: "The nature of a dandy's beauty lies in a frigid exterior which results from an unshakeable determination not to be moved." Wilde, in *The Picture*, proposes dandyism as a defensive psychological tactic: "To become the spectator of one's own life . . . is to escape the suffering of life."

Whom does the dandy love? Himself, obviously. What about others? Here, it gets more complicated. Barbey d'Aurevilly concluded that dandies have "double or multiple natures, sexually indeterminate when it comes to their intellects . . . they are the Androgynes of History." Montesquiou endorsed this idea of the double, or androgynous nature. He liked to quote the phrase: "Hybrids sigh for those who will devour them"—words you cannot read without thinking of Wilde and Lord Alfred Douglas.

This is hardly the gender fluidity of today, but it marks a strong resistance to the heteronormative. The (unscandalous) homosexual was welcome in Parisian society; the lesbian even more welcome. Sarah Bernhardt—of the unfashionably slim body shape—was often regarded as an androgyne. Montesquiou's biographer calls her "the hermaphrodite who haunts the end of the century." Pozzi was professionally interested in hermaphroditism. Which was no longer evidenced mainly by classical statuary. Around 1860 Nadar, at the instigation of a doctor friend from the Hôtel-Dieu, took the first photographs of a hermaphrodite. There were nine exposures in total, and he cannily copyrighted them at once.

Taste. Which often lies close to beguiling prejudice. It doesn't take much to put us off a writer; and it does save time. When it comes to nineteenth-century France, I've always had a scunner on Barbey d'Aurevilly. The reason is fairly simple: he was vile about Flaubert. So I long ago swore not to give him the posthumous pleasure of knowing that I had read him. And the occasional details I picked up—royalist, militant Catholic, pretending to be posher than he was—endorsed my aversion. He seemed from other people's descriptions of his books to write Poe-ish late-Romantic misogynistic fantasy fiction. Also this: he was born thirteen years before Flaubert, yet outlived him by another nine. How existentially unfair that seemed.

GEORGE SAND
FEMME DE LETTRES

I remind myself of his malfeasances. In 1869 Flaubert wrote to George Sand to complain about a review of *L'Education sentimentale*: "Barbey d'Aurevilly claims that I pollute a stream by washing in it." (What Barbey actually wrote is more interesting, though just as offensive: "Flaubert has neither grace nor melancholy: his robustness is like that of Courbet's painting 'Women Bathing'—women washing themselves in a brook, polluting it.") Flaubert would have winced further at this comparison: he was always very dismissive about Courbet's work.

Four and a half years later, Barbey reviewed *La Tentation de saint-Antoine* in terms of the difference between "the ardent, pious character of a very great saint . . . and the most frigid man of these times, the most materialistic in talent, and the most indifferent to the moral aspect of life." Naturally, Flaubert made no public response, but when, a few months later, Barbey published his best-known work, *Les Diaboliques*, Flaubert tells his old friend George Sand that he finds it "side-splitting. Perhaps it's due to the perversity of my nature, which

Jules Barbey d'Aurevilly, Charles Emile Auguste Carolus-Duran (1860)

makes me like pernicious things, but this work seemed to me extremely funny. Impossible to go further in the realm of the inadvertently grotesque." Right, that lets me off reading it all over again.

Still, Barbey did write a short biography of Beau Brummell, which I allowed myself to read while remaining suspicious of its factual accuracy. And then, perhaps "due to the perversity of my nature," I sent off for his *Memoranda*. These record, at great length and with very little filter, his daily doings over two six-month periods in 1836–38, and a shorter one in 1864. I note that he was an Anglophile, reading Wordsworth and Byron in the original. He decides that "apart from the great poets, I don't think the English write good books . . . the subtle genius of prose escapes them." Though he does later admire Bacon and Burke. He thinks "ethereal" a wonderful English word with no equivalent in French. And he cites with approval the Scottish proverb: "Never give a fool a pointed stick."

But then he gives himself a pointed stick to jab at—yes, here we go again—Englishwomen. "I have always distrusted women who *go for walks*—Englishwomen, for example, members of a cold race if ever there was one—not that this prevents them from being extremely corrupt. On the contrary: just one more reason for being so." Some pages later, Barbey goes to a soirée where he comes across "loads of Englishwomen (the most stupid women in the world are Englishwomen! Which makes the unpleasantness of the rest of the nation all the greater)."

Montesquiou acclaimed the counter-revolutionary essayist Antoine de Rivarol (1753–1801) as "the wittiest man in the world, even though few of his best remarks survive." Here is one of his cracks that did, and which the Count quotes in his memoirs: "Englishwomen have two left arms."

—

In 1893, Montesquiou sent Proust a photo of himself with the dedication "I am the sovereign of transitory things." Proust had already nicknamed him "the Professor of Beauty." He was also known as "the Commander of Delicate Odours"; while Yturri was the "Chancellor of Flowers." In his later, declining years, the Count used to console himself by repeating, "I am good, and have a beautiful soul," as if either matter were for him to decide. He liked to quote a couplet of his German fellow poet (and fellow Count) Platen: "He who looks Beauty full in the face / Is already dedicated to death." For Montesquiou, Beauty—whether the internal beauty of your own soul, or the concept and expression of beauty out there in the world—is something you retreat into, a manner of living that sets you apart, that holds the world at bay. It is something private, shared among initiates. Most of whom recognise who is the top initiate.

Wilde's concept of Beauty was more aggressive. It was—as Barbey's Scottish proverb has it—to be wielded like a pointed stick. Against whom? Against the Vulgar. And in Wilde's world, the Vulgar was everywhere. The Royal Academy is vulgar; Realism is vulgar; details are "always vulgar"; Switzerland is vulgar; "all crime is vulgar, just as all vulgarity is crime." Further, "Death and vulgarity are the only two facts in the nineteenth century one cannot explain away."

Arriving in America, Wilde explained to the natives, "I am here to diffuse beauty." The Artist as Aerosol, perhaps. Through Lord Henry Wotton, Wilde tells us that "Beauty is a form of Genius" and Beauty is "not as superficial as Thought." Beauty is no passive ideal or spiritual retreat, it is an active force. A weapon, also a purge—not unlike those "nourishing peptone enemas" which perk up Des Esseintes. Huysmans usefully provides the recipe for one of them: "29 grams of cod-liver oil, 200 grams of beef tea, 200 grams of Burgundy, plus the yolk of an egg."

It's tempting to think of all this as Divine Decadence, Darling, a last self-indulgent efflorescence as the century comes to an end. And much of the period can seem so, lying, as it does, back beyond the mountains of modernism. What we easily forget is how almost every period of art, even those which seem deliberately retrospecting—like neoclassicism or Pre-Raphaelitism—was thought at the time by its adherents to be definingly and defiantly modern. In America, Wilde proposed that he and his generation of young poets "move in the very heart of today." Beauty, in other words, is self-evidently modern. Dandyism, Wilde tells us in *The Picture*, is "an attempt to assert the absolute modernity of beauty." The dogma is thuddingly reprised, but no longer sways. Wilde's Beauty nowadays seems fanciful, decorative, egotistical, camp: the opposite of "modern." In the words of the old American hymn, "Time makes ancient good uncouth."

By the summer of 1881, the place Vendôme and its salon were up and running. Among the many fashionable painters who attended was Carolus-Duran (who had Latinised and hyphenated his name from a boringly baptismal Charles Durand). Henry James, writing from Paris in 1876, judged him "the fashionable portrait painter *par excellence*" and "of all the modern emulators of Velázquez decidedly the most successful." He also had a teaching studio, whose most brilliant pupil was a twenty-five-year-old American, John Singer Sargent. Carolus-Duran brought him to meet Pozzi, and *The Man in the Red Coat* was soon under way. Two years previously, Sargent had painted Carolus-Duran himself, and these two pictures would later be rated by Henry James as Sargent's greatest male portraits.

COLLECTION FELIX POTIN

CAROLUS DURAN

On the surface, everything looked perfect for Pozzi—professionally, socially and maritally; further, Thérèse was pregnant with their first child. And yet the marriage—only eighteen months old—was already deeply damaged, and Pozzi was writing to the Minister of Public Education, asking to be sent to Tunisia on a medical tour of the French army of occupation.

What went wrong, and so soon? We have no testimony from Thérèse, only explanations from Pozzi. In a letter to their matchmaker Henri Cazalis in April 1881, he writes:

Ah, if only Thérèse loved me! But she merely cherishes me, that's all, and she also cherishes her mother, and has been doing so for twenty years before I came on the scene . . . From the day my wife coldly weighed me in the balance against her mother, from the day she coldly imagined the possibility of a separation and only rejected it after much examination, my love for her was mortally wounded . . . Since then, despite what I've tried, and what she's tried, it has only languished, and is now dead . . . I shall always be the best of friends to her, but I wanted to be *more*, I wanted to be *everything* to her; why did she not want that? . . . So our marriage became merely a kind of addition to her life as a young woman, rather than a substitute for it.

In a journal he started keeping the following year, Pozzi elaborates on Thérèse's emotional makeup, as he sees it. He has talked to her, as most lovers do, about the part of the country he comes from, the Périgord; but a priori she has shown no taste for it, and no inclination to visit. "She is not in the slightest degree touched by all the childhood memories I laid before her. There is an absence of sentimentality in her which sometimes amounts to a larger absence of feeling."

Pozzi's reasoning, however lucid, is inevitably self-serving (how could it not be?). Would Thérèse's reading of the situation have been the same? It's hardly likely. Would any wife—there, then—say, "I didn't feel strongly enough and this made him stop loving me"? Many years later, that child then in the womb, Catherine, gets married herself. Looking back on her decision, she writes ruefully, "I married fairly late, as I was already twenty-five. I married 'in order to be married.' Many do the same, and attain a kind of happiness. It would have been better if I had stayed single and worked." But Catherine was Parisian, intense and intellectual; a career was a genuine alternative. Thérèse had been provincial, pious, unintellectual, brought up for marriage, and in recent receipt of a great fortune through the death of

Samuel, Thérèse and Catherine Pozzi at La Graulet

her father. Perhaps she and Pozzi went into the marriage with separate misconceptions: he with the romantic (English) delusion that love and marriage could be combined; she with the practical (French) delusion that being "established"—in society, in Paris, in the state of marriage—would bring its own happiness, regardless of whom she did the establishing with. Duty would in any case see her through. Pozzi imagined that Thérèse loved him when she married him; perhaps she imagined this too. But there can often be a lot of "thinking you love someone" before the loving truly begins. And if she had expressed prior doubts, the wisdom of generations might have reassured her that she "would come to love him." But what did she, a mere provincial virgin of twenty-three, have to go on? And then she became just another wife unable to love her husband as he expected and she hoped. It was not an original tragedy, but it was original to her.

Pozzi was convinced that Thérèse's mother, the powerfully possessive Mme Loth-Cazalis, had turned her daughter against him. "She has made my wife hate me, turned me into a kind of tyrant, almost an executioner." Mme Loth-Cazalis is as silent on the record as her daughter. But Pozzi's own words make it plain that the situation was more complicated than he later claimed; and that the trouble began very early. In December 1879, while the couple are still on their honeymoon, Pozzi writes from Madrid to Cazalis:

Thérèse is disconsolate at having been torn from her mother's bosom. I had to take vigorous, almost violent, action. I am more and more convinced that this was necessary. But the first part of our honeymoon was marked by a certain sadness.

It sits oddly in Pozzi's mouth that on their honeymoon he rebuked his wife for her attachment to her family, and yet complains about her lack of interest in his. Perhaps he imagined that once they established themselves in Paris, she would think about her family in Lyon with the same distant tenderness that he felt about his family in Bergerac. For a while he believed that her homesickness was just "a small cloud," as he put it, over their marriage. But he underestimated the depth of feeling between mother and daughter. The following year, Mme Loth-Cazalis moved to Paris, and—in Pozzi's view—her hold over Thérèse increased. Perhaps it was only ever the case that she simply loved her mother more, and there was nothing to be done about this. But would that in itself be enough to push a young bride in her early twenties to "coldly imagine" the possibility of a separation?

Pozzi wrote in his journal on 19 September 1882: "We have the best public relationship in the eyes of the world, but no intimacy." However, it is a sign of Thérèse's determination to keep up appearances that she had accompanied her husband on his working tour of Tunisia the previous year. Nor did "no intimacy" mean an end to sex. Thérèse was to have two more children: Jean, born two years after Catherine in 1884, and Jacques—the late child, the "miracle child"—twelve years later when she was forty and Pozzi fifty. Mainly, though, she ran the house, she hosted dinners and soirées, she went to church and she provided the money which funded Pozzi's collecting habits, his aesthetic shopping, his English tweeds and Liberty curtains. For thirty years they shared a public marriage, and endured private gossip.

When *A Rebours* was published, Huysmans was surprised to receive a fan letter sent by "an enthusiastic admirer" and containing a number of suggestive photographs. They showed the sender in various poses and different theatrical disguises, along with shots of his bedroom, which was "furnished with all the bad taste of a tart." The admirer signed himself Jean Lorrain.

Jean Lorrain, Antonio de la Gandara (1898)

Lorrain was a dandy, poet, novelist, playwright, reviewer, chronicler—in the mid-1890s he was reckoned to be the highest-paid journalist in Paris—scandal-monger, rumour-driver, etheromaniac and duellist; someone dangerous to be around, someone who deliberately went too far almost on principle, a homosexual more unequivocally out than most of the sophisticated aesthetes and dandies he mixed with. He was a habitué of bars and grog shops, clubs and dance halls, louche dives and funfairs. Like many in his world, his taste was for high and low—the salon and the street; he despised the middle—the middle being where he had come from. His father ran a marine insurance company and a brickworks in Fécamp. The young Paul Duval dropped both his names when reinventing himself as Jean Lorrain.

He is someone you half want to keep out of your book, for fear he might take over too much of it. He was extravagant, fearless, contemptible, malicious, talented and envious, a friend who couldn't help betraying you, and an enemy who would never forget. But Sarah Bernhardt introduced him to Pozzi, who for thirty years was his friend, confidant and doctor, as well as host at the place Vendôme. So here he is. As many biographers have discovered, you can't, unfortunately, choose your principal subject's friends.

Lorrain exemplified both the culture and the anarchy of the Belle Epoque. The Belgian poet Hubert Juin said that he "loved his age to the point of detestation." La Goulue, the famous Moulin Rouge dancer, nicknamed him "Prince Sleepy," as he had the glaucous eyes of a frog, over which closed heavy lids. Others elided physical description with moral (and homophobic) disgust. George Painter, Proust's biographer, called him "a large, flaccid invert . . . drugged, painted and powdered . . . [who] wore loads of jewelled rings on his fat, white, fish-like fingers . . . [He] belonged to that dangerous type of invert which tried to avert scandal by pretending to be virile and accusing everyone else of perversion." This last sentence seems particularly skewed, given that Lorrain openly nicknamed himself "The Ambassador from Sodom." Pozzi's biographer called him "that ugly, greasy, writer-poet-critic-journalist-homosexual-drugaddict-who-frightened little Catherine Pozzi."

Léon Daudet, who held back no more than Lorrain ever did, wrote:

Lorrain had the broad, chubby face of a vice-ridden hairdresser, his hair-parting soaked in patchouli, his gawping eyes greedily protuberant, his wet lips dripping and spraying as he spoke. Like a vulture, he fed off calumnies and filth peddled by salon-goers' servants, by kept women and fashionable pimps. Imagine the gurgling flow of the sewer outlet from a hospital. This special kind of maniac, who belonged to two if not three sexes, didn't lack a nose for a story, nor did he lack an artistic style . . . He filled the newspapers with poisonous allusions and pseudo-feminine bitchery about the houses where he was received, the houses where he was no longer received, and the houses where he was not yet received. The spinelessness of the times showed in the fact that Lorrain was tolerated, and did not each day receive his rightful due of kicks up the backside and caresses from walking sticks.

Lorrain dyed his moustache with henna and wore mauve powder; he was familiar with the passing whisper of "*He's* got the plaster on." He enjoyed the riskier side of homosexual life: the rough trade, and what Wilde called "feasting with panthers." Though, as with Wilde, the panthers were often alley cats. Lorrain would sometimes head off into the night with Yturri, Montesquiou's companion, to the dance halls of Point-du-Jour and other places of rendezvous. Lorrain, who in Goncourt's opinion had a "dark and reckless nature," was always getting into fights, being smashed in the face with a bunch of keys, coming back with his arm in a sling. Goncourt remembered him turning up once with a black eye and "a head wound which had required six leeches to clean."

He was a man to be both endured and enjoyed. He said: "What is a vice? Merely a taste you don't share." Like Wilde, he was someone whose excessiveness and noisy ego were exhilarating to some, embarrassing to others, and alarming to quieter homosexuals who valued privacy and feared the police van. Léon Daudet certainly thought so: "Apart from the final scandal, Lorrain's case is very similar to that of Oscar Wilde, whom English society tolerated, even adulated, regarding him as an 'original gentleman,' until such time as it came to realise that what it had on its hands was a true moral lunatic." Yet Wilde and Lorrain—who met when Wilde first set out to conquer Paris in 1893—didn't take to one another; perhaps it was too much like looking in the mirror. Wilde said: "Lorrain is a poseur." Lorrain said of Wilde: "He's a faker."

Many called Lorrain "the poor man's Montesquiou," which naturally enraged him. He was always trying to provoke the Count: in newspaper columns he nicknamed him "Grotesquiou" and "Robert Machère." In 1901, in his novel *Monsieur de Phocas*, he produced fiction's second shadow version of Montesquiou; though, being excessive, Lorrain put not one but three different versions of the Count into the novel. Even so, he couldn't get a rise out of Montesquiou; never a slapped face or a thrown glove, never the sought-after recognition or the sought-after aggression which would imply some kind of equality.

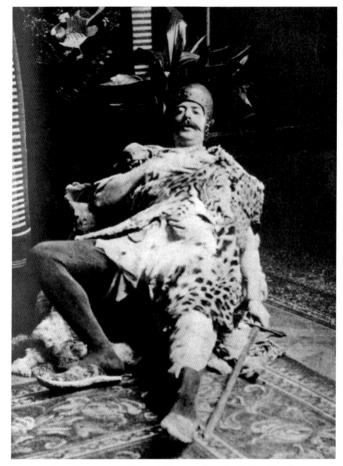

Jean Lorrain as a Dying Warrior, chez Sarah Bernhardt

Inevitably—and because of, or despite, his fan letter—Lorrain knew Huysmans; also that other Catholic novelist, Léon Bloy. With them, he went too far in a different sphere: religion. Lorrain more than dabbled in satanism and black magic; and he took Huysmans with him along the road of the occult, of evil spells, warfare against the Rosicrucians, and so on. A journalist sent to interview Huysmans was surprised when the novelist showed him some "exorcism paste," explaining that it was a mixture of myrrh, incense, camphor and cloves—"the plant of John the Baptist." But here, to the eyes of a Catholic novelist, Lorrain was doing more than shocking social convention; he was meddling with the immortal soul.

Eventually, Huysmans (like his creature Des Esseintes) felt the returning pull of the church, and in 1891, a year before he was received back, he wrote this rebuke to Lorrain:

> This evening, in the café, I've been looking through the back numbers of *Le Courrier français*. Lorrain! Lorrain! You are blaspheming with such deliberate intent that when the angels in leather jerkins and two-pointed hats take you "up there" to appear before the Definitive Assizes, you will undoubtedly be given the maximum sentence. Take care! Take care!

In March 1906, a few months before Lorrain's death, Bloy writes in his journal: "Someone brings me a book. It is *The Plays of Jean Lorrain*. With a contemporary portrait. It's the face of a reprobate, of a damned soul, of a stinking enemy of Glory and Eternal Life. What a horrible nightmare."

For all his social, moral, legal and metaphysical infractions, Lorrain, an only child, was also for many years an obedient son who lived with his mother in Auteuil. She was a lady of formidable appearance: Léon Daudet nicknamed her "Sycorax"—the mother of Caliban. There were three people to whom the quarrelsome Lorrain was always loyal (or as loyal as he could be): his mother, Edmond de Goncourt, and Dr. Pozzi.

Léon Daudet once asked Goncourt, who also lived in Auteuil: "Monsieur de Goncourt, how can you bear to put up with that frightful bloke? The very sight of him makes me feel sick." "What can I do, my dear boy," Goncourt replied. "Auteuil is a little out of town, and there are winter days when I am all alone. Lorrain amuses me with his tittle-tattle." Tittle-tattle which Goncourt would sometimes put straight into his diary. Where he would also observe that Lorrain was "a hysterical, duplicitous gossip." Lorrain would slander Goncourt to Alphonse and Mme Daudet, then slander the Daudets to Goncourt, knowing (in some part of his brain) that they would compare notes. He just couldn't stop himself. Goncourt often wondered at the source of this behaviour, and whether the dominant impulse within Lorrain was "malice, or the complete absence of tact." Lorrain also wondered about this: one explanation he found was that *le tout Paris* had malevolently deflected him from his true path as a poet. "Those pigs!" he once exclaimed. "They turned me into a journalist!"

The Goncourt Journal is one of the great documents of the age. It was the work of two brothers, Edmond (1822–96) and Jules (1830–70). They were inseparable in life (rarely spending more than a few hours

COLLECTION FELIX POTIN

EDMOND DE GONCOURT

apart, even sharing the same mistress at one time) and inseparable on the page, fusing themselves into a joint "I" to narrate the *Journal*. Aesthetes, collectors, dramatists, art critics and novelists, their curiosity ranged across the whole of society, low, middle and high. They were both sickly men, suffering from their livers, stomachs and nerves; writers disaffected by the age, preferring the elegant eighteenth century; men with high ideals and delicate sensibilities who were frequently wounded and outraged by the way the world operated. Edmond admitted that "We were temperamental, neurotic, unhealthily impressionable creatures, and therefore occasionally unjust." Jules, writing to Flaubert in October 1866, claimed that: "We three, with Gautier, form the entrenched camp of art for art's sake, of the morality of beauty, of indifference in political matters, and of scepticism with regard to the other nonsense, I mean religion."

Their opening diary entry was for 2 December 1851, publication day of their first book, *En 18..* Unfortunately for them (though good for the *Journal*) it was also the day of Louis-Napoléon's coup d'état, one of whose side effects was to make all printers and publishers extremely nervous, so that *En 18..* went unadvertised and undistributed, eventually selling a miserable sixty copies. The brothers formed the habit of writing their *Journal* late at night, after the day's excitements—apart from this last one—were complete, with Edmond standing while Jules wrote down their joint impressions and memories. Everything they recorded was truthfully done, even if what they had been told was not necessarily true. Edmond summed up their plan:

> What we have tried to do, then, is to bring our contemporaries to life for posterity in a speaking likeness, by means of the vivid stenography of a conversation, the physiological spontaneity of a gesture, those little signs of emotions that reveal a personality, those *imponderabilia* that render the intensity of existence, and, last of all, a touch of that fever which is the mark of the heady life of Paris.

Every great diary amounts to an undermining, if not betrayal, of the age it portrays. It is subversive both at the micro level—he/she was not as virtuous as he/she/they all pretended—and at the macro level:

it warns us against taking the age at its own estimation. *The Goncourt Journal*, richly detailed, funny, gossipy and blazingly unfiltered, remains the brothers' greatest work. Edmond thought of abandoning it after Jules's death from tertiary syphilis in 1870; but the need to record his brother's end, plus the disasters of the Paris Siege and the Commune, impelled him to continue. He did so until twelve days before his death in 1896.

However, not content with setting down the inconvenient truths of the age, Edmond went one step further and published them in nine volumes between 1887 and 1896. This was at a time when private letters were still routinely burnt on the sender's or receiver's death; and the *Journal* was greeted by some who featured in it with embarrassment, outrage and a sense of betrayal. The philosopher and historian Ernest Renan, author of *The Life of Jesus*, was famously and publicly furious when the fourth volume was published in 1890. He did not like being reminded—and having the reading public informed—that twenty years previously, with the Prussians encircling Paris, he had held forth at the Café Brébant on the superiority of the German mind and of German workmanship, ending with a cry of "Yes, gentlemen, the Germans are a superior race!" Goncourt defended his word-for-word account; he also agreed with a journalist sent to interview him as the row developed, that he was an "indiscreet individual." But he claimed that the only memoirs of interest were written by "indiscreet individuals," concluding with another prod at Renan: "Monsieur Renan has been so indiscreet about Jesus that he really ought to allow a little indiscreetness about himself."

A Rumour at Work

Edmond de Goncourt is talking to a lady whose name he has redacted. His *Journal* entry begins with the heading "A trail to follow."

Me: I dined on Wednesday with the Princess [Mathilde] and Mme Straus, who was looking in full beauty.

Mme ✳✳✳: And yet she's definitely suffering . . . I saw her on Saturday, and she'd just had a serious attack of nerves . . . Apparently she hasn't eaten for a fortnight . . . Something's definitely up . . . (*She is silent for a moment, then goes on*) Mme de Baignères, who knows her by heart, says that she is in love with love, and that at any moment, if Maupassant had asked her to follow him, she would have thrown up everything . . . Is she enamoured? And of whom? (*a silence*) The other day, I was asking her about her son, and she told me he had a job—he'd been accepted as one of Pozzi's interns. And at the name, the boy, who was there, looked at his mother in a certain way . . . Yes, there are a few little pointers which make me think it's him.

Me: Yes, yes, you could be on the track of it . . . How come that Pozzi, who doesn't normally go to the Princess's, was dining with her at the rue de Berri last Wednesday? . . . And I can give you a not unimportant detail. She [Mme Straus], who is so sensitive to the cold and always, when dining at the Princess's, wears a bit of lace or fur across her shoulders—because we're all freezing a bit since the Princess replaced her gas with electricity—in spite of all my neighbourly exhortations, absolutely insisted on remaining *décolletée*.

Mme ✱✱✱: That seems to confirm the thing . . . I must write and tell her that on Saturday I saw in her eyes such suffering that she must be in a state of moral pain . . . I'll keep you posted next Monday.

(But here the story, or the gossip, peters out.)

On Sunday 1 February 1885, five months before the "strange trio" set out for London, Edmond de Goncourt inaugurated his *grenier*—a "salon in the attic" of his house in Auteuil. It was to be a weekly meeting place for writers, based on the example of Flaubert, who had received each Thursday in the rue Murillo. "Writers," of course, meant "male writers"; though Mme Alphonse Daudet was welcome, and wives were admitted at the end to collect their husbands. And though this was a private gathering, Goncourt saw no harm in press publicity (if only to annoy those not invited). So he acceded to the request of Joseph Gayda to write up the event for the "Parisis" column in *Le Figaro*. But when Gayda turned up he brought embarrassing news. His section head was obliged to dine that evening in some remote suburb. So Gayda had been required to file his copy at three o'clock, two hours before arriving at the event he was paid to describe.

The next day, Goncourt complained to his *Journal*:

This morning, I read Gayda's article in *Le Figaro*. Apparently I had, yesterday, at my home, a gathering of *le tout Paris*, and amongst this *tout Paris* were people who had long quarrelled with one another, enemies who wouldn't even greet one another. The poor twentieth century! How it will be short-changed if it looks for reliable information in the newspapers of the nineteenth.

After this grumble, Goncourt goes on to note that there was talk at this first *grenier* of the "fantastical" Montesquiou, and in particular of his first loves—or rather, sexual experiences—which were "Baudelairesque":

His first amorous encounter was with a female ventriloquist who, while Montesquiou was striving away on the long road to happiness, suddenly threw her voice to make it sound as if a drunken pimp had just come in, and was threatening her aristocratic client.

Who wouldn't want to believe this? However, like much of the *Journal*'s more scabrous side—and like most sexual gossip—it is single-source; and, moreover, anonymous. The other problem is that it contradicts a more famous story, in which the Count's first heterosexual encounter was with none other than Sarah Bernhardt. And this story comes in two different versions. In one they rolled around on cushions together for a while, after which the Count vomited solidly (or liquidly) for twenty-four hours. In the second, they actually went to bed together, after which Montesquiou vomited for an entire week. We cannot know.

Montesquiou is routinely described nowadays as "a flamboyant homosexual." Flamboyant, certainly; and we can probably rule him out as being heterosexual. But not flamboyant as a (practising) homosexual, far from it; for all his camp extravagance, he was no Ambassador for Sodom. He was a great friend of Bernhardt's; they both loved the dressing-up box and were fascinated by their own fame. Her first hit, in Coppée's verse play *Le Passant*, was in a travesty part as a page. Nadar, the greatest portrait photographer of the age, dressed the Count and Sarah in matching tight male costumes from the play; then they improvised scenes from it for the camera. It was after this that they supposedly rolled around on cushions together.

Bernhardt (left) and Montesquiou dressed for *Le Passant*

What man, with the confidence of noble birth, money to spend, the ability if necessary to travel to shrouded lands, and no religious impediment in his mind, has not tried sex? Tried and retried it, more often than not. On the other hand, some try sex and decide it is not for them. One theory is that Montesquiou "wished to know everything and be involved in nothing." So Yturri would go out into the night, and report the next morning all the fragrant and whiffy details. The art critic Bernard Berenson wrote: "In my long acquaintance with Montesquiou, I never noticed the side for which Charlus is famous: sodomy. And Lord knows, at that time, young as I was, I made homosexuals' mouths water." He did too: Oscar Wilde once tried to seduce him at Oxford; when rebuffed, Wilde complained that Berenson must be "made of stone."

Though homosexuality had been legalised in France in 1791, there were still many associated dangers: of blackmail, of a related criminal charge (public indecency, the corruption of minors); also, of a squalid end. Montesquiou used to recall for the instruction of the young the story of a head waiter arrested in the Champs-Elysées during a "homosexual conversation." Put in a cell, he smashed his pince-nez and swallowed the broken glass, rather than face public shame and disgrace.

That Montesquiou was homoerotic, that his passionate responses were all to men, that he submitted to the male thrall of both Whistler and D'Annunzio, is indubitable. His biographer Philippe Jullian—no prude or moraliser—says that the Count grew to fear "the impulses of the heart as much as the nonchalance of pleasure." That second phrase is excellent. For such a Count, there might be something about pleasure (unless it is aesthetic pleasure) which could be grubby, open-ended, even middle class. Fastidiousness is also the enemy of pleasure. Jullian concludes: "Robert was always too French to go to the extremes for which the English are famous." It's true that in the Belle Epoque, fashionable Paris "preferred Sappho to Sodom"; but the French have always mistakenly assumed themselves to be less homosexual than the British (and so were surprised, and slow to act, when AIDS hit their country).

There was a seventeenth-century French saying about homosexuality: "In France the nobles, in Spain the monks, in Italy everyone." There was a more recent saying by Barbey d'Aurevilly: "My tastes incline me to it, my principles permit it, but the ugliness of my contemporaries repels me." This recalls Wilde's disastrous reply to Carson when asked if he had kissed Walter Grainger, the sixteen-year-old servant in Lord Alfred Douglas's rooms at Oxford: "Oh no, never in my life; he was a peculiarly plain boy." D'Aurevilly was being somewhat disingenuous, Wilde possibly perjurious; while the late-nineteenth-century French nobility had clearly not all shaken off the habits of the seventeenth century.

All that time medical science tried to tabulate reliable indicators of homosexuality: a mincing walk, an inability to whistle, a funnel-shaped anus, fatty deposits on the buttocks and thighs, the shape of the hand, a supposedly higher skin temperature (hence the double meaning in German of the expressions "warm brother" and "warm friend"), and so on. But also this: "a predilection for the colour green." It was a hint to the initiate, a curled lip to the ultra-straight. Hence the green carnation in the buttonhole; the frogged and furry green overcoat Wilde had specially made for his American tour; and Montesquiou's myrtle-green overcoat, which provoked Jean Lorrain to refer to him as "Monsieur Take-Your-Lute" and "Monsieur Haricot Vert."

And where could the colour's use be most overt, most provocative? Here are two green beds:

1) One of the few people who intimidated Montesquiou—and one of the few he unreservedly admired—was Degas. At an exhibition of decorative art, Montesquiou was sitting on an apple-green bed of his own design. The dandy caught the attention of the painter. "Do you believe, Monsieur de Montesquiou," asked Degas, "that one would have better children on an apple-green bed? Take care—taste can be synonymous with vice."

2) In May 1898, a year after his discharge from Reading Gaol, Wilde was in Paris, seeing much of Lord Alfred Douglas again. To fit out Douglas's new flat in the avenue Kléber, Wilde went to the Paris branch of Maple's and spent £40 on suitable furniture, "including a green bed."

One thing the dandy and the aesthete jointly disdained was sport. They might countenance popular entertainment of an athletic nature: thus Des Esseintes has an affair with a (female) American acrobat; while Lorrain's Monsieur de Phocas is imitatively excited by "some sensational acrobat, male or female" at the Olympia, the circus, or the Folies-Bergère, delights which result in "copious gossip." But sport as understood by men of the world was anathema to Montesquiou and Edmond de Polignac. They had a shared hatred of the sort of men who raced horses, and who hunted both animals and women with equal vigour. In the Count's case, there was a familial repugnance as well: his father was vice president of the Jockey Club. Polignac described it as a place where you were "blinded by the thick, smoky atmosphere and bewildered by the still thicker atmosphere of the talk."

If the Count and the Prince hunted anything, they hunted young talent. Both were patrons of musicians, the Count also of writers. The Prince would send the Count notes written in coloured pencil, barded with Latin quotations and English proverbs. The Prince invited the Count to concerts, and lent him Wagner scores; together, they travelled to Bayreuth. For many at this time, Parsifal was an exemplar: Parsifal, the holy knight whose bloodline was coming to an end. This was equally the case for the two aristocrats, who chose not to propagate themselves (not that either was active in holiness).

Polignac was fanstruck by Wagner, the living composer he revered above all. In 1860, the young Prince had met his hero in Paris, and invited him to lunch at his family's house in the rue de Berri. It did not go well from Wagner's point of view. "I lunched with [him] one morning," he wrote in his memoirs. "I heard him emit fantastical ideas that music provoked in him. He insisted on trying to convince me of the correctness of his interpretation of Beethoven's Symphony in A major [the seventh], whose last movement, he contended, described a shipwreck, stage by stage."

Polignac's own music was the opposite of Wagnerian: he sought to create a musical equivalent of *pleinairisme* and wanted his compositions to sound as if they were being sung "on the prairie." He also believed that he had invented the octatonic scale, unaware that it had been used in the folk music of various continents, and even introduced "officially" by Rimsky-Korsakov in his opera *Sadko*. Polignac's music is little played nowadays, except for an occasional song.

After Pozzi's death, Montesquiou wrote in his memoirs with uncharacteristic straightforwardness and self-knowledge:

> I have never met a man as seductive as Pozzi. I never saw him being anything other than his smiling, affable, incomparable self . . . For someone as devoted as I am to the aristocratic pleasure of displeasing others, it was a lesson to witness the unfailing smile of a man who made such good use of it, and who would take it to the grave with him. Pozzi had an art of pleasing that no one could match.

Pozzi's progress from Bergerac boy to Parisian high society was a triumph of intellect, character, ambition, professionalism and, yes, a seductive charm that worked on both men and women; he had a bedside manner as comforting to the mutilated *poilu* as to the hypochondriacal countess. What is surprising, given the frenetic, rancorous, bitchy nature of the age, is how comparatively few enemies he made for much of his career. It helped, of course, that he was a doctor (you never know when you might need one); that he was hospitable, generous, rich by marriage, clubbable, inquisitive, cultured and well travelled. But it wasn't just easy private charm behind closed doors. Pozzi was a public figure, a senator, a village mayor, a campaigner with a powerful mind and powerful opinions which many disputed. He was a scientific atheist at a time when the church was fighting hard against the state; a public Dreyfusard in a country split down the middle; a surgical innovator in a profession known for its conservatism; and a Don Juan in a society where not all husbands were complaisant. But it seems to be the case with him that a friend, once gained, was never lost. Montesquiou, whose temperament required a major quarrel every year or so of his life, inflicted only passing, minor *froideurs* on Pozzi.

Though for all their friendship, for all that they were "*Cher et grand ami*" to one another, the Count could never quite stop being a Count. In 1892, he published his first collection of poetry, *Les Chauves-Souris* (*The Bats*—Montesquiou styled himself "The Bat" in imitation of Whistler being "The Butterfly." It had a sumptuous two-tone binding, specially ordered Dutch paper, and a filigree bat as decorative motif. Naturally, it was a very limited edition, but he gave one copy to "my prestigious friend." Such—according to Montesquiou's account—was Pozzi's immense gratitude that he insisted the book should not be just a gift, but the first part of an exchange. And what could—did—Pozzi offer in return? Here is the signed certificate, preserved in Montesquiou's archive, and dated 25 July 1892:

I, the undersigned, associate professor at the faculty of medicine, surgeon at the Lourcine-Pascal Hospital, do hereby solemnly promise to keep Bed Number 1 in my hospital service at the disposition of any sick woman, whether needing surgical or gynaecological treatment, who presents herself as coming from the part of Count Robert de Montesquiou. This pledge will remain valid until 1909, the year when I retire from the hospital service.

S. Pozzi.

It sounds like a piece of late-night larkiness. But Montesquiou writes in his memoirs:

Naturally, I did not abuse such munificence by taking it literally, otherwise by now this man would have sacrificed to me half the fortune of Croesus. But I did make use of it. Many poor suffering women have rightly called me their saviour and do not know that an artistic fantasy which was successful enough to provoke the favour of a man of science is what they owe their recovered health to.

Is it the deal itself which makes one a little queasy; or the fact that the "poor suffering women" treat Montesquiou rather than Pozzi as their benefactor; or the rather smug pleasure the Count gets from his little poetic fantasies being transformed into tangible medical benefit? But there is something beyond this. Montesquiou always demanded gratitude—continuing gratitude—from those lucky enough to have received the imprimatur of his patronage or friendship; and perhaps Pozzi was clever enough to have intuited or observed this, and to have got in first, in a way that would keep the Count sweet for years to come. His son Jean was to become a diplomat, and there is no doubt which side of the family this gene came from.

By the way, that travelling bag Montesquiou gave to Pozzi, the one stamped with a coronet and the letter *R*. Is it aristocratic practice, when giving presents to us commoners, to mark the gift with their emblem and their initial rather than ours? Or might the bag have been an unwanted castoff?

In 1897, Pozzi's sharp-eyed fourteen-year-old daughter Catherine wrote in her diary: "Papa, who is *the* doctor *à la mode*, treats all the most fashionable women; princesses and queens want to be operated on only by him, because he is handsome and intelligent, and as kind as he is skilful." A decade later, a catty chronicler writing under the pseudonym of "Sparklett" in *L'Echo* ended his portrait of Pozzi thus:

> Surgeons are the masters of the universe in our time: what fashionable and famous ladies have they not opened up at least once? They correct and constrain nature; they trim, suppress, add, diminish, make straight. And it is often thanks to their timely intervention that we see women older than half a century giving—and sharing—the impression that they are in the bloom of youth.

Perhaps Pozzi performed some early plastic surgery (though the only example that has come down to us is the removal of a tiny cyst from Robert de Montesquiou's eyelid). More often it was a question of the psychological effect of the escape from danger thanks to surgery which not long previously would have been dangerous if not impossible. This was a time when you could die of appendicitis, and have an almost equal chance of dying from an appendectomy (one of Pozzi's specialities). In 1898, Sarah Bernhardt was diagnosed with a fast-growing ovarian cyst. Naturally, she wanted only "Docteur Dieu" to operate on her. By the time surgery took place, the cyst was "the size of the head of a fourteen-year-old." Pozzi wrote to Montesquiou that Bernhardt was "admirable in her decisiveness, her strength of mind, her courage and her docility . . . She'll be back on the boards in six weeks."

But Pozzi's fame wasn't confined to a coterie of grateful admirers. If, during the first two decades of the twentieth century, you bought a chocolate bar from the grocers Félix Potin, there was an outside chance that you might find in it a small photograph of Dr. Pozzi, the

size and shape of a cigarette card. Between 1898 and 1922 Félix Potin produced three series of *Célébrités Contemporaines*—with around five hundred in each batch—and also sold albums into which you could stick your cards. Pozzi featured in the second series, and was available in two different poses. I have both cards on my desk. Full-bearded and wavy-haired, with a marked widow's peak, he wears a dark jacket: in one, arms folded, he gazes off to our right; in the other, he stares straight back at us. Both poses exude dynamism and self-confidence; "Pozzi, Médecin" each of them proclaims.

The *Célébrités Contemporaines* albums illustrate the rich gallimaufry of fame: here are princes and poets, jockeys and politicians, actresses and popes. Here are Pius IX and Maud Gonne, Paul Verlaine and Mme Curie, Monet and Archduke Franz Ferdinand; the painter Félix Ziem (whose Venetian scenes Pozzi collected), the English swimmer Billington and the Italian cyclist Momo. British representatives include Kipling and Kitchener, General Roberts and Sir Campbell Bannerman, Tennyson, George Prince of Wales, and Percy Woodland, who won the 1903 Grand National on Drumcree.

Fame is predominantly male, and proud of its beards and moustaches: of the 510 featured in the second album, only sixty-five are women. Forty-three of these are "Artistes," in the sense of actresses and cabaret stars (Bernhardt had already starred in the first series); and eleven are members of foreign royal houses, including the Princess of Monaco, who memorably called Pozzi "disgustingly handsome." There are two women writers out of seventy-four (and one of these, George Sand, had been dead for a quarter of a century). It is a sign of medicine's celebrity that Pozzi is one of twenty-three doctors in the

second album: twenty French, two German, and one "Englishman" (i.e., Scot)—Pozzi's old friend Joseph Lister. Here too are Huysmans, Jean Lorrain, Alexandre Dumas *fils*, Léon Daudet and Robert de Montesquiou. There is something eternally satisfying about the notion of the dandyish Count—so superior, so exclusive, so aloof from the middle and lower classes, so removed from the normal materiality of the world—falling out of a chocolate wrapper as a free gift. And the anonymous drudge employed by Félix Potin to supply brief biographical notes sardonically observes that the Count "is the author of numerous verse pieces whose preciosity is only increased by the wilful oddity of the titles he chooses to supply them with."

On the afternoon of Saturday 11 December 1886, Walter Wingfield, who was either fifteen or sixteen, and the son of an English officer posted to Paris, went into the gunshop of M. Chapu in the 16th arrondissement. He was accompanied by his friend Delmas, who was either fourteen or fifteen. Delmas had bought a revolver from the shop the previous day, and was bringing it back for some unspecified reason. Wingfield handed the gun to the armourer without telling him (perhaps he did not know) that there was a bullet in the chamber. The assistant, while inspecting the weapon, pulled the trigger, and the bullet was released straight into Wingfield's abdomen.

As it happened, only two months previously the second Surgical Congress of France had discussed the question of gunshot wounds. Laparotomy—the surgical opening of the abdomen—had always been a hazardous business, but with advances in antisepsis, sterilisation and techniques for stitching, it was now regarded as feasible and appropriate in cases of ovarian and uterine tumours. But with gunshot wounds, there was much debate about its efficacy. Conservative surgeons—who were in the majority—believed that the procedure was more dangerous than simply leaving the patient alone. Younger surgeons, including Pozzi, believed that swift early intervention offered the best hope.

In part, it depended on where the bullet was. Some gunshot wounds to the brain, the lungs and the liver could mend themselves spontaneously. But this was not the case with the abdomen. It also, according to some, depended on the calibre of the bullet: wounds caused by a seven-millimetre bullet were often thought to be "benign," as long as they were left untouched. The calibre of the bullet in the English boy's body, when recovered, was between seven and eight millimetres.

The wounded boy was transported to his home. The doctor called in by the Wingfield family advised that Pozzi be summoned. Examination revealed no exit wound, so the bullet was still in the lower abdomen. A catheter was inserted and the urine came out bloodstained. The operation took place in the family's sitting room; Pozzi's assistants included his younger brother Adrien. He made an incision from navel to pubis, and quickly found the most obvious wound: a four-by-two centimetre rip in the small intestine. It required eleven stitches. Slowly extracting more of the intestine, Pozzi discovered five more lesions, which required a further eighteen stitches. At one point the boy stirred, and "vomited" out a further stretch of gut from the incision in his stomach. More chloroform was administered.

Pozzi proceeded to examine the liver, kidneys and spleen, the stomach, and the *bosselures* of the colon. The bullet's entry wound in the bladder was found and stitched. But the exit wound, if it could be located, would have had to be stitched blind—far too dangerous a manoeuvre. However, it was known that the bladder could cicatrise itself spontaneously. So, after two hours of surgery, Pozzi and his assistants sewed the boy up, leaving a rubber drain in contact with the bladder, and a Nelaton catheter in the penis. The boy was returned to his bed; he spent a peaceful Saturday night and Sunday, while complaining of a pain in his thigh, which was attributed to the presence of the bullet. But during Monday the patient's condition deteriorated, with vomiting and raised temperature; enemas were given, plus morphine and ether. Walter Wingfield died at two o'clock on the Tuesday morning, probably from a paralysis of the intestine leading to a reabsorption of toxic matter.

The epigraph to *A Rebours* is from the fourteenth-century Flemish mystic Jan van Ruysbroek: "I must rejoice beyond the bounds of time . . . though the world may shudder at my joy, and in its coarseness not know what I mean." Van Ruysbroek's context is purely spiritual, Des Esseintes' context is (initially) aesthetic; yet they run parallel. For Des Esseintes the world is packed with fools and scoundrels; he is besieged by a (Flaubertian) "deluge of human stupidity"; while the newspapers are full of "patriotic or political twaddle." His solution is "a refined Thebaid, a desert hermitage equipped with all modern conveniences, a snugly heated ark on dry land." This he creates for himself in the suburbs of Paris.

What do you do—as a writer—in the face of all this "stupidity" and "coarseness" and "twaddle" (unless you disagree, and redefine or replace those nouns)? For some, like Flaubert, you engage with it, expose it, mock it, make stories out of it: his final, unfinished novel, *Bouvard et Pécuchet*, is a great denunciatory engagement with human folly. Or you can take to the hermitage with or without like-minded others, and pull up the drawbridge. And the poems (for they usually are poems) that you write for your fellow initiates pride themselves on their exclusiveness, also their excludingness. Art becomes a refuge of and for the elect. Flaubert said that he had always tried to live in an ivory tower, but that "a tide of shit" kept breaking against its base and threatening to collapse it. This effluent, its presence and its stink, were important to Flaubert's art.

Others build their ivory towers higher, and either hold their noses or install extractor fans. This can be dangerous—for their art, and for them. Bad smells are good reminders. In 1867, the twenty-five-year-old Mallarmé, writing from Besançon, complains to a friend about the city. He describes a neighbour pointing to a window on the opposite side of the street and saying, "Goodness me! Mme Ramaniet certainly had asparagus yesterday!" "How can you tell?" "From the chamber pot she's put out on her windowsill." Mallarmé comments fastidiously: "Isn't that the provinces in a nutshell? Its curiosity, its preoccupations, and that ability to see clues in the most meaningless things—and such things, ye gods! Fancy having to admit that humanity, by dint of living on top of one another, has come to such a pass!!" Eight years later, Edmond de Goncourt complained about the poet in his *Journal*:

THE MAN IN THE RED COAT

"Among these exquisites, these dandies of word and syntax, there is a madman madder than the rest, and that is the fastidious Mallarmé, who maintains that one should never begin a sentence with a mono-syllable . . . This excessive fastidiousness dulls the minds of the most gifted of writers, and distracts them . . . from all the vital, great, warm things that give life to a book." The gulf between realist prose and symbolist poetry could not have been starker.

When Carson repeatedly asks Wilde if *A Rebours* is "a sodomitical book," Wilde first answers, "Most definitely not," then "No," and the third time asks Carson to describe what he means by the phrase. "You don't know?" asks Carson. "I don't know," replies Wilde. Though four years previously he had told a new friend, the Guatemalan diplomat and writer Enrique Gomez Carrillo, that "I have the same sickness as Des Esseintes."

From Huysmans to Des Esseintes to Wilde to Dorian Gray to Edward Carson QC, MP: it is a strange zigzag between fact and fiction, truth and law, France and England. But to answer Carson: *A Rebours* might be classified as "a sodomitical book" in the narrow sense that homosexuality is briefly referred to—and indulged in—by the pro-tagonist without explicit or implicit condemnation from a moralising author. Yet the novel is all much, much stranger than that. *A Rebours* is more about renunciation than indulgence; and indulgence of the sort Carson would criminally condemn is swiftly dealt with during an eight-page prologue covering thirty years. The story—though that is a blunt term for an exotic and wandering text—only starts when Des Esseintes has become disabused by both the social and the sexual life, by all the stupidity and twaddle and coarseness of the world. At one point, deludedly imagining that they live on a higher plane, he seeks out the company of writers. Another mistake: he is revolted by their spite and mean-mindedness, by their empty worship of success and money.

Des Esseintes' seclusion is not exactly austere—his "only" luxuries are rare books and fresh flowers (and having silent servants to wait upon his needs); but it is an attempt to live away from the world, surrounded not by false people but by genuine intellectual and artistic interests. His musings and his memories run alongside a growing spiritual crisis in which a return to the church is both completely impossible and the only feasible solution.

Barbey d'Aurevilly said that after writing *A Rebours*, Huysmans would have to choose between "the muzzle of a pistol and the foot of the Cross." Huysmans certainly never fought a duel, and probably didn't even own a pistol. Eight years later, in the course of a retreat at the Abbey of Notre Dame d'Igny, he was received back into the church. Wilde also went through a spiritual crisis during which Rome called, and he received the last sacraments on his deathbed. But Wilde, like his characters, was out there in the world, enjoying it much more than renouncing it. A dandy needs the eyes of others just as a great talker needs the ears of others.

A Rebours is largely plotless in any traditional sense, and virtually dialogue free; while its "characters" are memories of characters. Its "English" offspring, *The Picture of Dorian Gray*, is extremely talky—many of its exchanges read like stage dialogue rather than novelistic conversation—and stuffed with bits of plot, some of which are pure hokum. Leave aside the Wildean glitterdust, and the story might be by Stevenson or Conan Doyle.

Lord Henry Wotton, *porte-parole* of Wilde's artistic precepts in the novel, says at its end: "Art has no influence upon action." Auden would subsequently agree: "Poetry makes nothing happen." The line can be haughty—Art is above the mere mechanics of the world; or it can be modest and defeatedly pragmatic—no one takes any notice of Art, so let's not pretend. Lord Henry is specifically defending himself against Dorian Gray's complaint (or charge) that by giving him a copy of *A Rebours*, he has instigated his friend's corruption, leading him into vanity, sinfulness, debauchery, indifference and murder. No, no, replies Lord Henry: "The books that the world calls immoral are books that show the world its own shame." Even if this seems flatly contradicted by the very novel in which the line occurs.

Another riposte to the maxim that "art has no influence on action" might go like this. Wilde reads *A Rebours* on his honeymoon. He writes his own thematically derivative version, in the course of which Lord Henry gives *A Rebours* to Gray. The book corrupts the man (who does not, of course, "exist"). These two books, however, give Edward Carson QC key leverage in his forensic destruction of Oscar Wilde. *A Rebours*, *The Picture of Dorian Gray*, Reading Gaol. Another demonstration of the law of unintended consequence.

When Montesquiou met Whistler during that visit to London, the Count started imitating the artist, copying his facial hair, dress, gestures, voice, wit and taste. When Proust met Montesquiou, he started copying the Count, consciously or unconsciously, in his letters and gestures, and in a way of tapping the foot. Proust even began to raise his hand to his mouth when he laughed—though Montesquiou only did this to hide his unsightly teeth.

The dandy is self-created; the aesthete too. Both pursue taste, and the perfection of taste. Do they in this way complete themselves, or construct something inherently false? Or both at the same time? Count

Boni de Castellane, a heterosexual version of Montesquiou, and therefore one who, according to the Count's biographer, "lacked the detachment which true dandyism exacts," put it this way: "Robert pushes his gift for imitation to the extreme of imitating himself."

The dandy, the aesthete and the decadent all loved scents. *A Rebours* contains a whole chapter devoted to their history, manufacture, meaning and impact. Wilde gives a fat paragraph to them in *The Picture*. But their fascination lay not just in the arcane sensuous pleasure they provide. As Huysmans puts it: "One aspect of this art of perfumery had fascinated [Des Esseintes] more than any other, and that was the degree of accuracy it was possible to reach in imitating the real thing." A scent is as constructed, as plausible and as charming as a dandy.

However, it is not just the dandy who gets imitated. Pozzi was a friend of the Proust family: he invited the young Marcel to his first "dinner in town" at the place Vendôme, and later helped him avoid military service; while Marcel's younger brother Robert was Pozzi's assistant at the Broca Hospital from 1904 to 1914. He was a brilliant surgeon, who in 1901 carried out the first successful prostatectomy in France. In homage, generations of medical students used to refer to it as a "proustatectomy." After describing Proust's achievements, Pozzi's biographer adds drily: "Madame Robert Proust quickly came to the conclusion that her husband's admiration for his patron was excessive, when he pushed imitation to the point of seriously unsettling their marital equilibrium by his liaison with a certain Mme F . . ."

Pozzi with the heavily moustached Robert Proust

Life imitates life; art imitates life too, of course; but more rarely, life imitates art. According to the novelist and critic André Billy, "After Huysmans' novel appeared, [Montesquiou] took to frequenting that tavern near the Gare Saint-Lazare where one had the illusion of being transported to London." This is exquisitely satisfying for about three milliseconds, until we realise a) that the Count was annoyed by the shadow presence of Des Esseintes in his life; and b) would have thought it vulgar in the extreme to be sitting around in an English-themed pub hoping to be mistaken for a fictional character.

Some names and works recur pressingly in the fin-de-siècle litany, both as precursors and exemplars: Baudelaire, Flaubert, Antinous (Hadrian's lover), Salomé, Gustave Moreau, Odilon Redon, Parsifal, Burne-Jones, plus a supporting cast of androgynes, sadists, cruel mythological women and cruel English milords. The Flaubert cited and revered in the immediate decades after his death in 1880 was less the novelist of *Madame Bovary*, *L'Education sentimentale* and *Bouvard et Pécuchet* (in which guise he took us from the perfection of realism to the beginnings of modernism); rather, it was the author of *Salammbô*, *La Tentation de saint-Antoine*, and two-thirds of the *Trois contes*. This latter, technicolour Flaubert revelled in the historical exotic, in strange lands and bejewelled princesses, in cruelty and violence. Even Prince Edmond de Polignac wrote a suite of incidental music for *Salammbô*.

Flaubert's favourite living painter was Gustave Moreau, who also revelled in the exotic, the bejewelled, the violent. Flaubert saw in him something far more than a classy historical illustrator (which was the critical charge against Moreau from the beginning); he was a "poet-painter" whose work did not explain or describe, but rather "set you dreaming." The other side of Moreau that appealed to Flaubert was his ability (not unlike that of a certain novelist) to shut himself up in his studio, to ignore exterior goings-on, and create his own bustling, burnished visions. There was also a moment of creative conjunction: when Flaubert was planning his story *Hérodias*, he visited the 1876 Salon, where Moreau showed four pictures, two being of Salomé. It was less a moment of inspiration, more one of parallel endorsement.

In *A Rebours*, Huysmans has Des Esseintes assert what is doubtless his own opinion—that Flaubert's splendour is most fully expressed when

Leaving our petty modern civilisation far behind, he conjured up the Asiatic glories of distant epochs, their mystic ardours and doldrums, the aberrations resulting from their idleness, the brutalities arising from their boredom—that oppressive boredom which emanates from opulence and prayer even before their pleasures have been fully enjoyed.

L'Apparition, Gustave Moreau (1876)

Huysmans also devoted half a chapter to Gustave Moreau and (since anyone can own anything in fiction) grants Des Esseintes personal possession of those very two pictures of Salomé exhibited at the Salon eight years previously. One is an oil of the princess dancing—which Henry James judged one of the "lions of the Salon." The other is a watercolour called *L'Apparition*, which shows the scene after the execution. The Baptist's head has risen from its charger and hovers in midair, blood still streaming from its neck, and a grim, resentful look on its face; light sprays from a halo around it, irradiating the largely unclad Salomé, who extends an arm to ward off this rebuking vision. Only she sees it: executioner, musician, Herodias and Herod are impassive, reflecting on what they have just experienced. "Like the old King," Huysmans writes, "Des Esseintes felt overwhelmed, subjugated, stunned when he looked at this dancing girl, who was less majestic, less haughty, but more seductive than the Salomé of the oil painting."

Huysmans' novel came out in 1884; Lorrain's *Monsieur de Phocas* in 1901. In between, Moreau had died, in 1898, and left his house, studio and its contents to the state. So, rather than Monsieur de Phocas having to buy his own paintings to experience full rapture, he was able to visit the newly established Musée Gustave Moreau in the rue de la Rochefoucauld near the Gare Saint-Lazare. And there Lorrain's narrator discovers

the painter and philosopher whose art has always troubled me more than any other! Has any other man been so haunted by the symbolic cruelty of defunct religions and the divine debauchery that was once adored in long-lost lands? . . . The master sorcerer has bewitched his contemporaries, contaminating the entire fin-de-siècle of bankers and stockbrokers with a morbid and mystical ideal.

That last phrase is a dream-wish (like having Sarah Bernhardt appear in your play): most bankers and stockbrokers escaped the fin-de-siècle unseduced by Moreau. It's also true that few artists have lost their lustre, and their centrality, as quickly as he has done. Put Moreau beside Odilon Redon, as many did at the time, and more than a century on it is Redon who speaks the more strongly and directly. Moreau's work looks back to history, myth and scripture; it feels literary, grand, poised—"sad and scholarly" in Huysmans' phrase. But it is also inert; that first criticism of him has not gone away. Nowadays, he sets far fewer dreaming. Redon's work is spooky and free-floating, coming from and trained at our troubled unconscious. Moreau celebrates terror that comes from outside, from priest and Tetrarch and invader; Redon celebrates terror that lives within us, and that the twentieth century will learn to excavate. And in parallel, the Flaubert held in higher regard today is the "French" rather than the "Asiatic" one. Nothing dates like excess.

Dated: how the past must sometimes hate the present, and the present the future—that unknowable, careless, cruel, slighting, dismissive, unappreciative future—a future not worthy of being the future to the present. What I said at the beginning—that art always has time on its side—was mere hopefulness, a sentimental delusion. Some art has time on its side; but which? Time imposes a brutal triage. Moreau, Redon and Puvis de Chavannes: each once appeared to be the future of French painting. Puvis now seems—for a further historical period anyway—to be alone and palely loitering. Redon and Moreau spoke to their time with powerfully different metaphors, and the following century preferred Redon.

Huysmans greatly admired both Moreau and Degas. The two painters had been friends in Italy in the late 1850s, and their friendship had survived, if precariously, their artistic divergence. But Huysmans knew early on, before any other serious critic, that Degas was "the greatest artist we possess in France today" (*L'Art moderne*, 1882).

A barbed exchange between old friends. Moreau to Degas: "Are you really proposing to revive painting by means of the dance?" Degas to Moreau: "And you—are you proposing to renovate it with jewellery?"

At Moreau's funeral in 1898, Montesquiou sat next to Degas, and reported him as saying: "It was quite difficult to stay friends with a man who spent the whole time withdrawing his feet, out of fear that you might step on them."

Degas had been planning to establish a museum of his own work after his death. Then he went to the rue de la Rochefoucauld to see what Moreau had done. It struck him as something closer to a mausoleum than a museum, and he immediately abandoned his own project.

Eighty years after the publication of *Monsieur de Phocas*, and, like most beginners, unaware of the limits of my own originality, I set a key scene of my first novel in the Musée Gustave Moreau. It was one of the "favourite haunts" of my young male protagonist. He found Moreau's art "beguiling," especially when compared to Redon's "vapid, washy maundering." How little that young man knew. Now I realise that he was quite wrong—at least, for the time being.

Five Glimpses of Pozzi

Pozzi in the Saleroom

The libraries of two famous poets, Heredia and Emile Verhaeren, are auctioned off in Paris a week apart. André Gide writes in his journal:

> I go to the first day of the first sale and to the second sale. Between them a severe *grippe* keeps me in the house. In the auction room

I fight for a few books against Pozzi and Hanotaux . . . Most of the books are pushed way beyond their value. You let yourself be enticed into pursuing books that you only half want or don't want at all.

(A classic piece of self-consolation by a losing bidder. Overpriced—didn't really want it anyway!)

Pozzi in the Salon

Pozzi is sighted by Elisabeth de Gramont chez Mme Straus: "Professor Pozzi was . . . very serious, and busy Hellenising, having just come from chopping up the tender flesh of women."

Pozzi in the Smoking Room

Dr. Robin, a celebrated anatomist and professor of histology, of a previous generation, is invited to dine at the Pozzis'. He is astonished

3ᵉ COLLECTION FÉLIX POTIN

COLETTE
FEMME DE LETTRES

to discover an array of young painters, all with curls in their hair and gardenias in their buttonholes. They are joined by the actor Coquelin the Younger. As soon as they get to the smoking room, Coquelin, who has never met Robin before, asks him straight out what might be the secret, or the procedure, in order to be able to have sex for longer than anyone else in the world. Robin is shocked. Pozzi's contribution (if any) is not recorded.

Pozzi Abroad

Colette is at Bayreuth, in the procession of rustic carriages making their way towards the theatre, when she spots "Doctor Pozzi, dressed all in white, with the beard of a sultan and the eye of a houri, seated between Catulle Mendès— garrulous, beer-bloated, as reddish-blond as Siegfried—and Wagner the Younger, small, with a big head and a low-slung bottom, formidably ubiquitous."

COLLECTION FELIX POTIN

CATULLE MENDES

Pozzi at the Medical Students' Ball

The Ball is held in the "immense" salle Bullier and contained scenes of "orgiastic splendour," according to one of its participants; this despite the presence on a makeshift stage of various professors and hospital heads of service. "Pozzi makes his entrance, as magnificent as a Doge in his scarlet robe—there are cheers, shouts, clamours . . . At one point he gets up from his seat, and a certain silence descends on the room. But he doesn't give a speech. Instead, he takes advantage of the opportunity to reach down into the crowd, hoist a naked girl up on to the stage, kiss her full on the mouth, and then, turning to the rioting crowd, make a gesture as if to say, 'Do as I do.'"

The "scarlet robe" is not his famous "red coat," but rather his professorial attire, trimmed with ermine.

In 1884, three years after *Dr. Pozzi at Home*, Sargent painted an equally swaggery, and more openly erotic, portrait generally known as *Mme X*. Her name was Amélie Gautreau, the half-creole daughter of New

Orleans gentry, who was brought to Paris as a child and married off, at nineteen, to a banker twice her age. Sargent posed her in a black dress, standing by a side table against a brown background. Black, brown and flesh—plus the gilt of her shoulder straps—are the picture's only colours; though the flesh is not the normal creamy hue. Sargent noted that her skin was "uniform lavender or blotting paper in colour all over." Her hair is up, and she turns away to her left in disdainful, or at least indifferent, profile. But her body is turned towards us, and the erotic element is emphasised by this contrast of availabilities. Her dress is low cut, her shoulders and arms bare. Her left hand lifts her skirt very lightly (not enough to show even the end of a shoe à la Pozzi, but still suggestive); while Sargent cunningly poses her right arm twisting as it rests on the table edge, thereby turning the inside of her arm towards us, in a kind of intimacy. The gentle dents on the inside of each elbow are subtly accentuated. In its original form, the implicit eroticism was made explicit, because Sargent had painted her right

2° COLLECTION FELIX POTIN

HELLEU
PEINTRE

strap falling from her shoulder. This detail—which does sound symbolically blatant—caused outrage when the picture was shown at the 1884 Salon, and legend has it that the scandal caused the painter to flee from Paris to London. But 1884 was also the year Sargent met Henry James, who urged him to cross the Channel not to escape scandal but for richer commissions and better subject matter: this he did in late 1886.

Mme Gautreau sat—or stood—for other society painters: for Paul Helleu (whose fluency brought him the nickname "the steam-powered Watteau") and Antonio de la Gandara. She was by most accounts conventional and

Madame X, John Singer Sargent (1884)

rather dull, and Sargent was annoyed by her manifest boredom when posing: perhaps this at some level pushed him to elevate her into the siren she wasn't. After protest by both the subject and her mother, he repainted the fallen strap back onto her shoulder. Perhaps he also named her "Mme X"—when many would have known who she was anyway—as another hint of naughtiness. Amélie Gautreau and her husband had no great social standing, so it was easy for the smugly puritanical to disapprove. In the wake of the "scandal" (hardly much of one compared to what else was going on) Mme X retreated to Brittany and to an increasing melancholy.

It was not just her picture people stared at: she (and her looks) had become a kind of tourist site. While he was painting her, Sargent invited Oscar Wilde to examine her:

My dear Mr. Wilde,

Will you come to my studio tomorrow afternoon or Thursday morning?

You will find me still working at my portrait of Me [Mme] xxx which will go to the Salon . . . when it is finished and good . . .

You will see my sitter who looks like Phryne.

(Phryne was a fourth-century-BC Greek courtesan, wit and beauty, tried for impiety.)

A few months after *Mme X* was publicly shown, Pozzi invited Montesquiou and Edmond de Polignac to tea, where they might observe "Mme Gautreau of the swan neck." But Paris being Paris, and Pozzi Pozzi, the rumour grew—posthumously, it seems, in this case—that he had been Mme Gautreau's lover. It ran for most of the last century: the swaggery art critic Robert Hughes was still running with it in the 1980s when *Mme X* and *Dr. Pozzi at Home* appeared together in a show at the Whitney. Such evidence as we have suggests that the Pozzis and the Gautreaus were on light social terms with one another—which doesn't either exclude or imply anything.

One thing we can know, however, is that around this time Pozzi bought a much less notorious portrait by Sargent: *Madame Gautreau Drinking a Toast*, painted in 1882–83. It is informal, more freely painted, and charming rather than confrontational. Again the sitter is shown in self-absorbed profile, but facing the opposite way; her hair is again up, she wears a black dress with straps, and her shoulders are lightly veiled in a gauzy material. Her bare arm extends across the otherwise unoccupied centre of the picture towards a vertical pile-up of items on the left-hand side: at the bottom, a splash of pink flowers; in the

Madame Gautreau Drinking a Toast, John Singer Sargent (1882–83)

middle, a hand grasping a champagne glass; at the top, a bright square (either window or lighting). The work stayed in Pozzi's collection until his death.

We can also know that—as was often the case—Pozzi acted professionally with those he knew socially. He treated the Gautreaus' daughter Louise on several occasions, and operated on Amélie—possibly for an ovarian cyst—in the mid-1880s.

"We cannot know." If used sparingly, this is one of the strongest phrases in the biographer's language. It reminds us that the suave study-of-a-life we are reading, for all its detail, length and footnotes, for all its factual certainties and confident hypotheses, can only be a public version of a public life, and a partial version of a private life. Biography is a collection of holes tied together with string, and nowhere more so than with the sexual and amatory life. For some, there is nothing easier than understanding the sex life of someone you've never met, and easier still when they're conveniently dead; or in posthumously adding another conquest to the dance card of a known Don Juan. Others simplify things by maintaining that human sexual habits have always been more or less the same, the only variables being the degree of hypocrisy and cover-up.

But sex is a world in which self-deception can so easily present itself as objective fact, and "brutal honesty" is no more likely to be true than shy evasiveness or sentimental melodrama as an explanation of what really took place. Oscar Wilde may have been a "posing somdomite," but such evidence as we have suggests he preferred intercrural sex, and if so was not technically a "somdomite" at all. We cannot know. Sarah Bernhardt was a nymphomaniac. Oh, but she was also incapable of orgasm. Until she had the problem fixed by means of an ingenious surgical implant—which is reliably attested by that "hysterical duplicitous gossip" Jean Lorrain, and then recorded in the *Journal* of Edmond de Goncourt, whose views on women were old-fashioned to say the least. We cannot know. Robert de Montesquiou was a flamboyant homosexual, except that his biographer thinks he was too coldly fastidious to indulge his Hellenic urges, while Pozzi's biographer thinks he may have been impotent from around 1884, and remained so. We cannot know. Pozzi had a reputation as "an incorrigible seducer," a doctor who slept with his patients, who may even have used his consultations as foreplay. He also kept all the letters he had received from women over a sexual career of half a century or more. Yet after his death, Mme Pozzi instructed her son Jean to burn them all. So we cannot know a large amount. As to the failure—the amatory failure—of the Pozzis' life together, we only have his account. What exactly did Pozzi mean by taking "vigorous, almost violent, action" on their honeymoon? What did she make of this sudden behavioural change from the Pozzi of his wooing letters? Was this when she started coldly imagining the possibility of a separation? We cannot know. We may speculate as long as we also admit that our speculations are novelistic, and that the novel has almost as many forms as there are forms of love and sex.

"We cannot know"; but "This is what they said, anyway." Gossip is true in the sense that it repeats what someone believes, or what someone they know believes; or, if they have invented it themselves, what they would like to believe. So the gossip is true to the lie, at least, and truly revealing of the character and mentality of the gossiper. That ardent Francophile Ford Madox Ford habitually displayed a passionate disregard for what had actually happened. Sample lie: he claimed that he had attended Dreyfus's second trial at Rennes in 1899—where he might have run into Dr. Pozzi—and that this experience had helped him understand France more profoundly; whereas all through that time he was living quietly on the Kentish coast. Ford's biographer Max Saunders argues wisely and sympathetically that it is a question of "asking less whether what Ford says is *true*, and more what it means."

Goncourt used to ponder the source of Jean Lorrain's torrent of calumny; Lorrain himself was equally interested in the matter. Writing to Goncourt about a couple whose snobbishness had displeased them both (and they were both snobs themselves, of course, though in more refined ways): "I watch them, and whenever I get the chance, I shall show them my claws and my teeth. After the kiss there is no sweeter pleasure than the bite. Is it my fault that there is a small wild beast inside me which is unleashed by indignation and injustice?" The implicit smugness in this hints at a third motive: the pleasure the gossiper gives to the listener.

On the other hand, none of this means that the truth is negotiable. Wilde once declared that "between two truths, the falser is truer." But this is mere sophistry posing as paradoxical wisdom.

Montesquiou didn't like *Dr. Pozzi at Home*. Picking up on the fact that the doctor kept his image largely shrouded from both the light and prying eyes, the Count wrote: "The picture remained in the dark, and it was not wrong for it to do so. The painter, for some unknown reason, had dressed [Pozzi] all in red, and in addition, for no more apparent reason, made him look like a Valois of Gynaecology." Montesquiou's dislike of Sargent culminated in a printed attack in 1905 which drew applause from Bernard Berenson: "Your exquisite politeness is much more malicious than the brutal criticism of others. I am infinitely grateful to you for having been the first to attack this idol of the Anglo-Saxons." Montesquiou's biographer Jullian also joined in, writing of "this tiresome Bostonian . . . [who] let his talent go to waste, seduced by commissions from millionaires." The arbiter of fashion, the art historian and the biographer were all irked by Sargent's fame, his grand facility, and a public enthusiasm they could do little to deflect.

Montesquiou, while admitting that *Mme X* was a masterpiece, thought it Sargent's only one. He summed up: "Taste is a very special thing . . . Mr. Sargent, who is a great painter, does not have any." This is where the mere aesthete fails in the face of art: not understanding that to be "great" is in any case to travel way beyond "taste." But it was a common view.

Wilde, for instance, was quick to change his mind about Sargent. In Paris in 1882, he gave the painter a collection of poems by Rennell Rodd (with an introduction by Wilde). He inscribed it: "To my friend, John S. Sargent, with deep admiration of his work." And then (in French) Wilde's marketing tag: "Nothing is true but the beautiful." However, by the next year, in a public lecture, he was calling Sargent's art "vicious and meretricious."

But then others changed their mind about Wilde—and before his trial too. Conan Doyle met him at a small dinner party when the two of them were first being noticed. He remembered it as "a golden evening." Wilde, he wrote,

> towered above us all, and yet he had the art of seeming interested in all that we could say. He had delicacy of feeling and tact, for

the monologue man, however clever, can never be a gentleman at heart. He took as well as gave, but what he gave was unique. He had a curious precision of statement, a delicate flavour of humour, and a trick of small gestures to illustrate his meaning, which were peculiar to himself.

Doyle met him again a few years later, by which time Fame had struck: "He gave me the impression of being mad. He asked me, I remember, if I had seen some play of his which was running. I answered that I had not. He said: 'Ah, you must go. It is wonderful. It is genius!' All this with the gravest face. Nothing could have been more different from his early gentlemanly instincts."

In 1882, Sargent sent *Dr. Pozzi at Home* to the Royal Academy in London, where it made no impact at all. But time was on Sargent's side, not Montesquiou's. Henry James, who in the meantime had met and hosted the painting's subject, discussed the artist in an article for *Harper's Magazine* in 1887 (revised in 1893). He notes first that Sargent has been fortunate enough to paint more women than men, and "therefore that he has had but a limited opportunity to reproduce that generalised grand air with which his view of certain figures of gentlemen invests the model." This sounds like wily diminishment, but James immediately cites as the finest of Sargent's male portraits those of Carolus-Duran and of Pozzi; the latter being "splendid" and "an admirable example" of this aspect of the painter's art:

In each of these cases the model has been of a gallant pictorial type, one of the types which strike us as made for portraiture (which is by no means the way of all), as especially appears, for instance, in the handsome hands and frilled wrists of M. Carolus, whose cane rests in his fine fingers as if it were the hilt of a rapier.

Carolus-Duran, John Singer Sargent (1879)

In case there is any doubt, James goes on:

I have alluded to his superb *Dr. Pozzi*, to whose very handsome, still youthful head and slightly artificial posture he has given so fine a French cast that he might be excused if he should, even on remoter pretexts, find himself reverting to it. This gentleman stands up in his brilliant red dressing gown with the *prestance* of a princely Van Dyck.

In the same article, James also reflects on Sargent's *Mme X*. He calls it "an experiment of a highly original kind" in which "the painter has had . . . in regard to what Mr. Ruskin would call the 'rightness' of his attempt, the courage of his opinion." He dismisses the "unreasoned scandal" the picture excited when first shown as

an idea sufficiently amusing in the light of some manifestations of the plastic effort to which, each year, the Salon stands sponsor. This superb picture, noble in conception and masterly in line, gives to the figure represented something of the high relief of the profiled image on great friezes. It is a work to take or leave, as the phrase is, and one in regard to which the question of liking or disliking comes promptly to be settled. The author has never gone further in being boldly and consistently himself.

James's praise often seems too complicatedly expressed—and enshrouded, as it were, in what one might call bubblewrap—to be unambiguous; but in the present case this is—I am almost sure—a forceful endorsement.

—

If Montesquiou felt himself dogged and betrayed by the literary shadow versions of himself out there, a painted portrait ought to have been a less complicated matter. A portrait is generally both more accurate and more flattering to the sitter (who often, after all, pays the bill); it is entirely about the subject, who doesn't get mixed and mashed with other people, real and imagined. And sometimes sitter and artist are already friends, which helps. This was the case when Whistler painted *Arrangement in Black and Gold* (1891–92). The two men's aesthetic intimacy helped produce a marvellous image of the Count coming towards the viewer in a haughty, challenging fashion, right arm advanced and holding his stick, left arm draped with his cloak. And Montesquiou knew that Whistler knew that it was a marvellous image. He had watched the painter at work, watched how he seemed to draw the painted image out from within the canvas, rather than imposing it upon the surface from without.

Then, as Whistler saw this image he had created converging with that of the living man in front of him, he shouted "the most beautiful of all the sayings that ever came from a painter's mouth"—according to Montesquiou. It was this: "Look at me again for a moment *and you will look at yourself for ever.*" It was a high moment of self-praise, of course, but also a reassurance to a fellow aesthete: art will endure, and as long as my *Arrangement in Black and Gold* endures, you will not die, and neither shall I. The Count was so pleased with his portrait that he would stand beside it and lecture on its virtues to small groups of aspirant aesthetes—women more than men, usually.

But whatever Whistler shouted at Montesquiou, the American's portrait ceased at some point to be the best-known image of the Count. As a painting, it began slowly to collapse towards darkness, thanks to bitumen in the black paint. But it was also superseded in the public

Arrangement in Black and Gold, James McNeill Whistler (1891–92)

mind by the image Boldini created in 1897, in which the dandy looks even more dandyish (and hence perhaps less challenging). He is turned away from us in half-profile, exquisitely suited and gloved; he holds a walking stick diagonally across his body, and appears to be inspecting its blue porcelain handle, while twisting his left wrist towards us so that we may admire his matching blue porcelain cufflinks. He brandishes the cane like a sceptre—which might be a reference to that first line of one of his poems: "I am the sovereign of transitory things." This was the image on the cover of the Penguin edition of *Against Nature* which I bought in 1967—a seeming confirmation that Montesquiou "was" Des Esseintes.

Art may commemorate the sitter, but may also change him, even cancel him, despite the wishes of both parties. At the lowest level of competent representation, there is less of a problem. But when high talent, let alone genius, comes in, the painter is preparing an image which will represent the sitter after death, and thus in some way replace the living person. "Look at me again for a moment *and you will look at yourself for ever*"—yes, for ever, and as you are now, not as you will be tomorrow, and the day after, and on your deathbed. The painter is turning the look of a few days or weeks into something more powerful than the person left behind. Lucian Freud approached one potential sitter with the words: "I'd be interested in painting

from you." And he explained to another sitter the subject's relationship to the future finished object: "You are here to help it." As if the sitter were merely a useful idiot, temporarily present while the artist pursues a larger aim.

—

And Prince Edmond de Polignac? Where do we find him? Appropriately, given that he was the most invisible and unregistered of the original "strange trio," he is best located in a group portrait by Tissot, in the company of eleven other members of *Le Cercle de la rue Royale* (1868). Each of the dozen members of this gentlemen's club paid 1,000 francs to be included in it. The picture is competent but uninspiring, perhaps because Tissot had to be careful not to privilege one member over another. Some are standing, some sitting, while Polignac is the only one who is positively lounging. He reclines in an armchair, his hat, stick and gloves lolling beneath it; his right hand is in a strange clench, as if he is hearing secret harmonies (or riffing on the octatonic scale). The figure immediately behind the Prince is Charles Haas, the chief model for Proust's Swann. When the picture was complete, the twelve men drew lots to decide who should own it. It was won by Baron Hottinger, and is now in the Musée d'Orsay.

In *A Rebours*, Huysmans notes how the French aristocracy has sunk into either imbecility or depravity. It is dying from the degeneracy of its scions, whose faculties have deteriorated progressively with each generation until "they now consisted of the instincts of gorillas at work in the skulls of grooms and jockeys." Another cause of this noble rot has been "wallowing in the mud of lawsuits." Three aristocratic families are cited as examples of this vice: the Choiseul-Praslins, the Chevreuses, and the Polignacs. It is, of course, rarely easier to harden the heart than when told of the poverty of the aristocracy. There they are, down to their last castle, rain coming in, servants stuffing their shoes with newspaper, and so on. And such loss of lucre is usually produced less by revolution and taxes than by extravagant living, gambling, idleness and financial incompetence.

Montesquiou and Polignac came from equally distinguished families

Le Cercle de la rue Royale (detail), James Tissot (1868)

but had very different personalities. Montesquiou was supercilious, short-tempered and privilege-assuming: the sort of aristocrat who effortlessly encourages revolution. Polignac was gentle, whimsical and rather hopeless: the sort of aristocrat who seems to do little harm, and might even provoke a kindly pity. He was also quietly witty: "So-and-so," he once mused, "can't possibly be intelligent, because he's never ill." He had no urge for self-transformation, let alone self-imitation, like the Count. He was content, as in Tissot's painting, to sit at the edge of things, lost in thought. But he did have the old Polignac problem: money. He was by nature prey to swindlers and charlatans, and his final inheritance was soon lost on the stock market. By 1892, he was fifty-seven, and living in a small apartment in the rue Washington (yes, there was still an apartment, and it was in the 8th arrondissement, but even so). Two nephews found him sitting there in the only remaining chair after debt collectors had stripped the place of its furniture and fittings. The Prince had a knitted cap on his head and was wrapped in a shawl. Everything, he said, was gone, taken.

Yet he did have one inalienable, tradeable asset: his princeliness. And so, as in the novels of Henry James and Edith Wharton, there was an evident and familiar solution: find an American heiress. Montesquiou and his cousin the Countess Greffulhe considered the market and came up with a prime target: Winnaretta Singer, whose enormous fortune came from sewing machines. She had been previously married to a different prince, but Rome had granted her a divorce. As a foreign-born ex-princess, Winnaretta currently had dubious standing in the *beau monde*. Marriage would be a win for both parties: she would regain status; he would regain money.

There was one possible impediment, which might have been thwarting to those lower down the social scale: Polignac all his life had been a discreet but known homosexual. Yet, far from being an impediment, this proved to be his unique selling point, because Singer, in her turn, was a discreet but known lesbian. According to family legend, on the night of her wedding to Prince Louis de Scey-Montbéliard, Winnaretta Singer had climbed on top of an armoire and, brandishing an umbrella, shouted down at her ardent bridegroom, "If you come near me, I am going to kill you." The Vatican would have been informed of the non-consummation, but this piquant detail was probably suppressed. When Winnaretta and her new prince were married on 15 December 1893, he was fifty-nine and she was twenty-eight.

Montesquiou was well pleased with his negotiating strategy, and its result; but this now became a problem. The Count and the Prince had been friends for eighteen years; at the beginning, Polignac's biographer surmises, they might have been briefly, possibly (we cannot know), lovers. But as Montesquiou knew much better than Polignac, a friendship is only a stage on the way to a quarrel. The Count resented two things: first, that the couple (but especially Winnaretta) were not sufficiently grateful to him—and as the Count's circle knew, sometimes even unending gratitude was not enough. The second annoyance was that the couple, against all the normal rules and expectations of such an aristocratic horse trade, made a success of their marriage. The Polignac family had warned Singer that she would be joining herself to "an unbearable maniac." But the couple seemed genuinely happy with the arrangement—perhaps starting with low expectations helped. They liked and amused one another; they were passionate patrons of music; while the pieces Edmond wrote could be now staged in Winnaretta's atelier. And the Prince would go to Bayreuth with his Princess rather than the Count. But they also took separate holidays, which was socially acceptable, and allowed them space for their separate sexual explorations.

Couples are always comparing their own situations with those of

Self-portrait, Winnaretta Singer (1885)

other couples. Here were the Polignacs, beginning from a social and financial arrangement and ending in genuine affection; there were the Pozzis, beginning in what felt like passionate love, and quickly ending in social arrangement. And thirdly, here were the "Montesquious." In his relationship with Yturri, the Count was the hot-tempered boss and Yturri the emollient fixer; also organiser, explainer, middleman and reporter from the sexual hunt. Montesquiou also makes the point—twice—in his memoirs that Yturri lived "in the same street," rather than it being a matter of "two gentlemen sharing." This imbalance between the partners isn't surprising, let alone regrettable: given Montesquiou's temperament and self-regard, it was doubtless the only relationship of which he was capable. And he is unlikely to have felt anything as straightforward as envy for the Polignacs. But perhaps at some level he intuited that relationships could have an equality and a dynamic and a good humour to them which might be beyond his emotional skill.

If so, such feelings would have been subsumed into his anger at not being properly and lengthily thanked. Who did this American woman think she was? The Count's rancour expressed itself in poetic squibs and journalistic asides. It also had great longevity. In 1910, seventeen years after the marriage he helped fix, and nine years after Edmond de Polignac's death, another fashionable American lesbian in Paris, the painter Romaine Brooks, exhibited her portrait of Winnaretta. In a review for *Le Figaro* awash with cantankerous snobbishness, the Count wrote that Brooks had made the Princesse de Polignac look like "a Nero, a thousand times more cruel than the original, who dreams of seeing her victims pricked to death by sewing-machines." (Alas, the picture is currently missing.)

Perhaps Montesquiou, by birth and nature accustomed to using and commanding others, felt that for once, Polignac and Singer had somehow used and commanded him. And now, in another way, they did command him. Musical performances in the salon of the Princesse de Polignac ran for half a century. The first concert, on 22 May 1888, featured Fauré, Chabrier and D'Indy, played and conducted by Fauré, Chabrier and D'Indy. The last, on 3 July 1939, featured Bach, Mozart and Dinu Lipatti, played by Clara Haskil and Lipatti, with an orchestra conducted by Charles Munch.

The guest list glitters like a gold-painted tortoise studded with precious stones. Composers present: Wagner, Stravinsky, Prokofiev, Chausson, Fauré, D'Indy, Auric, Milhaud. Conductors: Klemperer, Beecham, Markevich, Munch. Fashionable painters: Boldini, Bonnat, Carolus-Duran, Helleu, Clairin, Forain. Writers: Edith Wharton, Proust, Colette, Valéry, Cocteau, Pierre Louÿs, Julien Green, François Mauriac, Rosamond Lehmann. Distinguished others: Mme Jeanne Lanvin, Diaghilev, Bakst, Lady Violet Cunard and Violet Trefusis. There were dozens of Polignacs and Rothschilds, Grand Dukes of Russia, and more Princes and Princesses, Marquesses and Marchionesses, Dukes and Duchesses, Counts and Countesses,

Viscounts and Viscountesses, and Barons and Baronesses than you could shake a stick at.

How an unquarrelsome Montesquiou would have felt at home. But he was invited (or at least accepted) only twice, in 1895. Whereas his friend and cousin Countess Greffulhe went eight times between then and 1903. Pozzi was not there (Pozzi was not quite everywhere), but his daughter Catherine was invited two weeks running in early 1927. On the second occasion she heard "admirable" Rameau, and Chopin "such as to take you out of your body."

Another who made the cut at the Princess's salon, three times, was Paul Hervieu, probably Pozzi's closest literary friend. He was a constant presence at lunches and soirées at the place Vendôme and later the avenue d'Iéna. Hervieu's work was concerned with contemporary moral and emotional dilemmas: adultery, divorce, remarriage. He wrote a novel called *Flirt*, which anatomised "the gently delicious state of soul in which one progresses dangerously from Virtue to Fault"; also a play whose curtain line (historic spoiler alert) was "For the sake of my daughter, I have killed my mother!" In private, he argued for the legalisation of abortion. And he would have studied

COLLECTION FELIX POTIN

PAUL HERVIEU

the Pozzi marriage very carefully. There is also a gnomic if exalted line in Catherine Pozzi's diary in December 1903, when she is twenty-one: "Oh Hervieu! Yes! Oh yes, Hervieu!" But he is not mentioned again, before or afterwards.

In 1905, when the *Code civil* was being rewritten, Hervieu was a member of the committee charged with examining and if necessary redrafting article 212: "Husband and wife owe one another the mutual duty of fidelity, assistance and support." Hervieu suggested to his colleagues the addition of a single word: "love." The committee, presumably content that those three requirements were the most any marriage could be expected to bear, declined to adopt his recommendation. In recent years an extra word has been added to that long-standing trio of duties. However, it is "respect" rather than "love." The romantic British, of course, have always promised to love.

Edmond de Goncourt wrote in his *Journal*: "Little Hervieu has a strange voice. It's like the voice of a sleepwalker made to speak by the man who has hypnotised him." He was no more impressed by Hervieu's work, and that of his colleagues. In 1890, he wrote:

> The novel of high society, as it is currently in vogue, and whose main practitioners are Bourget, Hervieu, Lavedan and even Maupassant, is of no interest: they are writing the monography of nothing. It could perhaps be interesting, but only if produced by a man who truly belongs to high society—born, nourished and raised within it—a man like, for instance, Montesquiou-Fezensac, who would reveal all the arcane secrets of this nothingness . . . As things are, my view is that the novel of high society hasn't even got three years left in it.

This was not a good prediction. Goncourt died in 1896, seventeen years before Proust published the first volume of *A la Recherche*.

Pozzi is remembered, described and painted as a "society doctor," treating foreign royalty, domestic aristocracy, famous actresses, novelists and playwrights. He was all this; but for thirty-five years he worked at the public Lourcine-Pascal Hospital (from 1893, the Broca), and in his early years was forbidden from taking on private patients. Later, he was to see them at weekends. In 1892 Ernest Hart, the journalist and former editor of the *British Medical Journal,* described the Lourcine-Pascal in a series called "Clinical Notes on the Paris Hospitals." He pointed out that ten years previously, when Pozzi arrived, the hospital had been entirely occupied by patients suffering from venereal disease, "for gonorrhoea is very common in the poor population, from which the patients of the hospital are drawn." But after Pozzi took control in 1883, he added a series of wooden constructions to the original buildings, and began giving lectures on gynaecology in non-venereal cases. He built an operating theatre, with a special room for laparotomies. "Since that time a regular course of gynaecological teaching has been carried on with demonstrations, and this hospital is now one of those most visited by foreign practitioners." Such progress is set against a wider French context: "There is, however, no chair of gynaecology and no official gynaecological clinic in the faculty of Paris, which is, in this respect, behind other faculties throughout the civilised world." In other words, Paris, thought of as the world capital of Sex, was slovenly in dealing with constituent mechanisms and its consequences.

Hart's report is full of praise: for the "numerous and intelligent staff," "the great cleanliness of the wards," and Pozzi's views on antisepsis—"His motto is, Intra-abdominal asepsis, extra-abdominal antisepsis." Hart notes the surgeon's "extremely small incisions" and "extreme rapidity" when performing laparotomies: "By this mode of procedure he avoids the exposure of the viscera to the air and the escape of the intestines through the wound, and the surgical injury is considerably lessened."

Pozzi supplied the *BMJ* with full statistics for the previous eleven months at the Lourcine. "Sixty-two laparotomies [with] only four deaths . . . twelve ovariotomies [with] two deaths . . . Vaginal hysterectomy . . . twenty-two times with two deaths . . . Curetting for endometritis, eighty-one cases, no deaths." The total was 243 operations, 148 of which were major, with ten deaths. Hart also observes that in cases of colpoperineorrhaphy and Lawson Tait's perineal operation, "M. Pozzi has abandoned catgut and only employs silver wire." He concludes his survey by noting

> how thoroughly imbued the present generation of French surgeons is with the antiseptic and aseptic principles, with what logical accuracy and perfection they carry them out, and how excellent are their results. It need hardly be said that the anatomical knowledge, the neatness of hand, the perfection in surgical procedure which has always distinguished the Paris school of surgeons is not, and are not, less striking than heretofore.

Pozzi was, in these years, transforming French gynaecology from a mere subdivision of general medicine into a discipline in its own right. In 1890, he published his two-volume *Traité de gynécologie clinique et opératoire (Treatise of Gynaecology)*: over 1,100 pages, with more than five hundred diagrams and illustrations, mostly based on his own drawings. There had been nothing remotely like it in French before (fat volumes on gynaecology were normally in German). Pozzi had studied British, German and Austrian practices as well as using his own observations and experiences at the Lourcine-Pascal. His *Treatise* covered antiseptic procedures, anatomy, examination, surgery and post-operative treatment; it remained the standard textbook in France into the 1930s, well after Pozzi's death.

It also contained a humane side often lacking in books about women's health written by men—as they all were at that time. It was not long since the American Charles Meigs (who knew that "gentlemen's hands are clean" and therefore didn't need to be washed before surgery) had warned that vaginal examination of a patient by a male doctor should only be performed "out of some direful necessity to the woman," because it might result in "a lax moral sense in the patient." Now here is Pozzi, writing about bimanual examination versus (and in addition to) examination by speculum, and recommending that, for the woman's comfort, the speculum should first be warmed in sterilised water. He also stresses that the patient's modesty must always be considered; so, for instance, the doctor should avoid eye contact while making examinations.

Pozzi's *Treatise of Gynaecology* was quickly translated into English, German, Russian, Italian and Spanish, and soon recognised worldwide as a standard text. In Britain it was published by the New Sydenham Society in three volumes (1892–93). The *Lancet* reviewed each volume separately (and anonymously). The reviewer(s) applaud Pozzi's "studiously moderate attitude toward disputed points," his "very complete account of abdominal hysterectomy for fibroids," his "excellent account of the relation of micro-organisms to metritis," his "interesting sketch of the history of ovariotomy" in what is, they conclude, "a valuable work." But there is also something prissy and antiseptic about the reviews (*"Pas trop de zèle!"*) which might come from an Englishman reviewing a Frenchman. And the opportunity is not missed for a minor cross-Channel nitpick:

Antisepsis is dealt with in great detail . . . the extreme importance of rendering the hands and nails aseptic is very rightly insisted on and minute directions for the purpose are given. As regards the nails, we should, however, consider the plan of keeping them short and thoroughly brushing them with soap and water preferable to cleaning them with a pointed nail file, as here advised.

Gilles de la Tourette trained at the Salpêtrière Hospital under the great neurologist Jean Charcot. Tourette had—literally—made his name by examining, at Charcot's invitation, nine similar cases of physical and verbal mannerism. He termed the condition *la maladie des tics*, but Charcot preferred to publicly credit his assistant and we still know it as Tourette's syndrome. Now, nine years later, in December 1893, a twenty-nine-year-old woman by the name of Rose Kamper called on

COLLECTION FELIX POTIN

DOCTEUR CHARCOT

him. She asked if he was indeed Dr. Gilles de la Tourette, the man who had written books on hypnotism. He said he was. She told him that she had agreed to be the subject of hypnotic experiments while confined at the Salpêtrière the previous year. As a result, she explained, she had lost all her willpower and developed a split personality. Unable to work anymore, she was destitute. She asked him for fifty francs.

What she did not tell him was that she had made a list of three doctors she held responsible for her condition, and was planning to kill the first of the three she encountered. In fact, neither of the two doctors specifically in charge of her supposedly harmful treatment was on the list; while Tourette himself wasn't sure if he even faintly recalled the woman. Nonetheless, he was number three. Her first choice had been out of the city, and the second had refused her entry. As Tourette turned to show her out, Rose Kamper fired a revolver three times. One bullet hit the bookcase, a second the leg of a table, while the third went into the back of Tourette's neck.

The doctor was lucky. When he put his hand to his head, he felt blood, but also a hard object lodged between skin and bone: the bullet had glanced off the occipital bone at an angle. Meanwhile, Rose Kamper sat calmly at his desk, waiting for arrest. The bullet was safely extracted, and Tourette lived on until 1903. Rose Kamper was found to be suffering from persecution mania, and deemed unfit to plead. She was confined to a series of institutions, from some of which she escaped, and from some she was released. She spent the last twelve years of her life incarcerated in the Hôpital Sainte-Anne, where she died in 1955 at the age of ninety-two.

The Belle Epoque was a time of vast wealth for the wealthy, of social power for the aristocracy, of uncontrolled and intricate snobbery, of headlong colonial ambition, of artistic patronage, and of duels whose scale of violence often reflected personal irascibility more than offended honour. There wasn't much to be said for the First World War, but at least it swept a lot of this away.

Artistic patronage might seem the most benign aspect of this *ancien régime*, though it was also a kind of domestic colonialism. At the Princesse de Polignac's salon the guests were glamorous, but the musicians were underpaid. Or consider the case of Léon Delafosse. He was a piano virtuoso from a modest background (his mother still gave piano lessons), who had won first prize at the Conservatoire at the age of thirteen. A willowy, charming boy, he had been taken up by Proust around 1894. The novelist planned to offer Delafosse to Montesquiou as—what?—*bonne bouche*, plaything, Ganymede, Antinous? The stratagem would benefit all parties, Proust imagined. He would gain the Count's gratitude, and their friendship would be strengthened. The Count, whose younger intimates had lately been proving troublesome, would have a new object of attention. And Delafosse, by performing at the Count's house, would enjoy such a career bounce that concert halls would open up to him.

Léon Delafosse, John Singer Sargent (1895–98)

The plan succeeded for a while. The Count was pleased. As his biographer puts it: "After the fashion of those who are not really musical, Montesquiou liked music for the image which it invoked in him. It was a gentle opium." So Delafosse would fill his patron's pipe with Fauré, and his patron would close his eyes and dream. Montesquiou referred to him as "the Angel," and made a public show of his attachment. They travelled together; and for a few years it worked. But angels fall. Delafosse foolishly forgot that perpetual gratitude was the Count's normal expectation and demand; there was an incident with a musical princess who was herself a fine pianist (and friend of Paderewski). So Montesquiou grew bored with his musical toy, and in a fit of pique decided to smash it. Why? Because he could. He wrote to Delafosse:

> Little people never see the efforts one makes to descend to their level, and never climb up to one's own . . . All the houses that have been opened to you by my sovereign protection will be shut to you and you will be reduced to strumming some Moldavian or Bessarabian clavichord for a pittance. You have only ever been an instrument of my thought, you will never be more than a musical mechanic.

Delafosse was cut adrift. Some friends remained: Sargent arranged concerts for him in London; while the Princesse de Polignac—presumably on the principle of "my enemy's enemy"—invited him to play at her salon. But his wider career stalled. Montesquiou also seems to have infected his protégé with snobbery. He declined invitations to play in America, that land without duchesses. In his memoirs, the Count writes that Delafosse, "In frustration, and perhaps *faute de mieux*, threw himself, not into the arms, for she can hardly be said to have had any, but at the feet—which were enormous—of an aged Swiss spinster." Who, in all probability, had better moral values than Count Robert de Montesquiou-Fezensac. The Count continues: "When I decided to execute him [Delafosse], Yturri advised me to reconsider, assuring me that I would never find his like again; and this was true. I have often quoted the words of the old lady who used to say, 'You only love one curé in your lifetime.'"

Delafosse was leery of America, that boisterous and unaristocratic country: onetime colony, long-term idea, currently both a lure and a threat. But America was coming to France. In some ways, it was already there, in the shape of John Singer Sargent and Henry James and Edith Wharton; of Mary Cassatt, who was helping American millionaires back home buy up Impressionist paintings before their French and British equivalents woke up; in the shape of transatlantic heiresses brought over to shore up impoverished aristocratic houses; and of zealous and fashionable lesbians like Winnaretta Singer and Nathalie Barney and Romaine Brooks. But, more threateningly, it was coming (was already there) as an idea: the future. Huysmans originally imagined Des Esseintes as someone who has "discovered in artificiality a specific for the disgust inspired by the worries of life and the American manners of his time." In the novel itself, his character is more outspoken, referring to "the vast brothel of America," the land which contains multitudes, and so provokes a multitude of responses.

The Goncourt brothers had no doubt about the future destiny of Old Europe. Just as in a former age the "uncivilised barbarians" had destroyed the old Latin world, so, before too long, "the barbarians of civilisation" would swallow up the modern Latin world. They saw evidence of this "death-blow to the past" at the 1867 Paris World Exhibition:

The *Americanisation* of France, industry awarded priority over art, the steam-driven threshing engines whittling down the space for pictures, articles of vulgar domestic use under cover and statues exposed to the air; in a word, the Federal Republic of Matter.

But this isn't—or isn't only—an aesthete's lament. The Goncourts recognised the attraction as well as the inevitability of that coming Americanisation. Marianne and Britannia had grown frumpish, and the new American spirit was going to be represented not by a symbolic woman but by a real one. In that same year—1867—one of the brothers found himself sitting next to her at the French Embassy in Rome. She was

> the wife of an envoy from the United States in Brussels, and seeing this free-and-easy, jaunty grace, this tireless energy proper to a young nation, this hint of coquettishness that still retains the compelling charm of a flirtation in the young maid who has become a wife, and calling to mind the vivacity and insinuating ways of certain Americans in Paris, I said to myself that these men and women seem destined to become the future conquerors of the world.

Of course, Old Europe didn't go down without a fight. Oscar Wilde arrived in America in January 1882 for a yearlong, coast-to-coast tour; Count Robert de Montesquiou in January 1903 for a briefer, four-city engagement. Both saw themselves as being on *missions civilisatrices*. At the national, imperial level this involved land and God and loot; at the personal, cultural level, this involved self-promotion, fame and loot. Wilde, on his return, boasted to Whistler that he had "civilised America" (adding that this left only Heaven to conquer). His tour was theatrical in manner and often in location; it was also, in its deliberately provocative aestheticism—and to use one of his favourite adjectives—vulgar.

Montesquiou's tour was private, geographically limited, and more socially exclusive. "The beautiful Count is coming to Boston," wrote one newspaper. "This gentleman of France is now a reigning divinity in New York due to his good looks and good clothes. He does not lecture but gives 'conferences' at $5 a ticket." These events were held in large hotels and the drawing rooms of fashionable houses. After New York and Boston he went to Philadelphia and Chicago, where he was received by Mrs. Potter Palmer, the art collector and wife of a famous manufacturer of biscuits. (These American Palmer's Biscuits are not to be confused with the "Palmer's biscuits" which Des Esseintes sees on display at the Bodega in Paris during his failed expedition to London. These would certainly have been British, and made by Huntley and Palmer.)

When Wilde visited the States, the deal was that he should be promoted as a fashionable member of British society as much as a writer or thinker: he would proclaim the new aesthetic ideal of Beauty, while also publicly embodying that ideal. In England he had become famous by being inflated into the figure of Bunthorne in Gilbert and Sullivan's *Patience*; in America he was to become famous by being inflated into the figure of "Oscar Wilde." It is a moment when a shift in the nature of literary fame occurs. Previously, a famous writer was a writer who became famous by writing. Wilde pioneered the idea of becoming famous first, and then getting down to the writing. By the end of 1882 he was "still" only a minor poet and diligent lecturer. But he was also famous on two continents and therefore primed for a literary career. By June of 1882 the takings from the Wilde Experience were over $18,000, with his profits after expenses about $5,600.

Wilde also established another prime rule of fame in the modern age: that there is no such thing as bad publicity, there is only publicity. Success is better measured in column inches than by what those columns contain. Wilde understood that the "penny newspapers" were "the nineteenth-century standard of immortality." Having the aesthetic ideal mocked by Philistines was just as good an advertisement for that ideal as a lecture hall full of solemn applauders. He learned to outface those who hissed him, who called him "a penny Ruskin," who sneered that "she's a Charlotte-Ann." Yet the price of fame is rarely a simple transaction. If Wilde was treated in France as an upper-class

THE ÆSTHETIC CRAZE.

Whats de matter wid de Nigga ?   Why Oscar you's gone wild !

Englishman, in America he was merely an Irishman—indeed, a low-status Paddy. Furthermore, in a weird crossover of caste stereotyping, he was caricatured as being black as much as Irish. It came as a shock to the Oxford double-first to be drawn as a gangly African-American youth brandishing a sunflower.

When Whistler was painting Montesquiou, the artist warned the Count about the danger of living so worldly an existence: "If you continue to go about in society, your fate will be to meet the Prince of Wales." There is no evidence of Montesquiou meeting the Prince, though they swam in the same waters; and the Count's cousin, Countess Greffulhe, stayed with the Prince at Sandringham. As for Wilde: during his tour of America, and despite republican convictions, he liked to let drop allusions to "my friend the Prince of Wales."

Wilde and Montesquiou went to America and came back with money. Prince Edmond de Polignac, by nature more indolent, stayed in France and let money come to him, in the form of Winnaretta Singer. It's strange that the term "gold digger" is reserved exclusively for women who attach themselves to men for upward financial mobility. The biggest gold diggers of the Belle Epoque were English and French male aristocrats who married American heiresses to renew their bloodline, revive their sense of entitlement, and bolster their bank balance.

Samuel Pozzi's attitude to America was not based on either social superiority, paranoia or cupidity. It was inquisitive, open-minded and professional. As he had written in his *Treatise*, "Chauvinism is one of the forms of ignorance." In 1893, he was invited to the World's Fair in Chicago as part of the official French delegation. He sailed on the liner *La Touraine* to New York, where he met his American editor, then took the "Michigan Central" Pullman train—twenty hours of it—to Chicago. There, alongside his official duties, he had the chance to see four of the city's hospitals. He was amazed by the efficiency of the American system, and by its private funding; also by the higher social status of the nurses, and their higher pay (three or four times that of their French equivalents). On his return, he immediately began raising private money for the Lourcine-Pascal, and founded a Comité des Dames to provide support and entertainments for the patients.

His second visit to North America came in 1904, when he was invited to "represent French surgery" at a two-venue congress, in St. Louis and then Montreal, spread over May and June. By now, Pozzi's fame and social weight were considerable. Though booked to sail on the liner *La Savoie*, he was scooped up at the last minute by Gordon Bennett Jr., an American socialite, newspaper owner and sportsman. They had first met when Pozzi stitched Bennett up after he had fallen off the running-board of a car. Now they crossed the Atlantic on Bennett's 2,000-ton steam yacht, whose luxuries included a Turkish bath and two milking cows.

In the States and Canada, Pozzi was feasted and fêted; now fifty-eight, with his charm and excellent English, he was the perfect face of French surgery. Despite the attractions of the St. Louis World's Fair, his main discovery on the American leg of his trip was that the pioneering centre of American surgery was not in one of the great cities, but in Rochester, Minnesota, where the Mayo Clinic had been founded in 1889 by an Englishman from Lancashire; the 300-bed hospital was now run by Mayo's two sons. This was the first of many contacts: on his return to Paris, he sent his assistant Robert Proust on a follow-up mission.

From Rochester he went to Montreal, where in his plenary address he recalled reading about Canadian fur trappers as a boy in books by Fenimore Cooper and Gabriel Ferry; while the next day he demonstrated his "speed and skill" in performing a laparotomy and hysterectomy. Though he was everywhere at his diplomatic best, the

English-language *Montreal Medical Journal* couldn't help observing that "Prof. Pozzi, who is not a Catholic in religion, is distinctly 'rouge' in his politics, as we say in Quebec."

There was only one other French delegate in Montreal, a junior one, Alexis Carrel, and the two of them seem not to have met; certainly Pozzi didn't attend his compatriot's presentation. Carrel was then an obscure thirty-one-year-old, but only eight years later would win the Nobel Prize for Medicine. He described to the congress his early experiments in organ transplantation—of the thyroid and the kidney—in dogs. The operations themselves had been successful, though the animals had died from subsequent infection. And the key to it all was the successful suturing of blood vessels, a matter in which Pozzi was and would remain deeply interested.

Sarah Bernhardt loved touring America as much as Oscar Wilde did. She went nine times: the last trip, when she was already in her early seventies—and with a leg amputated, and in wartime—took her to ninety-nine cities in fourteen months. Wilde and Bernhardt—those two great national self-inventors—were made for one another, and they recognised it. When she came to play *Phèdre* in London in 1879, he met her off the boat at Folkestone and strewed lilies at her feet. When she came to perform in *Fedora* he brought her an enormous bunch of wallflowers from a street vendor. On his honeymoon in Paris, he saw her as Lady Macbeth, and lauded her to the *Morning News* interviewer. Both of them dealt in extravagant praise, and were unblushing in receipt of it. Wilde had written her a sonnet, but longed to dress her in a full-length play. His first idea was Elizabeth I; his later, better one—committed Flaubertian as he had always been—was *Salomé*. Started in Paris, finished in Torquay, and written in French, it was prepared for the London stage in 1892. When Oscar asked Sarah how she would do the dance of the seven veils, she replied, with an enigmatic smile, "Never you mind."

At that time, the Parisian theatre was like Hollywood a century later: a money machine that showed no sign of exhaustion. And as novelists today pantingly hope their books will be adapted for the screen, back then the play was the thing. To have Sarah Bernhardt in your play raised it to being a news event; while to have her in an

original role specially tailored for her was a dramatist's dream come true. Wilde wrote *Salomé* for her. Alexandre Dumas *fils* wrote *La Dame aux camélias* for her. Edmond Rostand wrote *L'Aiglon* for her. His elder son Maurice Rostand wrote *La Gloire* for her, in which she made her final appearance, with a part allowing her to remain seated throughout. Pozzi's friend Paul Hervieu wrote *Théroigne de Méricourt* for her—a six-act Revolutionary drama which left Pozzi "discreetly bored."

But it didn't work out for all. Edmond de Goncourt spent a long stretch of 1893 in the hope, verging on expectation, that she would take the lead in his play *La Faustin*. As long as he hoped, he found her delightful, charming, natural, straightforward, adorable. When he heard nothing for two months, he sent a telegram asking for the return of the script. It came back another two months later, without even a note.

The extremist Jean Lorrain inevitably had a more extreme experience. He wrote a number of plays with Bernhardt in mind, but knew that *Ennoïa* with its fashionable exoticism would be perfect for them both. He had done all the preliminary buttering-up: each time she presented a new role, he would devote his entire "Pall Mall" column to it. Lorrain finally lost confidence and temper when Bernhardt—who had been sitting on his script for months—appeared "instead" (as he would have put it) in Rostand's *L'Aiglon*. Rostand was one of Lorrain's top bêtes noires. Bernhardt took the lead in this play about Napoleon's son, and Lorrain noticed—or at any rate persuaded himself—that its third act suspiciously resembled the second act of his own play. And then, after holding on to *Ennoïa* for five years, the actress sent it back to him. In a letter to Pozzi, Lorrain complained about Bernhardt's snooty preference—both literary and social—for Rostand and Montesquiou over him. "She has become Rostandised . . . They call her The Good Sarah-mitaine. But as for me, I'm dropping her now," he concluded. However, it was she who was dropping him—indeed, already had.

Yet playwrights faced other obstacles besides the headstrong actress. The London cast of *Salomé* was two weeks into rehearsal when the censor withdrew permission for the play. Not, as we might assume, on grounds of sex, or of violence, or of decadence, or of simply being French, but under an ancient but suddenly useful law which forbade the portrayal on the British stage of biblical characters. *Salomé* was eventually given its premiere in Paris four years later, by which time the staging had become an act of solidarity, since its author was now in Reading Gaol.

In 1895, after Wilde's conviction and incarceration, petitions were circulated in both London and Paris asking for mitigation of sentence. But signatures were harder to acquire than expected and the petitions were never presented. In London, Bernard Shaw and Walter Crane signed; Holman Hunt and Henry James declined. In Paris, Gide and Bourget signed; Zola refused. So did Jean Lorrain, claiming that *Le Courrier Français* would sack him if he signed. The French were also more satirical in their responses. Jules Renard, obstinately original as ever, declined thus: "I would willingly sign the petition in favour of Oscar Wilde, on condition that he gives his word of honour . . . never to pick up his pen again." The poet François Coppée offered to sign not as a writer but as a member of the Society for the Prevention of Cruelty to Animals: "A writer pig is still a pig."

The name of Wilde was suddenly tainting. Alphonse Daudet refused to endorse the petition on the ground that "I have sons." He had two: Léon (already twenty-nine), who had trained as a doctor, then became a novelist and one of the age's most violent chroniclers: "poisonously amusing," as Edith Wharton put it. Alphonse was more likely to be worrying about his younger son Lucien (then eighteen), known as Zézé, who was much the gentler. Renard described him in his journal as "a pretty boy, curled, pomaded, painted and powdered, who spoke in a low voice." Montesquiou thought him a golden lad and a possible disciple; but Lucien, like many, was to disappoint. He was a deep and daily friend of Proust, and on one occasion the pair of them were invited by Montesquiou to hear Delafosse play. As often happened, Lucien and Marcel set one another off into paroxysms of hysterical giggles. The Count never forgave this "gross breach of decency." He once sent Mme Daudet a rose, with the message, "You are a rose, your children are the thorns."

Lucien was the cause of the Belle Epoque's unlikeliest duel, which took place in February 1897 between Proust and Jean Lorrain. Under his known pseudonym of Raitif de la Bretonne, Lorrain reviewed Proust's *Les Plaisirs et les jours* in *Le Journal*, implying as he did so a homosexual relationship between Lucien and Marcel. Proust challenged him, and three days after the article appeared, they met on a cold, rainy afternoon in the Bois de Meudon. Twenty-six years previously, while Marcel was still in the womb, his father had escaped a stray bullet; now Marcel escaped his own. Pistol shots were exchanged from a distance of twenty-five metres, and it seems both men deliberately fired in the air.

And Lucien Daudet? He wanted to be a writer, then a painter, and had all the necessary connections but lacked the necessary talent. He succeeded, however, as a courtier to the Empress Eugénie, who had gone into British exile after the debacle of 1870: first at Chislehurst, later at Farnborough. Lucien would visit her there, and also stay in the house she still owned in the south of France. Proust described his friend's life as a genial merry-go-round: "Farnborough and Cap-Martin, the end of spring and summer in Touraine, and staying with friends. He spends only three or four months in Paris, when he goes out a lot." George Painter describes Lucien's later years rather differently: he indulged in "unhappy relationships with young men of the working classes." This probably can't be blamed on Oscar Wilde.

How to Be a Guest

1) Count Robert de Montesquiou-Fezensac often went to dinner chez Proust. Guest lists would first be submitted to the Count—or rather, to Yturri—to discover who was currently in or out of favour. Flowers would be ordered, the cook harassed by Mme Proust, and to keep their principal guest in good temper, he would be asked to lecture about art and taste over the dessert.

Proust's father was a brilliant doctor, a specialist in cholera and international hygiene, widely travelled, world famous. The Shah of Persia once thanked him with some sumptuous carpets. Proust's mother was rich—her dowry being 200,000 gold francs—very beautiful and highly cultivated. She was an accomplished musician, "chose fine furniture for the family home," knew English and German, and helped Marcel translate Ruskin. But when the Count came to dinner, the parents would be placed at the bottom of the table. On one occasion Montesquiou, "with a mixture of wit, insolence and good taste," turned to Marcel and commented, "How ugly it is here!"

2) In 1891, when Oscar Wilde was what Paris called "*le great event*," he met Proust, who invited him to dinner. On the appointed evening, Proust was a few minutes late arriving home. "Is the English gentleman here?" he asked the servant. "Yes, sir, he arrived five minutes ago; he

had hardly entered the drawing room when he asked for the bathroom, and he has not come out of it." Proust ran to the end of the passage. "Monsieur Wilde, are you ill?" asked the anxious host through the door. "Ah, there you are, Monsieur Proust," replied Wilde, appearing majestically. "No, I am not in the least ill. I thought I was to have the pleasure of dining with you alone, but they showed me into the drawing room. I looked at the drawing room and at the end of it were your parents, and my courage failed me. Goodbye, dear Monsieur Proust, goodbye . . ." Afterwards, Marcel's parents told him that, while looking around the drawing room, Wilde had exclaimed, "How ugly your house is!"

"A man can be happy with any woman, as long as he does not love her." This cute paradox from Wilde's *porte-parole* Lord Henry Wotton did not apply to Samuel Pozzi's life with Thérèse—unless you redefine "happy" as "able to operate socially." But at some point in the mid-1890s he met Emma Fischoff, with whom, all the evidence suggests, he could be happy. Born Emma Sedelmeyer in Vienna, she was the daughter of a Parisian art dealer, who had shown Sargent among others. Sixteen years younger than Pozzi, also with three children—indeed, a matching set of two boys and a girl—Emma was cultured, confident, rich, and keen on intellectual and decorative shopping. Her husband Eugène, also Jewish, also born in Vienna, was a member of the Jockey Club, and owner of Dandolo, one of the most famous racehorses in France. It was named after the Venetian doge who, during the sack of Constantinople in 1204, sent back to Venice the bronze horses that have adorned St. Mark's ever since—except when they were looted in turn by Napoleon and lived in Paris from 1797 to 1815.

For some years Pozzi had travelled alone for work and pleasure, though also with friends: as when spotted at Bayreuth by Colette in

The Sedelmayer Family (detail), Franz Rumpler (1879)—Emma is on the right

1896 with the poet Catulle Mendès by his side. The following year, however—and to complicate our reading of his marriage—he took Thérèse to Bayreuth to hear *Lohengrin*. Their fifteen-year-old daughter Catherine, who loved music and had begged in vain to be taken with them, was not happy—annoyed to be treated as a child when she was a *jeune fille*. She wrote a letter of rebuke to her absent mother "in which I rather naughtily put all the reproaches I had piled up in my heart, and all the anger at her indifference to what I had so much desired." Replying from Bayreuth, Thérèse calls her "a wicked little girl," the more so since at the very time Catherine was writing her letter of complaint, her mother had been looking to reserve an apartment in the town with a sitting room, two bedrooms and three beds. Not for the following year, but the one after, 1899: "By then you will be in a better condition to support both the profound emotions and the bad food."

But when 1899 came around, Catherine (and Thérèse) were to be disappointed. Pozzi set off for Bayreuth alone; and when he got there, he joined up with a circle of friends: Mme Bulteau, the Rostands, the La Gandaras, abbé Mugnier . . . and Emma Fischoff. They heard *Parsifal, Meistersinger* and the *Ring Cycle*. And when the music stopped, he and Emma set off together for Venice. This was no sudden romantic escapade: while there, they visited the lagoon island of San Lazzaro, where—presumably by prior arrangement—they had their union officially blessed by an elderly Armenian monk, Father Mimikian.

The following year, on 17 August, with Thérèse and the children safely away in the country, Pozzi boarded the sleeping car for Munich at the Gare de l'Est with a veiled woman at his side. He and Emma spent three weeks in Germany, Austria and Italy: no Bayreuth this time, but *The Magic Flute* at the Munich Opera House, and the Oberammergau Passion Play. Also Hohenschwangau, Neuschwanstein, Innsbruck, Verona and Venice. They quickly discover that "abroad" does not equal "incognito"—certainly not if you stay in the best hotels and book the best theatre seats. In the dining room of their hotel in Salzburg, they run into Mme Maurice Ephrussi, who is "extremely embarrassed." The next day, setting off for an excursion to Schafbergspitze, they cannot avoid the Marquis de Saint-Sauveur.

We presume Eugène to have been complaisant. Thereafter, the couple travelled together every year—mostly in the summer, occasionally spring or winter—until the outbreak of the First World War. Most years the itinerary included Venice. By their third trip, Father Mimikian was dead, but a younger monk took up the task of renewing their morganatic vows. In her travel notebook, Emma recorded: "Our first stop is always at the Armenian Lazzaro, it's our Love Pilgrimage. That evening, despite the heat, we went to the Goldoni Theatre, but didn't stay long as we had better things to do!"

San Lazzaro was a literary island—its visitors' book contains the signatures of Browning, Longfellow and Proust. They were all following in the steps of Byron, some of whose literary relics are in the library. This would have felt appropriate to Pozzi, who viewed himself, and was often viewed by others, as a Byronic fig-ure. He would sign letters (to women, obvi-ously) "Your Giaour" in reference to Byron's poem of that name; and among his treasures in Paris was a Turner watercolour of *Childe Harold's Pilgrimage*—quite possibly sold to him by Emma's father. Pozzi collected paint-ings of Venice by Bellotto, Guardi and the French artist Félix Ziem. And there is, in ret-rospect, something doge-like about that red coat in which Sargent pictured him.

Pozzi, whom even his sympathetic French

biographer refers to as "an incorrigible seducer," did not flop into some quasi-marriage with Emma Fischoff, whatever their Armenian vows contained. Here he is in 1900, writing seductively to another potential conquest, signing himself "Your Giaour," and, furthermore, addressing her as "Mme Pozzi II." However, had Mme Pozzi I agreed to a divorce—which her Catholic faith forbade—the likeliest candidate for the position would have been Emma. As long as Monsieur Fischoff I agreed in his turn.

But there can be something settling, even cosy, about a continuously impossible—or at least, insoluble—situation. And so, each year, the two of them would depart on another European journey, which would often include Bayreuth as well as Venice. In 1903, when Pozzi had the excuse of a gynaecological conference in Athens, they travelled by wagon-lit to Marseilles, and then on by steamer to Piraeus, with tickets booked in the name of the Baron and Baroness de Pozzi. In 1904, in Syracuse, their guide shows them his autograph book: it contains the signatures of Jules Verne, Maupassant . . . and Jean Lorrain. In 1906, their ninth journey together, they go by Orient Express to Bayreuth for *Tristan* and *Parsifal*, then on to Venice and Fiume, down the Dalmatian coast to Cetinje (where the French Consul gives them a bottle of Saint-Emilion as thanks for a spontaneous consultation), followed by Sarajevo, Zagreb, Zurich, Basel and Paris. The next year it is Paris–Munich–Venice–Corfu–Patras–Constantinople–Budapest–Vienna–(where they see *The Merry Widow*)–Paris. In 1908 they set off in April for Barcelona, then Palma de Majorca, Reixa, Madrid, Cambo-les-Bains (to visit Edmond Rostand), then back to Paris. While they are away, at Auteuil, Dandolo wins the Prix du Président de la République, a handicap steeplechase. Eugène Fischoff of the Jockey Club receives the prize of 50,000 francs plus a work of art from the Sèvres porcelain factory, to be chosen by the winning owner.

—

By the time Pozzi had finished all the renovations and innovations at the Broca, it represented a map of his travels and consultations across the world. The low-pressure steam radiators were based on those at the chief hospital in Leipzig. The ventilation system, showers and mains drainage were American in origin. The bed linen, however, was French, being in Pozzi's judgement finer than any available even in Vienna or Berlin. The operating wing, derived from sketches Pozzi made on his travels, was revolutionary for France. It had separate rooms for antiseptic procedures, for sterilisation, for instruments, and even— "an astonishing innovation"—a chloroform room where patients were anaesthetised before being taken in to surgery. This new gynaecological service was inaugurated in 1897, fourteen years after he became Head of Surgery.

But Pozzi was also aware that a hospital was not just a hygienic location for effective surgery and good nursing. He always insisted on healing's moral as well as physical side. So he installed a library at the hospital; and called on painter friends to decorate the corridors and wards. Girard, Bellery-Desfontaines and Dubufe provided frescoes in gentle colours of calm, bucolic landscapes. But the pièce de résistance was a spectacular allegory by the society painter Georges Clairin. He was an old friend of the Pozzis, and had decorated a ceiling and several walls at the place Vendôme shortly after the couple moved in. Clairin was also a lifelong friend and (brief? occasional? we cannot know) lover of Sarah Bernhardt; he had accompanied the actress on her first and only balloon flight. Now, for the Broca, he painted a grand fresco, 4.40 metres wide and 2.75 metres high, called *Health Restored to the Sick*. In a scene at the edge of woodland, with flowers bursting over the picture's frame, an exalted female figure in a flowing white gown soars above mere mortals representing the sick and weary. A small girl

A ward at the Broca Hospital, with frescoed walls

Health Restored to the Sick, Georges Clairin

kisses her hand; a female acolyte sits in a meadow holding a bouquet. Health looks as if she has dropped from the skies—perhaps by balloon. The recognisable model is, of course, Sarah Bernhardt.

On 1 January 1899, Pozzi and the Broca received the highest official accolade. The President of the Republic Félix Faure came to open his renovated and modernised hospital. Two years later, after a long campaign and long conservative resistance, the first chair of gynaecology in Paris—and therefore in the whole of France—was established. And Pozzi sat in it. On 1 May 1901, he gave his inaugural lecture. He chose to deliver it not in the great amphitheatre of the Faculty of Medicine, dressed in the academic robes of theory, but in the smaller amphitheatre of the Broca, wearing the white robes and skullcap of practical work. Thérèse was there, alongside family and friends, including Montesquiou and Countess Greffulhe. Pozzi placed the members of his Comité des Dames—the support group whose idea was copied from Chicago—in the front row.

"A great poet," he began, "who was also a great philosopher, once said that the ideal life for a man is to be able to realise in maturity an idea that he has conceived in his youth. And so today you see me a happy man." He gave appropriate thanks to those who had created the chair of gynaecology "so long asked for without success." He described the bad old days, at the start of his career, when treatments were primitive: patients were not so much healed as uselessly tortured with repeated vesicatories and deep abdominal cauterisations. Ovarian cysts would be treated by evacuatory puncture: there were patients obliged to return several times a year for such treatment, until they became completely worn out. Then came Pasteur, and Lister, and the flowering of laparotomy as a now benign operation.

Great advances had been made, and they were all to be applauded. However, Pozzi went on—to the surprise of some listeners—it was in his opinion now time to pause and reflect. "In the enthusiastic fervour which followed the introduction of the antiseptic and aseptic procedures, therapeutic gynaecology perhaps took a turning which was too exclusively and radically interventionist." In a warning which may sound very contemporary, despite coming from more than a century ago, he cautions against what he calls *furor operativus*: the rage to operate. He gives as an example Battey's Operation, in which healthy (or only mildly affected) ovaries were removed in order to provoke an artificial menopause and thus cure nervous troubles of various kinds (it was a procedure popular in mental hospitals). Also, there were technically brilliant interventions in the uterus, and amputations of the neck of the womb, which succeeded in the short term but often led to serious consequences for the patient in subsequent pregnancies. "I know for a fact that among many members of the public the name of consultant, and even gynaecologist, has become synonymous with surgeon." An operation should be a final, unavoidable procedure, rather than an automatic way of dealing with an immediate problem. "There is the matter of conscience for each of us who holds the power of life and death over a fellow human being—and conscience must be the first characteristic of a doctor, especially one who wields a knife."

He concludes this deeply felt and rousing *profession de foi* with these words: "I would like to teach the young doctors who will train at this clinic how to examine the sick so as not to scare them, how to examine them without needlessly wounding their modesty, and how to talk to them in words which, according to the occasion, might need to be indulgent or severe, but without either over-familiarity or harshness." He quotes Shakespeare on the milk of human kindness, and ends: "However empty the heavens above us might have now become, we should always be able to recognise amongst them the divine figure of Pity."

—

Jean Lorrain might have fought a duel with Maupassant, until sanity prevailed. He nearly fought one with Verlaine, who sent his seconds round after Lorrain had reported (mistakenly) that the poet had been committed to an asylum. He did fight one with Marcel Proust, even if it was just a matter of discharging pistols in the air. But the writer he deeply and persistently wanted to fight was Robert de Montesquiou. The Count's biographer maintained that "Jean Lorrain hated Montesquiou with the hatred that a middle-class woman who has lost her reputation has for a great lady who is above scandal." This seems as absurd as it is snobbish: the Count, going around for twenty years with his companion Yturri, while having public crushes on attractive young men like Delafosse and Lucien Daudet, was hardly ungossiped about.

2ᵉ COLLECTION FÉLIX POTIN

VERLAINE
HOMME DE LETTRES

Despite—or perhaps because of—being ignored, Lorrain never stopped snapping and sneering. When Boldini painted the Count's portrait, he reviewed it snootily:

> This year Monsieur de Montesquiou has entrusted the task of reproducing his elegant silhouette to Monsieur Boldini, the habitual deformer of over-excited and grimacing women, otherwise known as "the Paganini of the Peignoir."

But always Montesquiou declined to rise—even in excessive circumstances.

On 4 May 1897, at 4:20 in the afternoon, fire broke out at the Bazar de la Charité, an annual event organised by the Catholic aristocracy of

Paris. It began during a cinema show, and was caused by the projectionist's equipment, which used a mixture of ether and oxygen rather than electricity. The site, in the rue Jean-Goujon, was packed, the blaze rapid, and many of the victims so unrecognisable that dental records were used for the first time to identify them. Of the 129 or so dead (numbers vary), 123 were women, mostly from the upper classes, notably the Duchess of Alençon, sister of the Empress of Austria.

Catherine Pozzi, then fourteen, wrote in her diary:

> At 5 o'clock, we dropped Papa off at the Bazar de la Charité; it's an enormous bazaar where scores of charities sell side by side. Papa was going there to buy something. We saw an enormous crowd. Without asking why, we returned to the place Vendôme. It was only there we learnt that there had been a terrible fire; 150 dead, as many injured.

The Pozzis lost six friends in the fire. "All Paris is in mourning," she continued. "They've closed all the theatres." The Baron de Mackau, who presided over the bazaar, was fined 500 francs. The cinematograph projectionist and his assistant were tried for murder, receiving, respectively, a year in prison and eight months. But this being Paris, there was soon a popular song—"Au Bazar de la Charité"—out as sheet music. It was sung to the tune of "Dors, mon Chéri."

Jean Lorrain, as if this were normal journalistic comment, insinuated in one of his columns that Montesquiou (who had been provably nowhere near the scene) had used one of his famous walking sticks to beat a path to safety through the ranks of terrified society ladies. Did the Count respond to this most false and libellous of accusations? Still not. Perhaps he was disdainful not just of Lorrain but of duels themselves? Not at all. He would only fight a worthy opponent. And

Baron DE MACKAU
HOMME POLITIQUE

DE REGNIER
HOMME DE LETTRES

one soon presented himself at a Rothschild reception: his fellow poet Henri de Régnier. They had a verbal scuffle around the walking-stick rumour, the question of honour, and the chastisement of women; at which point Régnier remarked provocatively that the Count probably preferred a fan or a muff to a sword. Montesquiou called him out; de Régnier chose swords, and the Count was wounded in the hand. The doctor who bandaged him up was, of course, Pozzi.

The next morning, the front page of *Le Figaro* featured an adulatory portrait of Montesquiou by Proust. Written as a sonorous pastiche of Saint-Simon, it was a literary tongue-bath which did young Proust no harm with the Professor of Beauty. Seven years later, the Count was to fight a second duel, with the son of Mme Ernest Stern, an enormously fat socialite who wrote poetry under the name of Maria Star. It is not clear if Montesquiou had mocked her size or her verses. This time the Count received three wounds; again, Pozzi was in attendance. The writer Marcel Schwob begged Montesquiou to call it a day: "You are too rare a man and too exquisite a poet to put your life in jeopardy for a banal distinction that should be reserved for journalists." The Count's faithful Yturri, as if not wanting to be left out, also challenged and fought a journalist who had accused him of, well, the usual.

An afterthought. Jean Lorrain hated Montesquiou not as a fallen bourgeoise hates a great lady; more as a homosexual who is (bravely) much more out than in might hate a homosexual who cautiously plays society's game, and places manners above truth. Lorrain put the Count into his novel *Monsieur de Phocas* three times: as himself, under his own name; as Comte Muzarett (who maltreats his musical protégé Delabarre much as Montesquiou maltreated Delafosse); and also in the general outline of the title character, Monsieur de Phocas. It is a strange name over which scholars have puzzled. Might it relate to *Phoca*, the generic Latin name for a seal (but why?); or even to the word "focus"? Alternatively, there were two historical Phocases on whom Lorrain might have been focusing. One was a Byzantine emperor who murdered his way to the throne in 602 before being tortured and decapitated in 610. The second was a fourth-century Christian martyr who helped the poor and who, when denounced for his faith, first dug his own grave, and then handed himself over to his executioners. None of these explanations makes convincing sense. So consider this. Lorrain knew English very well; Montesquiou knew English not very well. Lorrain was always excessive, and by 1901 knew that Montesquiou would never challenge him to a duel, no matter what the offence. Was "Phocas" meant to be pronounced "Fuck-Arse"? There is also the French phrase *"pédé comme un phoque"* (as gay as a seal), though when the expression came in is unclear.

There is gossip, and then there is sexual gossip. The thing about sexual gossip is that more or less everyone believes it (even when they pretend not to) because it always seems plausible. Not necessarily because the gossip confirms some pre-existing pieces of circumstantial evidence (though it may); but rather because the sexual habits of human beings are a mystery, yet one which, when "solved," appears to solve the wider mystery of the human personality. Oh, *that* explains it—now I see, of course, now it all makes sense.

And there is a further aspect—to do with time. The past is the present's toy and plaything, gratifyingly unable to answer back (let alone sue for libel, or challenge the present to a duel). And nowhere more so than in the sexual life. We know more and better, don't we? We can see through their façades and their hypocrisies, their self-deceptions and their lies; we can read their hearts and their genitals. We see them clearly for what they are, as they stumble anxiously along the dusty, potholed track which leads towards us. And that is why we understand them so well, because deep down, what those dead people always wanted was to be *us*.

Then, as now, sexual gossip about a woman was more judgemental. A man who had many affairs was made more of a man by it; a woman claiming similar freedom was viewed as a serious danger. Sarah Bernhardt was an actress, in any case—a very bad start when it came to reputation. She had many lovers, and an illegitimate son with whom she openly travelled. To decent society, this made her no less than a whore. And it's true, even when famous, Bernhardt took jewellery and large cash sums from her richer admirers. The fact that she travelled not only with her bastard son but with a menagerie of animals (including a chimpanzee called Darwin, perhaps in honour of Pozzi's translation of the Englishman) merely confirmed her animalistic nature. As did the fact that she slept with women as well as men. Oh, and on top of all that, shouldn't we mention that she was . . . Jewish?

Why did she go to bed with so many? Obviously because she was a nymphomaniac, shameless about slaking her lust. Additionally and alternatively, as the lawyers liked to say—since male accusation of woman rarely rests on a single charge when another can be added—it was alleged that Bernhardt was frigid and unable to reach orgasm. Perhaps this was why she was a nymphomaniac: a medical case running away from her diagnosis. Evidence for this second accusation comes from a well-known letter she wrote in 1874 to her actor-lover Mounet-Sully:

> You must realise that I am not made for happiness. It is not my fault that I am constantly in search of new sensations, new emotions. That is how I shall be until my life is worn away. I am just as unsatisfied in the morning after as I am the night before. My heart demands more excitement than anyone can give it. My frail body is exhausted by the act of love. Never is it the love I dream of . . . What can I do? You must not be angry at me. I'm an incomplete person.

This is an astonishingly frank and touching confession; but is it necessarily a confession of anorgasmia, as it is now routinely taken to be? She is not made for "happiness" (daily, bourgeois, monogamous happiness); she seeks new sensations; she dreams of such extreme pleasure that reality inevitably fails her, and she moves on to the next lover. If any man had made such a statement, would he not be acclaimed as, say, a horndog, rather than judged a sexual inadequate? Further, for Bernhardt to accuse herself of being "an incomplete person" might well have been a generous way of bringing to an end two years with the melodramatic, exhausting and impossible Mounet-Sully (who came from Bergerac, just as Pozzi did). Henry James, sending a dispatch from Paris in 1876, described him as a "lurid star" who "has no conception of the proper way to treat beautiful lyric verse" and whose "rantings

SARAH BERNHARDT

MOUNET-SULLY

REJANE

and splutterings and contortions are altogether beside the mark." James adds, understatingly, "I believe he is a very wilful young man." With such a partner, blaming yourself might be the most tactful and least rancour-provoking form of exit.

But of course, an actress must always be acting, mustn't she? So she must act in bed as well? So she fools and flatters men in bed by pretending to orgasms she doesn't feel: why not? The male sexual ego has always been threatened by the notion that, while there is clear physical evidence for the male orgasm, there is none for the female. Sarah Bernhardt, frigid dissembler! False nymphomaniac! So it was rumoured that "instead of a clitoris she has a corn." The actress Marie Colombier, once her friend, later her denouncer, called her "an untuned piano, an Achilles vulnerable everywhere but in the right place." Her more immediate rival Réjane once referred to herself as "a complete woman," which may or may not be pertinent.

In 1892 Edmond de Goncourt records the rumour—fed him by the "hysterical" gossip Jean Lorrain—that Bernhardt had been able to reach orgasm only in the last ten years, thanks to an operation by Dr. Odilon Lannelongue, who provided her with "a surgically implanted gland which lubricated her formerly dry vulva." Unsurprisingly, this rumour is single-source. Does this sound like a probable operation (in which case, why would she not have asked Pozzi to perform it?) or the likelier result of Chinese whispers? You hardly need a machine to lubricate a vulva. And though Lannelongue is known to have treated Bernhardt, he was a specialist in bone diseases, particularly osteomyelitis and bone tuberculosis. We cannot know, but we can certainly doubt.

My first encounter with Dr. Pozzi was in the form of his tremendous image by Sargent. The wall label told me that he was a gynaecologist. I hadn't previously come across him in my nineteenth-century French reading. Then I saw in an art magazine that he was "not only the father of French gynaecology but also a confirmed sex addict who routinely attempted to seduce his female patients." I was intrigued by such an apparent paradox: the doctor who helps women but also exploits them. The man of science who brings comfort and relief from mental and physical pain, whose innovations and techniques saved women's lives, who helped the poor numerically more than the rich, but who in his private life behaved like a caricature of a sophisticated Frenchman. Even his grandson, Claude Bourdet, called him, "A man difficult to live with . . . whose extraordinary charm and profession as gynaecologist certainly threw accumulated temptations into his path." At the same time, I paused over the phrase "confirmed sex addict," which made him sound like he'd been admitted to some rehab clinic in Arizona. Who "confirmed" his condition? And where did that "routinely" come from?

Still, to begin cautiously: there was, for almost his entire life, very little scandal attached to Pozzi's name. His activities were heterosexual, legal and (as far as we know) consensual. But they also depended on the discretion and tact of his partners. It's not clear when and where he had his assignations; how long his liaisons lasted; whether and how often they overlapped. But there is not a single recorded note of female complaint against him. Do we allow his lovers no agency? You could say that this silence is just another aspect of the way male power played out; but there were other men who ended up in the scandal sheets and libel courts, and on duelling grounds—his own son Jean found himself, in 1912, wielding a sword as a consequence of a three-way love entanglement. Pozzi makes it into the diaries and letters of the time, as a surgeon, society figure and collector; but even Edmond de Goncourt, whose *Journal* is as good a guide to sexual habits (and sexual gossip) as we have, notes only minor evidence for possible affairs. There is also the danger of getting overexcited about other people's sex lives. Pozzi never emerges from documents of the time as the kind of ruthless libertine—indeed, "sex addict"—into which he is being transformed by a twenty-first-century coarsening of language and memory.

What is it about the present that makes it so eager to judge the past? There is always a neuroticism to the present, which believes itself superior to the past but can't quite get over a nagging anxiety that it might not be. And behind this is a further question: What is our authority for judging? We are the present, it is the past: that is usually enough for most of us. And the further the past recedes, the more attractive it becomes to simplify it. However gross our accusation, it never replies, it stays silent. When, in my twenties, I was studying law, I was taught that there were, historically, two different ways a defendant's silence could be interpreted. The accused might be "mute due to visitation of God" (physically unable to speak); or "mute of malice" (able to speak yet unwilling to do so for fear of self-incrimination). If the defendant was mute of malice, then—in the old French phrase—*peine forte et dure* might be applied. Torture, in other words. The past is mute by visitation of God, but we often behave as if it were mute of malice.

There is another factor. Repetitive affairs, even if we have the details, often make for dull reading—and dull living. Not dull at the point of action, obviously, but dull in terms of reflection and self-reflection. The lotharios, Don Juans and *coureurs de femmes* I have come across in my life have invariably confirmed the wise observation of François Mauriac in his novel of literary jealousy, *Ce qui était perdu*: "The more women a man has known, the more rudimentary an idea he constructs for himself of women in general." This dictum, soon to be a century old, has lost little of its truth.

So I became less interested in Pozzi the amorist, and more in Pozzi the fraught family man, Pozzi the ever-curious doctor, Pozzi the traveller, Pozzi the urbane figure (Pozzi the snob?), Pozzi the internationalist, the rationalist, the Darwinist, the scientist, the modernist. Pozzi, the man who never lost a friend (unless they were an anti-Dreyfusard). Pozzi, a sane man in a demented age.

But whatever we might decide to think of him, Dr. Pozzi doesn't care, that's for sure. He doesn't care mainly because he's dead. But he also doesn't care because the present—the past's present, in this case—rarely thinks about the future's judgement. It used to think a great deal about the future's judgement when this was represented by heaven and hell and divine reckoning; but Pozzi was a man of science and reason, not religion. He looked to the future in terms of medical advances: how to improve the success rate in treating gunshot wounds to the abdomen, how to make appendectomies and proustatectomies routinely safe operations—and soon—rather than what the future's opinion of him might be. This is what we all mostly do: it's bad enough worrying about the present's verdict on us, let alone the future's.

Claude Vanderpooten, Pozzi's 1992 biographer, assures us from a complacent distance that Pozzi "was always sincere" in his affairs, and that he remained on good terms with all his lovers afterwards. Pozzi's fourteen-year-old daughter Catherine writes in her diary on 15 February 1897: "My father is one of those men, one of those Don Juans who just can't help it. How many hearts has he wounded? How many broken?? Without counting that of Maman, who sees the amorous glances given him by Mmes B. S., T, S. B., X, Y, Z, etc." Somewhere between these two verdicts, the truth lies. Unless the truth can contain them both.

One of the problems of telling Pozzi's story—let alone of attempting to judge him in some late-assembled court of morals—is the lack of female evidence. His wife Thérèse was mocked in society as "Pozzi's mute" (the nickname adapted from the title of Auber's opera *La Muette de Portici*), and has remained largely silent, apart from some touching letters to her son Jean after Pozzi's death. The influential Mme Loth-Cazalis has left not a syllable on the biographical record. All Pozzi's archived love letters were burnt, including those from Emma Fischoff; so her voice is heard only in the travel diaries she co-wrote with Pozzi, which consist mainly of awed annotations of European and North African sites. Sarah Bernhardt, who knew and loved him for half a century, never mentions him once in her autobiography. Some of her letters to "Doctor God" survive, but as that sobriquet suggests, they are theatrically intense in tone. "Much loved man! It was a great joy to see you! When will you read me a thesis again?"

The closest female witness we have is Catherine Pozzi, who kept extremely personal diaries from 1893 to 1906 and from 1912 to 1934;

Catherine Pozzi at eighteen

she also published, in 1927, a transparently autobiographical novella, *Agnès*. All diaries need to be approached with caution until their underlying biases and motivations can be grasped. Adolescent diaries need approaching with even more wariness. They look so bright-eyed and clear-seeing, so uncorrupted by the hypocrisy and double dealing of the world. And so they are. But in their clarity of judgement on their elders, they are at the same time both absolutist and volatile. On one page Catherine Pozzi adores her mother, on another she cannot bear her; on a third page she adores God and wants to lay down her life for Him; on a fourth she doubts He even exists. She is precocious, ultra-sensitive, painfully self-conscious, emotionally and spiritually oscillating. As a child, she is asthmatic; as an adult, tubercular. She is death-haunted, and even names her chihuahua Tod. She believes herself ugly, though in photos she looks remarkably like her mother, who was, we remember, when young and very rich, consequently "beautiful." But Catherine seems unaware of having (now or in the future) an inheritance. She vacillates between wanting either a "*grand amour*" or nothing—and thinks that "nothing," plus an early death, would be the best outcome to her life. She longs to be "*un être pur*, genuine not all made-up." Those last words were written in English, as are stretches of her diary. Like her father, Catherine was an Anglophile.

The child diarist also does not have the full context, and cannot be aware of the hinterland all relationships contain. "How stupid parents are," writes the sixteen-year-old Catherine, "to believe that young girls are little ignorant saints." True; but sometimes parents want to make their children believe that this is what they believe about them so that the children will have a model to live up to (and feel guilty about diverging from). Specifically, children cannot know what went on between their parents before they were born, and before they came to sentience. Did Catherine know (and if so, when) that Thérèse had "coldly" considered a marital separation while she was still in her mother's womb? It seems very unlikely—if she did, she would surely have mentioned it in her diary; so she was unable to factor that in, and account for its continuing effect on her parents' relationship.

As a small child, she is deeply attached to her father. But that time of innocent daughterly devotion soon passes. Aged eleven, she is lying in her parents' bed between them; Thérèse is reproaching Samuel over something; he is responding ironically; they bicker—and all of a sudden Catherine realises that "[they] don't love one another and are going to divorce." She flees to her own bedroom, breaks into sobs, is comforted by her mother, while her father is remorseful. At least she does not appear to believe (as is often the case) that their breach is in some way her fault; but from this moment on, her eye misses little.

She notes her father's flirtatiousness with other women; her mother's bad moods and neuralgia; their constant rows. There are some good times: aged fourteen, she has her first proper outing as a grown-up girl, alone with her father; he takes her to the Opéra-comique to see *Don Giovanni* (perhaps, in the circumstances, not the most tactful of choices). But by the time she is eighteen, she is writing that:

> I could have loved Papa even more than Maman, because he is made of the same stuff as me, and I admire him as I get to know him. He is what I could have been if circumstances had been favourable to my moral development, and if they had bothered with it . . . Well, now I detest him just in thinking what we could have been to one another, and what, thanks to him, we have not been.

At twenty-two, she writes: "And yet, I did love him, this *moral wreck* of a father." A month or so later: "this incomplete and phoney being" who "suffers from a plague of lying . . . Alas, alas, which of the three of us has ever been his child? Oh, the inexpressible moral poverty of this man whom all of Paris admires or envies!"

In 1899, Catherine had an appendectomy. In advance of this still-perilous operation, she rather melodramatically wrote farewell messages to her family. To her mother, her brother Jean and her grandmother, she expresses love and apology. Her note to her father reads:

My Father, You haven't loved me very much, and I felt it cruelly, but perhaps it wasn't your fault, and I was clumsy in trying to find the way to your heart. I have admired you from afar, and know that I resemble you.

The sentimental (!) memory you will hold of me will be worth more, I am sure, than the cold little disdainful friendship which is all that I have known from you.

I do love you all the same.

This diary of mine isn't exactly [Anatole] France, but I know that it will surprise you.

How could you imagine that at sixteen one could have such thoughts—and suffer from them.

It's not evident that Pozzi ever saw his daughter's scathing judgements on him. But it was he who had the courage (or responsibility) to carry out the operation, and it passed without complication. It is a sign of Catherine's spirit and wit that when, afterwards, the anaesthetist Dr. William Cazenove says quietly, "Are you awake? I think she's awake, but she doesn't want to talk," she carefully ponders her first words (as opposed to her last words), and eventually replies slowly, through bruised lips, "You're nothing but a filthy anti-Dreyfusard."

Her (almost) final words to and about Pozzi, in his lifetime, come in a diary entry of October 1913. She is thiry-one and married, but it seems that he has somehow outwitted a young man who had designs on her. She calls him—and the poet in her finds a nice double internal rhyme, "*le cher père si bien adultère.*" The diary entry, without the rhymes, is: "And there is my dear father, the well-known adulterer, still sternly defending my hymen . . ."

And if English readers are firmly on Catherine Pozzi's side (and why should they not be?) it's worth noting that, despite her Anglophilia, she was as capable as any other French person of banal Anglophobia. In Venice, aged eighteen, she runs into a group of Cook's tourists, and rages to her diary about "those tall Englishwomen, dried-up, harsh-skinned, stingy and vain, with absolutely *no* grace or softness; and those proud, cold, insensitive Englishmen, egotistical, idiotic and Oh so pleased with themselves."

And while we are on the subject, here is what the poet Jules Laforgue (1860–87) claimed: "There are three sexes: the male, the female, and the Englishwoman." But despite such unthinkingness, the year before he died, Laforgue married an English governess, Leah Lee.

In October 1899, after twenty years in the place Vendôme, the Pozzis moved to 47 avenue d'Iéna, near the Arc de Triomphe. They had commissioned the four-storey house for themselves, and Pozzi studied the plans as meticulously as when extending the Broca. The layout reflected the internal split in the family. Thérèse and her mother had the left wing of the house, Pozzi the right; they continued, in Catherine's phrase, to "live together as enemies." Pozzi's quarters, reached by a grand flight of steps, reflected his divided professional life: one part for medicine—office, surgery, examination room—and more formal quarters where he received political visitors. He also had his own bedroom overlooking the garden, and it seems probable (we

Pozzi among his treasures

cannot know) that bed-sharing had now ceased. Upstairs, the dining room seated thirty, and the salon continued as ever. The writers, painters, composers, aesthetes and politicians (except Dreyfusards) were still loyal; and it was here that Catherine Pozzi, soon to turn eighteen, made her first entry into literary society.

As the century turns, Pozzi is in his prime. He is rich, famous and successful; he has been elected senator for the Dordogne and mayor of his village. He is the holder of the first chair of gynaecology in France, which has been specifically created for him "via a whole set of procedural games to which Pozzi himself could not have been a stranger." His *Treatise of Gynaecology* has earned him European and American renown. He has celebrity patients and celebrity friends. He hunts at Rambouillet with the President of the Republic and the Prince of Monaco. Anatole France dedicates a book of speeches to him. He has many affairs, but has found a life companion in Emma Fischoff. He looks every inch a prime example of a successful man with his life held in balance between his delicate surgeon's hands. Soon, his photographic image will start falling out of Félix Potin chocolate bars.

He receives fan mail not directly related to his surgical skills. In December 1902, he forwards to a female friend "an epistolary pearl" he has just received from "a female Ibsenite harpist" (Ibsenite being the key word, a denominator of free thinking). She tells him that each evening she plays her harp while gazing at his photograph. Of course, there is gossip. There is always gossip: and it increases as fame increases. A satirical magazine claims that in one of his cupboards Pozzi keeps a lineup of bottles containing the appendices of some of Paris's best-known actresses. But this is the kind of rumour that, in many circles, burnishes a man's reputation.

At the same time, all is not well with Pozzi. He has discovered that even a masterful man cannot bend everyone to his will; still less can he bend money, and religion, and certain expectations of society, to his will. Thérèse has kept house for him, has organised and presided over lunches and dinners and their salon for twenty years. She is discreet, and knows how to put on a social face. She is also aware of his public relationship with Emma Fischoff. In the privacy of their home, first in the place Vendôme, then the avenue d'Iéna, they quarrel and shout—in front of their seven servants, and also in front of their three children.

And then there is Thérèse's mother, who lives with them. She and Pozzi are no longer on speaking terms. And charm—that very charm which works so well on society women—is never going to mollify a pious, provincial Catholic widow. Thérèse's mother continues to have more influence on her than Pozzi does. She is also watching over the spiritual welfare of her granddaughter Catherine. Grandmother, mother and daughter take communion together at the Eglise de la Madeleine. Religion and money do not change—and here both are held on the female side of the family.

Pozzi complains to a friend about being torn to pieces by "marital maenads."

In 1927, nine years after her father's death, Catherine Pozzi, then forty-four, publishes a brief novella, *Agnès*, about the emotional and spiritual turmoil of a seventeen-year-old girl. Agnès is writing a series of love letters (or, more exactly, soul-explaining letters) to the man of her dreams, whom she has yet to meet. She has also set herself a training regime—divided into three sections, Body, Mind and Soul—so that she will be in perfect condition for equal love when He comes along. *Agnès* is touching, tranced, Rilkean and blindingly autobiographical. In her own solitary, misunderstood adolescence, Catherine had written similar letters to The Future One, many of them in English. She had also set herself a similar training regime.

On 1 February 1927, Catherine notes in her diary: "*Agnès* has come out. Mother is in heaven." The book was published under the fairly transparent initials "C-K" (Catherine's closest friends called her Karin), which seem not to have been penetrated. Five months later, she is received by the society poet Comtesse Anna de Noailles (in bed, unpowdered, hair loose). Catherine is asked if she wrote *Agnès*; she denies it. Interrogated for half an hour, she does not yield. Back home, in the company of her diary, she writes: "One thing that pleased

3ᵉ COLLECTION FÉLIX POTIN

COMTESSE DE NOAILLES
FEMME DE LETTRES

me: in *Agnès*, she recognised Papa, 'the father.' She is the only one who recognised him; also, the only one intelligent enough to do so . . . Alas!"

Anna de Noailles' savvy should not be over-praised. "The father" is a fashionable doctor who lives and works in a grand apartment while the rest of his family (wife, daughter, mother-in-law) live precisely fifty-six steps higher up, as in reality. The father is very successful, his quarters filled with tapestries and books and curios. "All the rays of life seemed to come to me from his direction," writes Agnès, "and yet he is inaccessible, like the sun." Too often, when she needs his attention, he is busy with his correspondence or on the telephone. "Yes, Princess . . . ?" is how he answers a typical call.

As an intransigent seventeen-year-old, Agnès observes that grown-ups lie all the time; but "Papa always lies less than the person he's speaking to." Her father has given her the complete works of William James, and lent her his Darwin. He is an atheist, but when she begins to suffer religious doubts, he fails to back her up and puts family peace above intellectual truth. "Don't be a nuisance to Grandma," he tells her. "Go to communion with her." This is felt as a further quiet betrayal, and by the end of the novella the tormented Agnès is praying to the Virgin at the fountain in Lourdes. Her thrice-repeated request is: "Give me love or make me die."

Catherine Pozzi's first experience of love—of love's feelings, that is—was with a young American woman, Audrey Deacon, in 1903. They spent two intense months together in Engadine, young women each with a melancholy streak and a sense of abandonment. For Catherine it was partly a grand existential loneliness—she endorsed Musset's formulation that life was a "sombre accident between two infinite sleeps"—and partly familial: she was used to an absent father, but now it seems her mother is "constantly away on visits" as well. Audrey's childhood was marked by her father shooting dead her mother's lover in 1892: she and her three sisters were shuttled transatlantically at first, then put in European convents while their mother travelled with her new prince-lover. There was also mental instability in the family: her father died in an American asylum in 1901; while her sister Gladys, who fulfilled her mother's ambitions for her by marrying the Duke of Marlborough, also ended her life in confinement.

These two months of fierce love–friendship were followed by a fierce love–separation, with Catherine addressing her letters to Audrey (in English) "My dear Ship"—as if to one sailing away from her. In fact, Audrey was sailing away from her definitively: she was diagnosed with heart disease, and put under the care of English nurses in Rome, with a Dr. Troisier in charge (who was, somehow inevitably, a good friend of Pozzi's). She died in the spring of 1904 at the age of nineteen; Catherine kept a photograph of her lying in her padded coffin, eyes half-open, as if staring out at lost life.

Her next attachment was another young American woman, one

Audrey Deacon in her coffin

much more confident and outgoing: Georgie Raoul-Duval. This was
a more dangerous love–friendship, and closer to becoming carnal.
Georgie was already the mistress of Colette's husband, and "probably"
already part of a threesome. Her seductive intentions were evident, and
she did an analysis of Catherine's handwriting which proved that the
writer wanted to submit to them. For the first time, Catherine knew
she was desired. The problem was that others knew, or saw, this too,
and her parents were alerted. They asked their daughter to keep her
distance from Georgie; and Catherine complied.

By the time she wrote *Agnès*, Catherine had also twice experienced heterosexual love—of very differing degrees. In 1909, aged twenty-six, she married the twenty-two-year-old Edouard Bourdet. She had known him for a number of years as one of a gang of friends, more playmate than aspirant lover. Determined to impress an older, and seemingly more sophisticated woman, Edouard boldly wrote to tell her that he had rented a bachelor apartment and would be waiting for her there. Retaking the initiative, Catherine replied that she would come to him, but "not as your mistress, as your fiancée." (In fact, they did little more than cuddle on the two occasions she visited his *garçonnière*.) On their honeymoon in Cannes they played golf together, and their lovemaking, from Catherine's point of view, was like a continuation of their adolescent games, less than oceanic. One structural problem to their relationship was that Edouard could passionately express his love in letters when he was away from her, but was tongue-tied in her presence. Another was that he quickly became successful as the author of the sort of boulevard plays she despised. Bourdet was a man who preferred life (and love) to be uncomplicated, and found Catherine's intense, self-punitive nature hard to take on a daily basis. Unsurprisingly, she also disapproved of Bourdet making the lead actress in one of his plays his mistress. But—like her mother—she was pregnant by the time she fully realised that the marriage was not going to be a success.

Her second love had all the complication, intelligence and intensity she had always craved: the poet Paul Valéry, whom she met in 1920. Here at last was the soulmate her adolescent self had dreamed of, written to and schooled herself for. A man of the highest intellect and sensibility, someone to match (and master) her. Violent passion was declared on both sides. They were together (except in the sense of cohabitation) for eight years. The relationship oscillated viscerally, her hours of greatest fulfilment matched by the most painful

Edouard Bourdet

disappointments she had ever known. Valéry was both her "Very High Love" and her "Hell." She reproached him for his worldliness, his egotism, his cynicism—and his attachment to his family. All of which might have been enough to dish any relationship, however exalted.

Agnès, addressing her unmet future love, writes, "Women's fate depends excessively on chance. You [men] meet them either too soon or too late, and those you do meet are never there at the time which would be the most delighting. In vain do they prepare themselves, and wait, and say, 'Now, now . . .'" This was certainly the case with Catherine Pozzi's two adult loves. But the very first love to disappoint her was her charming, busy, distracted, selfish, careless, absent, adored father. As soon as she was able to write, Catherine started sending him notes and letters; he always replied. This correspondence, "copious, ironic, happy and witty," went on for several years. Much later, when

Thérèse discovered and read it, she exclaimed, "But these are love letters." Of which she had received none herself for a long time.

In May 1929, eleven years after Pozzi's death, Catherine is reading an old volume of Swedenborg from his library. When she reaches page seventy-seven, a letter from her much younger self falls out. It begins, "I shan't go, dear Father . . ." (which sounds like a reference to church attendance). On the back of her letter Pozzi had scribbled some unrelated medical annotation. The older Catherine finds her younger self's letter "tragic"; in that moment, she rediscovers "all my youth and all my foolish courage, which never worked out." But "there is some sweetness nevertheless in my words, and in his a magnificent pride . . . And my wise, determined little letter is, after all, a love letter. Which he also felt, because he kept it." And even all these years on, "There is still a touch of Father's scent on the paper."

In 1901, sixteen years after the "strange trio" went to London, Edmond de Polignac lay dying. Winnaretta hired an English nurse to sit with him through the night. Delirious, Polignac imagined that this white-collared woman was one of the "unpleasant" English nannies who had attended him as a child. So he dismissed her from his bedroom with the words, "I have nothing to say to the Princess of Wales at three o'clock in the morning."

He returned to England for the last time in his coffin, and was buried, at his request, in the Singer family tomb, on the cliffs above Torquay, looking over to France. His inscription reads "Composer of Music." Winnaretta, when she died forty-two years later, had herself described as "Wife of the Above." This unlikely couple, whose connubial contentment so annoyed Montesquiou, shared a joint epitaph—"Happy in Faith, Happy in Love"—from *Parsifal*.

Jean Lorrain, always one to enjoy spoiling another's party (or funeral), managed to publish *Monsieur de Phocas* within a week of the Prince's death. Winnaretta makes a small but instantly recognisable appearance as La Princesse de Seiryman-Frileuse, "the Yankee multi-millionairess whose wealth has imposed her on Parisian high society." Here are two (male) onlookers observing her at a party:

> "It was clever of her to marry the old prince—in name, but little else—and settle eighty thousand francs on him so she could bear his title while parading before the world her depravity and her independence. She is at least honest and passionate, that one . . . and beautiful in her perverse way—look at the harsh wilfulness in her proud profile, her hard and mournful grey eyes the colour of melting ice, which conceal such energy of thought, and such obstinacy . . . Do you know the Princess's nickname?"
>
> "Lesbos?"
>
> "Yes, absolutely. 'Lesbos, land of warm and langorous nights.'"

(The line is from Baudelaire.) There is a circularity to Lorrain's cattiness. He spent a long time trying to get a rise out of Montesquiou; the Count simply ignored him. Montesquiou spent a long time trying to get a rise out of Winnaretta; the Princess simply ignored him. Now Lorrain was targeting Winnaretta, who had more important things on her mind.

Ten years after Polignac died, the Princess, in a nice gesture of (Americano)-Franco-British friendship, set up in his memory the Edmond de Polignac Prize, to be administered and judged by the Royal Society of Literature in London. It was to be awarded annually, and was worth £100. The intention was to honour young and promising writers rather than the established. And one condition specified by Winnaretta was that women should not be excluded from the award.

They may not have been excluded, but they never won it. In its first year, 1911, the prize went to Walter de la Mare; then to John Masefield (1912), James Stephens (1913) and Ralph Hodgson (1914). Indigent writers of poetic prose were most grateful for the £100. Stephens noted that when the news came through, his "total wealth in visible and moveable goods was one wife, two babies, two cats and fifteen shillings." Definitely poorer than Polignac sitting in the rue Washington in his shawl and knitted cap. In Masefield's year, the ghost of Oscar Wilde came on the scene: Lord Alfred Douglas denounced his prize-winning *The Everlasting Mercy* as "nine-tenths sheer filth." But patronage is always implicitly conditional. In 1915 and 1916 the Princess failed to send the RSL any money from Paris, whereupon her loyal if brief attempt to keep the Prince's name alive in British literary circles came to an end.

The *roman à clef* has obvious attractions for a novelist—the joy of malice, the wink of non-secret secrecy, the vanity of being in the know and sharing it with others. But the dangers are more evident. It can seem arch and self-involved; it can lead to lawsuits and even duels; but the main danger is that it comes time-stamped, like the dandy, like the butterfly. Also, place-stamped. Jean Lorrain's first novel, *Les Lépillier*, is a *roman à clef* about his natal Fécamp, a novel of "rain, mud and cupidity." It was said that everyone who lived within thirty kilometres of the town could recognise all the main characters disobligingly portrayed therein. The downside being that few living beyond that boundary knew (or cared) who was being mocked. *Monsieur de Phocas* was sent out to reviewers with a publicity flyer claiming that the novel was "a telephone directory of all the great Parisian vices and of all the *Femmes Damnées*." Here, the latent enemy is less geography than time. What happens when everyone in the telephone directory is dead? Needing footnotes to work out who a character "really is" in a novel is like going to see a classic play and needing the antique jokes explained to you.

The reason we turn to *A Rebours* more willingly than to *Monsieur de Phocas* is mainly because the former is the stranger and more original novel; but also because, despite its reputation, *A Rebours* isn't "really about" Robert de Montesquiou. Huysmans spins off from a few pillaged details about the Count's ménage, but then focuses on his own thematic obsessions. Whereas Lorrain knew Montesquiou, the Polignacs and others all too well, and had scores to settle; so his novel becomes the prisoner of real people and their real lives. It is also a *roman à clef* in a different, odder way: a novel which refers back to a previous novel, which draws some of its scenes and subjects from *A Rebours*. A *roman à roman à clef*? A *roman à clef à clef*?

Even Edmond de Goncourt, who knew Lorrain well, and liked him, couldn't decide whether to attribute his friend's reckless use of words to malice, or a complete absence of tact. (It could be both, of course.) This is one of the central problems of having him in your book. You often can't work out his motivation, and you doubt that he can either. He knows everyone and seems to have quarrelled with most of them. He feeds off aggression. He wants to be an outsider but also an insider. He feels he isn't really accepted, but only half wants to be. He believes he hasn't had his literary due. He senses that he is tolerated rather than valued. He wants to be a dandy but is outclassed by Montesquiou. He wants to be a novelist but is outclassed by Huysmans. He wants to be a poet, a dramatist, to write words for Sarah Bernhardt to speak—and he is known as a journalist. He doesn't know when to stop, and such excessiveness must be part of his charm. At a time when libel law was weak, editors loved his provocations. Is it simplistic to suggest he was filled with self-hatred (and therefore sought out rough trade and enjoyed getting beaten up)? Or is that too modern an explanation?

2ᵉ COLLECTION FELIX POTIN

JEAN LORRAIN
HOMME DE LETTRES

Certainly, it is hard to know the basis of his friendship with such a committed rationalist as Dr. Pozzi. Lorrain spent years dabbling in satanism and the occult. Sexually, they were at opposite ends of the spectrum. Lorrain was a reckless gossip; Pozzi very discreet. The attraction of opposites? That feels too pat. Both were great talkers by repute; but talk dies. Perhaps the fact that Pozzi rarely quarrelled with anyone (except his family) and rarely disapproved of anyone (ditto) helped. Probably he found Lorrain amusing. And each might have enjoyed the fact that the other was not in his professional world.

The problem of working out just exactly what happened in Lorrain's life, and head, and heart, can be illustrated by the case of Jeanne Jacquemin. She was a pastellist, symbolist and satanist, a friend of Verlaine's who lived in an artistic-occultist commune in Sèvres with an engraver called Lauzet. Various poets were naturally in love with her. She also had serious health problems which left her, in the ever-ungallant words of Edmond de Goncourt, "with a body as bereft of its internal female organs as a fish prepared for salting." She and Lorrain seem to have first met among the bohemian cafés of the mid-1880s. He was drawn to both her art and her occultism, and wrote a serious appreciation of her work which helped launch her.

After several years of shared satanism and bohemia, something went wrong between the two of them. According to Lorrain's biographer, "Jacquemin became very jealous; perhaps she was truly in love with the writer and he experienced the belligerence of the invert for a woman who wants to ravish him; or perhaps she wanted to marry him to get out of her own irregular situation; either way, he was frightened, this man who regularly braved the roughest of rough trade." He complained that "She is a ghoul, feeding off my substance." In 1893, he told Pozzi that Jacquemin was stalking him. Pozzi diagnosed strained nerves (his, not hers), and advised him to take a calming voyage to North Africa. Which he did, travelling to Algeria and Tunisia.

Pozzi's diary for 15 March 1894 reads: "Lunch Lorrain—Mme Jacquemin." Did it have a specific purpose? Was Pozzi playing the peacemaker? Lorrain's biographer calls it "lunch with two of his operatees" (so it's possible Pozzi had performed a hysterectomy on Jacquemin). But then he ascribes to it a purpose, on no obvious stated evidence, writing of Lorrain: "The patient's gratitude often expressed itself in giving dinner for the doctor with an as yet unknown beauty." Except that this was lunch—and Pozzi already knew Jacquemin if he had operated on her. But the biographer persists: both Jacquemin and Liane de Pougy (whose ambition was to be the most fashionable and expensive whore in Paris) were offered up to Pozzi by Lorrain "in order to keep him sweet." Yet why did Pozzi need keeping sweet? This is not explained. But it is typical of what happens when Lorrain enters the story: things become less rather than more clear.

As does the next development. You are Jean Lorrain. Jeanne Jacquemin has been stalking you and trying to feed off your substance; you have been close to nervous collapse, and have taken a restorative African break; you are back in Paris lunching with her and your mutual surgeon. What do you *not* do next, immediately, and for much of the following decade? You do not start and continue mocking her in print, presenting her under the most permeable of disguises. Except that you are Jean Lorrain, and therefore this is exactly what you do.

Here she is portrayed as a quarrelsome nymphomaniac with the air of a saint; there she is as a fallen Rosicrucian who has wallowed in all the filth of satanism; she is also "a spider-crab with the head of a jellyfish." And so on. Lorrain even turned against her art in print, disparaging "the monotony of her pastels, which have a wilful oddity and an overwhelming ugliness." It must have come as a great surprise to him when, in 1903, the bohemian ex-satanist finally responded not in a bohemian or a satanical fashion—no voodoo dolls stuck with pins—but in a properly bourgeois one: she set the lawyers on to him. And they found a choice array of articles on which to base a libel action.

In the witness box, Jacquemin reportedly played the ravishing libelled martyr to perfection. The court found that she was transparently recognisable in many of Lorrain's pieces, and that he had attributed "depraved morals" and "shameful adventures" to her. It awarded 100 francs against *Le Journal,* 2,000 francs against Lorrain, plus punitive damages of 50,000 francs split between the paper and the writer, and two months in prison for Lorrain. He appealed against the verdict, but strangely—though also confirming that you never know what's going to happen next with Lorrain—on the day his appeal was to be heard, Jacquemin withdrew her complaint.

Lorrain escaped prison, but even so was bust. He asked Huysmans for help, and when his former friend declined, Lorrain wrote an article accusing Huysmans of corrupting the public by popularising occultism and black masses. Then he got back to work. He started a satirical novel about women writers and the recently created Prix Fémina, to be called *Maison pour femmes*. But he sensed things closing in on him, and in 1905 began signing his chronicle in *La Vie Parisienne* with the pseudonym "*Le Cadavre.*"

2. COLLECTION FELIX POTIN

DE LA GANDARA

Lorrain certainly kept Pozzi busy as a doctor. He was a committed drinker of ether, which gradually destroys the gut, and his recreational behaviour was rarely influenced by sound advice, medical or otherwise. In June 1893, Pozzi removed nine ulcerations of the intestine (which some thought syphilitic in origin). On Sunday 11 November 1894, Lorrain attended Goncourt's *grenier* and told him he was very ill, and was booked in for a double consultation with Dr. Pozzi and a colleague who specialised in gastric pathology. Lorrain added that whenever he was ill, his childhood always came back to him, and the writer within him wanted to speak of nothing else.

This latest consultation led to surgery the following May, in which "a few centimetres" of gut were removed. On the 26th the artist De la Gandara went to see him at Pozzi's clinic and reported to the *grenier* that he was in enormous pain from his tightly wound bandages. On 30 June the poet Henri de Régnier (Montesquiou's opponent in the Bazar de la Charité duel) described Lorrain "lying on a chaise longue, wrapped in white flannel and surrounded by flowers sent by Otero"— Mlle Puentovalga Otero, the famous flamenco dancer. Finally, on 7 July, Lorrain himself turned up at Goncourt's door, looking remarkably cheerful, and full of semi-treacherous stories:

He tells me about this house of death, where four women died during his stay there, where the talk is of nothing but the removal of ovaries and uteri, where there is a training course for women so that they may learn the Pozzi method of suturing, which leaves not the slightest trace that might repel either a husband or a lover.

Lorrain says he has suffered dreadfully for two weeks, each night reliving the operation and in such pain that he was constantly given morphine. He has anti-Semitic nightmares, shouting, "Maman, there are Jews in my bed." He still has to go back twice a day as an outpatient; after washing him out with an enema of alcohol and boiling water, an intern then feeds into his body big fat tubes, like garden hosepipes . . .

The following April, Lorrain laughingly complains that Pozzi's "butchery" of his body has produced a kind of phosphorescence; that it has set off in him a mad desire for sex; and that all the excesses he is currently practising, instead of making him thinner, are making him fatter.

Did Lorrain really pimp for Pozzi? Did Pozzi need anyone to pimp for him? Perhaps Pozzi, whose life and work were all about control and precision, enjoyed mixing with someone whose life was lived with the opposite priorities. And perhaps the lifelong rationalist enjoyed studying those for whom black masses held appeal. The nearest Pozzi ever strayed from the scientific was when an actress asked him to prescribe something for stage fright. He recommended a homeopathic remedy (briony, if you're interested). But maybe this wasn't even a minor straying from rationality: Pozzi might well have calculated that a placebo would work as effectively, if not better, than a pharmaceutical product.

There is also an undated letter from Pozzi to Montesquiou inviting him to a soirée at the place Vendôme, where he would be able to witness hypnotism, magnetism, braidism (a version of mesmerism) and somnambulism. But this would have been a scientific demonstration rather than hocus-pocus. These subjects were of medical interest at the time: Paul Broca had tried hypnosis as an anaesthetic during surgery (with mixed results); while Charcot had been experimenting with it since 1878—indeed, there was an ongoing public dispute between the "school of Nancy" and Charcot's own "school of La Salpêtrière." As it happened, Pozzi was then living only three doors away from the house in which, at the end of the previous century, Mesmer had set up his practice of magnetic healing. Patients were connected by steel rods to bottles of magnetised water standing in oak tubs. Many regarded this as a true scientific procedure; and for some, indeed, it seems to have worked.

It was hard to pierce Robert de Montesquiou's carapace—and he wouldn't have wanted you to. He was perhaps at heart a melancholic: he liked to say that his mother had "given me the sad present of life." His restlessness and furious acquisitiveness might have been a response to this. He was vain without being especially self-reflective, one of those who, rather than look inside to discover who they are, prefer to see themselves in the reflections that come back from others. He often describes clothes and decor with more loving and attentive detail than the people who inhabit them. He said: "I prefer the parties I give to the guests who attend them" (and perhaps the guests noticed). He was devoted to his houses, of which he had many.

His favourite was built during the Second Empire, in Petit Trianon style, at Neuilly, on the edge of the Bois de Boulogne. He christened it the Pavilion of the Muses, and lived there from 1899 to 1909. Yturri had found it for him, and it was the perfect setting for parties. The rooms "were not really decorated as one understands the term today, but arranged either by caprice or by affinities more subtle than those merely of colour or style." As well as fine bindings, the library contained aesthetic and literary relics: a lock of Byron's hair, a sketch by Baudelaire of his mistress, and so on. One room was dominated by Whistler's portrait of the Count; another by Boldini's portrait of him. There was also a drawing by Boldini of Yturri's legs clad in cycling breeches.

One day, the Count was down in an "ugly" spa town in the Pyrenees, tending the "intermittently valetudinarian" Yturri (who suffered from diabetes), when he received a telegram from his *gardien* containing the worst news. The Pavilion had been burgled. He set off immediately, leaving Yturri to recover by himself. As he travelled north, the Count's apprehension deepened. He imagined his Whistler slashed to pieces. He remembered Flaubert's phrase from *Salammbô* about the mercenaries destroying objects "whose meaning escapes them, and which, because of this, exasperate them." When he got to Neuilly he found, to his relief and amazement, that his treasures were all intact and the "mercenaries" seemed to have left without any loot. Shortly afterwards, the burglars were arrested. At their trial, one of them was asked why they hadn't stolen anything. He replied: "Oh, there wasn't anything for *us* there." Montesquiou described these words as "the most flattering of all that have been addressed to me in my entire existence."

In November 1904, Elaine Greffulhe, the daughter of Montesquiou's "cousin" Elisabeth, married the Duc de Guiche, a long-term friend of Proust's. When the writer asked the groom what he would like as a wedding present, the duke jestingly replied, "I think I have everything except a revolver." Proust took him at his word, buying him a Gastine-Renette. He commissioned the fashionable painter Coco de Madrazo to decorate its leather carrying case. This he did with gouaches illustrating poems written by Elaine Greffulhe when she was a young girl: they were about seagulls, white ships, mountaintops and tigers.

As far as I can remember or ascertain, nobody shoots anyone in Proust.

The Dreyfus Affair was the most violent event—politically and morally—of the Belle Epoque, so it's hardly surprising that guns and bullets also featured. During the second trial at Rennes, in 1899, Dreyfus's lawyer, Maître Labori, was walking to court when he was shot by a young man who ran away. The exact dimensions of the incident are unclear. By one account, Labori was gravely wounded; by another, he didn't need to be operated on. Dreyfusards found it deeply suspicious that the attempted assassin, revolver in hand, found no difficulty in escaping from a city filled with troops and police. Anti-Dreyfusards countered that it was all a put-up job, fake news. "Have you seen the bullet / The bullet that went into Labori?" ran a satirical song which quickly hit the street.

In 1908, after the long national agony—what Romain Rolland called the "holy hysteria"—was theoretically over, Zola's remains were transferred to the Panthéon. It was a grand state occasion: the President of the Republic was there, also Clemenceau, Jaurès, Mme Zola, Dreyfus himself and Dreyfus's doctor, who was, of course, Dr. Pozzi (Pozzi was everywhere). After a musical tribute but before the military march-past, the journalist Louis Grégori, a great friend of the violently anti-Semitic Edouard Drumont, fired two shots at Dreyfus, hitting him in the hand and arm. Dr. Pozzi was there to provide first aid.

When Grégori was brought to trial, French justice showed itself at its Frenchest. Grégori's lawyer argued that his client had not actually been shooting at Dreyfus the man, but rather at "the idea of Dreyfusism." Astonishingly, the assize court of the Seine accepted this argument, and Grégori was acquitted. Six years later, Jaurès was assassinated; his assailant was also acquitted.

French justice was always more open to abstract ideas than British justice; also, to the deployment of wit on the part of the defendant. In 1894, Félix Fénéon, art critic, journalist, literary and artistic insider—the only dealer Matisse ever trusted—was caught up in a police sweep of anarchists. It was not by mischance: Fénéon was a committed anarchist, by both word and deed. A police search of his office turned up a vial of mercury and a matchbox containing eleven detonators. Fénéon's the-dog-ate-my-homework explanation was that his father—who had recently died and was therefore sadly unavailable to give evidence—had found them in the street. When the judge put it to him that he had been observed talking to a well-known anarchist behind a gas lamp, Fénéon coolly replied, "Can you tell me, Monsieur le Président, which side of a gas lamp is its behind?" This being France, his wit and cheek did him no disservice with the jury, who acquitted him.

The following year, Oscar Wilde, perhaps imagining himself in France, engaged in his battle of wit and cheek with Edward Carson QC, only to discover that it did him no good in an English court, before an English jury. Coincidentally, this was also the year Toulouse-Lautrec portrayed Wilde and Fénéon in, respectively, plump and cadaverous profile, elbow to elbow, watching La Goulue do the Moorish Dance at the Moulin Rouge.

When Wilde reappeared in Paris in 1898 after his release from prison, Fénéon was one of those who openly welcomed him back, taking him to dinners and the theatre. But Wilde's spirits were often low, and he admitted to Fénéon that he had been tempted by suicide and had gone down to the Seine with that intention. On the Pont Neuf he had encountered a strange-looking man gazing down into the water. Judging him equally desperate, Wilde asked, "Are you also a candidate for suicide?" "No," the man replied, "I'm a hairdresser!" According to Fénéon, this non sequitur convinced Wilde that life was still comical enough to be endured.

At his trial, Wilde rebuked Edward Carson QC for the juvenile fantasy that a book can be either moral or immoral: it can only be well written or badly written. Nor does a work of literature do anything as simplistic as put forward a point of view. The aim of art is purely, simply, Beauty. And Wilde would agree with his own Lord Henry Wotton that "art has no influence on action."

These ideas are either refinements or vulgarisations (depending on your point of view) of Flaubert. The young Wilde was very Flaubertian: while he was at Oxford, Walter Pater lent him his copy of the *Trois contes*. Wilde planned to translate *La Tentation de saint-Antoine*. He said that in order to write English prose, he had studied the prose of France (it doesn't particularly show). He also claimed that his "recipe" for stimulating composition was to read twelve pages of *La Tentation* and then take "two or three haschich pills."

As a young man—ten years before he wrote *Madame Bovary*—Flaubert described himself as "merely a literary lizard basking the day away beneath the great sun of Beauty. That's all." He later wrote: "You cannot change humanity; you can only know it." He also said,

"You don't make art out of good intentions." These may sound like quietist principles, but aren't. Flaubert was always sternly against the sentimental, meliorist view of literature: the notion that an uplifting story with a happy ending (though weepie-happy would do just as well) might inspire readers to behave better and improve their lot. But "knowing humanity" and describing it accurately is an essentially corrective action. Things are not like that, you are saying, things are like this. People operate like this; society runs like this; religion (and sentimental literature) affect human sensibilities like this; what you have read in other novels is wrong. And this corrective function—oh, and by the way, love and sex and death aren't like that either—has an effect, the effect of truth, of restored vision. Though what people—readers—choose to do with this truth is not up to Flaubert. Some close the book in their hands, and simultaneously close their minds; others leave it open, and are filled with a form of grave reverie.

Which leads to another gun, and a couple more bullets. In March 1904, while Proust was collecting his artistically packaged revolver for the Duc de Guiche, a murder trial was beginning at the Seine assizes. Six months previously, a man and a woman had gone to the man's room at the Hotel Régina in Paris. The man was Fred Greuling, a Swiss national with a Württemberger father and an English mother, one Louisa Dewhurst of Northampton. He was small, blond, neatly turned out, plausible and loquacious—"vaguely intelligent and deeply stupid," as *Le Matin* cruelly put it. The son of hoteliers, he first dreamed of becoming a lawyer; instead, he sold postcards and became skilled at obtaining loans without ever repaying them.

On 7 October 1903, Greuling met Elene Popesco, a Romanian "artiste," and fell instantly in love with her—or so he claimed. He also claimed that she claimed that he was her first lover. For two days they took drives in the Bois, ate in fashionable restaurants, and went to the Comédie-Française, all on borrowed money. At one point, Greuling mentioned owning a gun. In his hotel room, they had a quarrel, supposedly about whether they should run away together to Nice or to Bucharest. Popesco then searched for Greuling's revolver, but in doing so came across a packet of love letters addressed to him. Feeling herself betrayed by a man who had so recently taken her virginity, she shot herself. Twice. Once in the back of the head, and once in the right eye. Or so he said.

If this sounds like a cheap, implausible novelette, it pretty much was; Greuling had spent his six months on remand writing out the story of his life in twenty notebook volumes, and he relied on this roman-fleuve for his defence. Perhaps he hoped the "penny newspapers" would bring him "immortality." Unremarkably, the court declined to believe much of his story. The prosecution claimed that the case was no more than the squalid matter of a pimp killing his mistress; while the judge was robustly and publicly sceptical that Elene Popesco, moving in the circles which she did, could possibly have been a virgin.

But there was a further, literary aspect to the case, and a possible refutation of Wilde and Lord Henry Wotton's belief that art has no effect on action. "M. Jean Lorrain has always had a great influence on my destiny," Greuling said in evidence. As a young man "I used to put on either a blue or a pink dressing gown to read his books, and he awakened in me unrealisable desires . . . I wanted to get to know him. But I was greatly disappointed when I finally set eyes on this man with the gaze of a viper, and his fingers ornamented with rings. He was an eccentric of the first water." Despite such predictable disappointment—writers in person routinely fail to satisfy or gratify a reader's expectations—Lorrain's influence continued. By now Greuling had switched from postcard-selling to gold-dealing, and was able to afford a dream he had first entertained while reading Lorrain: that of seeing Venice.

Once there, he told the court, he had a "perfect platonic romance" in a gondola with a petite and "very poetic" Russian woman. "And it was here," *Le Matin* commented sardonically, "that Lorrain, without his knowledge, presided over this marriage of souls." In Greuling's account, the writer's name came up in conversation, whereupon he expressed his admiration for *Monsieur de Phocas*. "What!" exclaimed the petite Russian woman in the gondola. "And you don't say anything bad about him! At last I have met a man who doesn't say anything bad about Jean Lorrain!"

This joyful escapade seems to have been irrelevant to Greuling's legal defence, which was two-pronged. On the one hand, he was innocent, because Elene Popesco had cleverly managed to kill herself in a way that looked remarkably like murder. And on the other hand, and in any case, his reading of Jean Lorrain had undermined his moral sense and diminished his responsibility. Strangely, the court declined to believe either of Greuling's explanations, and sentenced him to ten years.

Lorrain was disturbed by this trial, and the evidence given. The previous year, he had not only incurred ruinous libel damages in the Jacquemin case, but had also been dragged into another unedifying prosecution. Two aristocrats in their early twenties, Baron Jacques d'Adelswärd-Fersen (a descendant of Axel von Fersen, supposedly Marie Antoinette's Swedish lover) and Count Albert Hamelin de Warren, were convicted of "inciting minors to debauchery." The two men had lured young boys from some of Paris's best schools to their bachelor apartment, where—twice weekly—quasi-satanic practices led to "Neronic" sexual behaviour. The press, true to type, delighted in the

"Black Masses Scandal," which it took as evidence of the end of civilisation. While the court addressed the case in strict legal terms—sodomy not satanism being its concern—the newspapers preferred to lament the wider, deplorable state of the nation. The aristocrats' *garçonnière* was compared to Des Esseintes' suburban retreat (not that he got up to anything there). Literary names, from Baudelaire onwards, were cited as helping promote a climate of Decadence: prominent were those of Huysmans and Lorrain. Literature could poison, the press insisted. The matter was made worse for Lorrain because he had actually met Fersen in Venice in 1901; while the Baron, in his defence, blamed Lorrain's writings for his behaviour. As proof of influence, he had even published some of his poems under the pseudonym "Monsieur de Phocas."

As in the Greuling case, the court was uninterested in the defendant's literary excuses. But Lorrain was alarmed: being publicly accused of having such a noxious literary effect that one man had been led to murder and another to the sexual abuse of minors was, even by Lorrain's unconventional standards, pushing it too far. He appealed to his writer friends for public support. Colette came to his aid, but most declined to help, or simply ran for cover.

This was not surprising: the boldest may grow prim and scandalised when fire wafts in their direction. In 1895, at the time of the Wilde trial in London, the journalist Jules Huret, in *Le Figaro littéraire*, named three French writers as "intimates" of Wilde. They were Marcel Schwob, Catulle Mendès and Jean Lorrain. Schwob had, in Lorrain's description, been Wilde's "*cornac*," or elephant driver, during his 1891 visit to Paris. He and Mendès both challenged Huret to a duel; while Lorrain forced the journalist to publish a retraction.

Catherine Pozzi, like her father, was an Anglophile; and like him, spoke excellent English. In March 1918, when it suddenly seemed possible that Germany might win the war, she found herself lacking in furious patriotism:

> Do I really give a damn about the future of my country? Do I not like France? Frankly, I don't like it any better than England, my second spiritual home. England has given me so much, so many precious things: a sense of the ineffable, a religion of striving towards the divine, Browning, [George] Eliot, the holy anguish of Shelley and of Swinburne. Oh, there are so many of them, and so great.

England was also a place of physical refuge for Catherine, especially after two violent family crises. In April 1905, aged twenty-two, she had a furious row with her father, denouncing his adulteries to his face, specifically his public liaison with Emma Fischoff. Addressing herself in the second person in her diary, she writes: "Your father cursed you, Katie, the other day, and heaped blows upon you, because you allowed him to see, just for a second, that you didn't respect him." As a consequence, she was despatched to spend time in London by herself, and then three weeks in Hove, visiting her younger brother Jacques, who had been sent there to boarding school in order to learn self-discipline.

But this being Catherine Pozzi, it was far more than just a censorious daughter provoking a self-righteous father to violence. The event is swathed in existential crisis. Her diary entry begins: "You are weeping, you are weeping . . . Is it because you have understood that nothing, nothing human, would ever satisfy the immense longing in your soul?" And ends: "My God! My God! My God! Give me the right to die, and to sleep . . ." So this was more than something that could be resolved by family counselling. In between these two outbursts, Catherine is terrestrial and punitive, spreading her contempt beyond her errant father. Her brother Jean, she writes, "shamelessly displays every day the most banal and the most narrow of egotisms." And her mother, whose side she always takes against her father, is more to be pitied than despised:

Catherine and Jean as children   Jean and Catherine, *c.* 1903

Your mother is just a small child found standing by the wayside, on whom pity has been taken, because she has entrusted herself to you, and whom one loves because she is sweet-tempered and because harm has been done to her—but who will never be able to console you for anything, and whose eyes can look into yours for a long time without ever divining the despair behind them.

It's clear that this family explosion has been building for a while, and this is a rare occasion on which we hear from the middle child, Jean.

Now twenty-one, the future diplomat is already practising his skills. Two days before the crisis, and responding to a suggestion from his sister that their parents might divorce, he writes:

> Consider how regrettable a *violent* solution would be for all of us at this moment in time: for Mother, who loves him despite everything, and who would have to put up with the existence of a *second* Mme Pozzi; and for you, given that the world doesn't entirely accept divorce . . . I can't speak for him, but he already has many enemies, and this fall, this loss of social status, would put him into the category of adventurers: *and he is worth better than that.* Can't you two understand that he doesn't absolutely love Mme F: what he seeks from her is what he doesn't get at home—a smiling face, friendly words, *admiration*, words which flatter his amour-propre, and the respect due to someone who has attained the position that he has in the world . . . You mustn't expect that our father will now drop Mme F: he makes it a point of honour that he owes her gratitude for the *love* she has shown him. But do you not, for your part, think that Mother ought to have been able to tolerate this inevitable liaison . . . and show him, instead of recrimination, a smiling face, and to make for *us*, with him or if necessary without him, a house, a home, a family . . .

It makes for an intense quartet: a proud father, an intransigent mother, a fiercely moral daughter, a diplomatic son; a family split along sex lines. Thérèse Pozzi, up to this point, is still not directly heard from; in that respect she remains, domestically as well as socially, "Pozzi's mute." In 1932, Catherine noted: "Yesterday, I reread some letters from 1909. I was astonished to discover a letter to me from my father in which he writes of Mother's harshness, of her pride, and of her commitment to 'all or nothing.'"

Catherine Pozzi, in Parisian fashion, among her fellow students at Oxford

In the spring of 1907—a time not covered by Catherine's diaries—there was a second fracas. This one is less annotated, but the grounds remained the same; at one point, Catherine flung herself between her parents and was slapped and "half-strangled" before Pozzi was calmed down. Again, she fled to England, where friends found her a temporary place at St. Hugh's College, Oxford. She spent the spring term there, experiencing rain, cold and loneliness, as so many have done since. She also upset her feminist fellow students by declaring in a public debate that a woman is "only an inchoate mass of possibility waiting to be moulded by a man's hand." Still, her work impressed the dons, who offered her a permanent place from the autumn term. She rented a flat against her return, and confidently went back to France for the holidays. She was imagining for herself an English future: as a student, a thinker, then later as an essayist or perhaps journalist and critic. She would make a serious life in this cold, harsh country full of fine poets. Her tutor, Miss Miller, assured her that she was capable of succeeding in her goals. But she had reckoned without her mother. Thérèse, with a mixture of flattery, tears and emotional blackmail, persuaded her to abandon her academic career before it had begun. It was a matter of long regret that this English life was taken away from her. Thérèse also convinced Catherine to be reconciled with her father, after months of mutual silence. Mme Pozzi, however mute, is far from a passive actor in these family dramas.

An artist paints a likeness, or a version, or an interpretation, which celebrates the sitter during life, commemorates him or her after death, and perhaps sparks curiosity in the spectator centuries and more later. This sounds straightforward, and sometimes it is. I was drawn to Dr. Pozzi by the Sargent portrait, became curious about his life and work, wrote this book, and still find the picture a true and dashing likeness.

But it doesn't take much for this collusion between dead painter, dead subject and live spectator to go wrong. One of the greatest of French nineteenth-century portraits is Ingres's *M. Bertin*. I've seen this picture many times over many decades. It was painted in 1832 and lives in the Louvre. A large, powerful man with suspicious eyes and a down-turned mouth sits in a chair. As with *Dr. Pozzi at Home*, the hands are key: fiercely grasping the knees, pulling the man's torso and head towards us, so that he looms and dominates. I knew somehow that Bertin was a banker, and for many years he embodied for me a certain side of French nineteenth-century life: the hard, acquisitive, smug side, pandered to in the 1840s by Prime Minister Guizot when he urged his compatriots to concentrate on making money. *"Enrichissez-vous!"* he is said to have declared (though the phrase, like many such, seems to be apocryphal). In any case, they did; and this portrait, monumental despite its medium size, always filled me with a fascinated disgust. Bertin was an enemy, an enemy of what I stood for (if I stood for anything); and also, I feared—were I to meet him in real life—more brutal, more powerful than me.

However, about ten years ago, I bothered to read the label beside the picture and discovered that Bertin wasn't a banker after all, but . . . a journalist. Of course, journalists can fill us with fascinated disgust as well, but still. Then I read that Bertin—editor of *Le Journal des débats* and, like Pozzi, a collector—was "warm, wry and engaging," qualities apparently brought out by Ingres in his portrait, even if not previously visible to me.

This was, admittedly, my entire fault. But it is hard for us not to see with modern eyes, and to read modern emotions into those who gaze out at us. Sitters rarely smile in early photographs, because having your picture taken was a serious (often once-in-a-lifetime) event, but also because of the long exposure required. When we look at a portrait—of an Elizabethan child, a Georgian worthy, a Victorian matron—what we are doing in part is trying to bring them back to life, to have an ocular conversation with them, as we look at them looking back at us. And in this exchange we may mistakenly assume that their feelings are versions of our feelings—or what our feelings might be if we were in their place; also, that they are, somehow, as interested in us as we are in them. We draw conclusions from their pose, their clothes, their accoutrements and their backdrop which might well be mistaken; we

Louis-François Bertin, Jean-Auguste-Dominique Ingres (1832)

may be ignorant of prevailing artistic conventions, or there might be a formal decision imposed on the sitter by the artist (or on the artist by the sitter). Though Pozzi and Sargent clearly got on, and enjoyed lunch together after each sitting, the portrait might still, in Sargent's mind, have been "all about the coat"; and in Pozzi's mind, less about swank and swagger than it turned out. Perhaps he was anxious that Sargent's manner might outweigh his matter; perhaps he was silently computing the difference between the scientific and the artistic eye; perhaps thinking about lunch (or his mistress). What did they talk about in their sessions together? We cannot know.

Sometimes it boils down to this: Who's in charge? And are they doing what they think they're doing? Here is Wilde's artist Basil Hallward:

> Every portrait that is painted with feeling is a portrait of the art-
> ist, not the sitter. The sitter is merely the accident, the occasion.
> It is not he who is revealed by the painter; it is rather the painter
> who, on coloured canvas, reveals himself.

This seems at first close to Lucian Freud's gruff assertion that the sitter is merely there to "help" the picture, and that what the sitter is "like" (in character, even physiognomically) is of minor interest to the artist. But Freud would not have gone so far as to say that when he painted a splayed female nude he was "revealing himself"; rather, he would say that he was using a person to make a picture, and by doing so was replacing that person—and their existence—with a new reality.

In any case, Hallward's contention is undermined by the very novel in which he (and Wilde) make that claim. Because the picture of Dorian Gray is, as everyone agrees, a compellingly accurate physical representation of the titular young man. And further—which is what drives the plot—it turns out to be a compellingly accurate moral representation as well, in his increasing degradation.

Those who generalise about the human condition often find their truths overturned by the obstinate individualism of reality. And the high point of the generalisation is the Wildean epigram. It is intended to be piquant, to stun and amuse and make the reader (or theatre-goer) feel inferior: in this, the Wildean epigram is a verbal dandy. And like the dandy, most epigrams, except the greatest, come with a "best before" label. Time is equally the enemy of the butterfly, the dandy and the epigram. "Work is the curse of the drinking classes" now seems no more than a glib inversion, and also tremendously snobbish, designed to entertain the idler who can afford to drink without concern for family or money. Mr. Erskine of Treadley, "an old gentleman of considerable charm and character" in Wilde's novel, tells us that "the way of paradoxes is the way of truth. To test reality we must see it on a tightrope. When the Verities become acrobats we can judge them." This is very Wildean. He was, socially and intellectually, a juggler, a tightrope walker, a trapeze artist, quick on his feet and quick in his head, a whirl of rhinestones caught in a spotlight while the rising clatter of the snare drum urges him and us towards that final cymbal clash. And then the applause—oh yes, the applause is vital.

"The way of paradox is the way of truth." When I was a young man, I first heard Wilde's epigrams on the lips of actors who knew exactly what effect they would have. I was startled by their elegance and confidence and therefore assumed their truth. Later, I began to notice how many of them relied on a slick reversal of a normal assumption or *idée reçue*. Then, in middle age, I began to doubt their essential truth, or even their moderate truth, or even their vestigial truth, and a fierce literary moralism set in. Finally, I realised that the Wildean epigram (whether in dramatic or prose form) is actually a piece of theatrical display rather than any serious distillation of truth. And then, post-finally, I discovered that Wilde was aware of this all along. As he once wrote to Conan Doyle: "Between me and life there is a mist of words always. I throw probability out of the window for the sake of a phrase, and the chance of an epigram makes me desert truth."

If it's true that we die in character, then we might expect the excessive to die excessively. Jean Lorrain was viewed as a French version of Oscar Wilde by Léon Daudet and others.

COLLECTION FÉLIX POTIN

RODIN

Wilde died in Paris on 30 November 1900. In the morning, "foam and blood" began coming from his mouth; at two in the afternoon, he expired, whereupon "his body exploded with fluids from the ear, nose, mouth and other orifices. The debris was appalling." Lorrain died in Paris on 30 June 1906, two days after being found on the stained linoleum of his bathroom, having perforated his colon with a self-administered enema. He was taken to a clinic in the rue d'Armaille. Pozzi and his colleagues conferred. Lorrain's intestines were in such a collapsed state—from ether or syphilis, the debate continued—that surgery would have been pointless; though they allowed the patient to believe otherwise, and hope for a recovery. He spent two days agonising. No visitors were allowed; but he received flowers and letters. He was greatly cheered when Rodin (without knowing Lorrain was ill) wrote and compared the subtlety of his prose to the smile of the Mona Lisa. Finally, his mother—Sycorax—arrived to watch over the death of her only child. At one point in his delirium, Lorrain cried out: "Paris! You have defeated me!"

The previous year, Lorrain's fellow night-prowler Gabriel Yturri had died from diabetes, also in character: dutifully, quietly, subserviently. Montesquiou responded to his final decline in the only way he could, shutting up any feelings within his bright carapace, keeping up his social obligations, often returning only to change clothes and go out again, as if dying were an act of bad taste. At one point, Yturri was pushed to complain to their mutual friend the Marquise de Clermont-Tonnerre, "The Count is leaving me to die like a dog." When the Marquise dared to remonstrate with Montesquiou, he replied: "If I go, he wishes it, and if I stay, he wishes it." He buried Yturri beneath an eighteenth-century lead statue in a cemetery at the gates of Versailles, and a year later celebrated and mourned his friend with a memorial volume, whose title was Yturri's anointed nickname: *The Chancellor of Flowers*.

1909 was the year when Pozzi's family life finally succumbed to the fissile pressures from within. He began it cohabiting at the avenue d'Iéna with his wife, mother-in-law, daughter and younger son; he ended it alone. First to go was Catherine Pozzi on 26 January, marrying, as she later put it, "in order to be married." By the time the newlyweds returned from their honeymoon, Catherine was pregnant and her husband had written a three-act play in ten days. It was called *The Rubicon*.

Three months later, at the avenue d'Iéna, a domestic rubicon was finally crossed. Thérèse demanded, and Samuel accepted, the legal separation she had first considered at the very start of their marriage. She would have charge of thirteen-year-old Jacques, whose education Pozzi would pay for. She would resume "complete command" of her fortune. Pozzi would pay rent to Thérèse for the continued occupation of his quarters. The only demand at which he jibbed was that Thérèse, her mother and the children be allowed to spend their holidays at La Graulet, the Pozzi family house in the Bergerac countryside. He insisted that his "personal room" there be available for his sole use in the summer. On 15 July, Thérèse and her mother moved out, to 33 avenue Hoche. The marriage was officially at an end. But at the same time, there was no question of a divorce: Thérèse's faith forbade it. Pozzi and Emma would have to get by with an Armenian monk's repeated blessing.

What caused this official rift, only a few months before the couple's thirtieth wedding anniversary? Perhaps this very fact: the date would commemorate something sham at its heart. Further, Catherine and Jean had left home. Jacques, the younger boy, was mentally frail and would require psychiatric treatment throughout his life. Perhaps Thérèse thought it was time to retrench and concentrate on essentials.

But there was another factor. Pozzi had occasionally been attacked and satirically treated in the newspapers before; but now *La Libre Parole*—one of the vilest papers ever printed—began to target him and was getting ever closer to home. The newspaper was edited by Edouard Drumont, in turn one of the vilest journalists ever, whose two-volume *La France juive* was a ranting codification of every anti-Semitic thought and feeling and paranoid "fact" ever entertained in the human mind. Thérèse sought help from one of their anti-Dreyfusard friends, the wonderfully named Sibylle Aimée Marie-Antoinette Gabrielle de Riquetti de Mirabeau, Comtesse de Martel de Janville, who wrote humorous novels under the decidedly snappier pseudonym of "Gyp." The Comtesse asked Drumont to do something to arrest the campaign against the private life of Dr. Pozzi. Drumont declined.

You can see why Pozzi had become a natural target for the anti-Dreyfusard, anti-Semitic, royalist, nativist, Catholic right. He was, for a start, "not really French," as his name admitted. He was not

COLLECTION FÉLIX POTIN

DRUMONT

COLLECTION FÉLIX POTIN

GYP

at all Catholic, being a Protestant turned atheist. He was a known freethinker who had the audacity to sit in the Senate. He was a committed Dreyfusard who spent a week taking notes at the second trial in Rennes. To blood-and-soil patriots, the final outcome of those years of "holy hysteria" was not in any way "a victory for justice," but rather "a victory for the Jews." Pozzi could pretty much be considered a "rootless cosmopolitan" himself. He had had a long affair with the Jewish nymphomaniac Sarah Bernhardt. For the past decade he had further flaunted his philosemitism by humiliating his wife and parading his mistress—his Jewish, married mistress—across the fashionable cities of Europe. And this was a man who, on a regular basis, examined with his bare hands the naked private parts of good French Catholic wives and daughters, some of whom, as everyone knew, he went on to seduce. What more need be said about such an enemy of the people? And how could Thérèse—reserved, religious and morally correct Thérèse—bear to live with him any longer?

That summer, Pozzi wrote to a friend from Venice, saying his life was "unstitched at the seams, yet currently bearable." Not least because

Pozzi by Léon Bonnat (1910)

the unmentioned Emma Fischoff was present at his side in the Grand Hotel Britannia. And further, because his career continued and his international fame was undiminished. That spring, he had spent six weeks in America, on his third and final visit. The official purpose was to attend the centennial celebrations in New York of the first successful ovariotomy, performed by Ephraim McDowell on Christmas Day 1809. Jane Crawford was held down in a chair by two burly men while, without anaesthetic, she was emptied of fifteen litres of fluid, turned on her side to drain the blood, and then stitched up again. All in twenty-five minutes. She was forty-seven at the time, and lived to be seventy-nine.

This was indeed something to celebrate. Within the lifetimes of the American and European delegates the streets had been largely cleared of the sight of women tottering painfully along behind grotesquely inflated stomachs, with many assuming they must be pregnant (and all the confusion that might entail). Nor is this an entirely historical matter. While I was writing this book, British newspapers reported the case of twenty-eight-year-old Keely Favell, who went to her doctor in Swansea after putting on weight and suffering blackouts. Three home pregnancy kits had returned negative results, and when asked by friends about the baby's due date, Keely now replied that she was "just fat." Blood tests were inconclusive; her GP decided she could only be pregnant and sent her to hospital. Whereupon a scan revealed an ovarian cyst weighing 26 kilograms—the equivalent of seven babies combined—which was removed during four hours of surgery. Fortunately, with anaesthetic.

Pozzi, speaking in English, addressed the New York conference on the subject of "French Successors to McDowell." He was not without his national pride: the idea of ovariotomy had been first raised in France in 1755. Further, it was the French invention in 1865, by Koeberlé and

Péan, of the haemostatic clamp—a "solid and reliable" instrument for compressing blood vessels—which made the operation viable. Still, the occasion was festive and fraternal, rather than competitive, and a relief from the "marital maenads" and poisonous politics of Paris.

Pozzi then took his second trip to the Mayo Clinic, where he spent three days with the two brothers and their now ninety-year-old father. Back in New York, he finally got to meet Alexis Carrel, whom he had missed in Montreal five years previously. Carrel was now installed in a laboratory on the top floor of the Rockefeller Institute on East 60th Street. He was thirty-six: small, tanned, balding, and "entirely clean-shaven in the American style" (this was a manifest transatlantic difference: every one of the twenty representatives of French Medicine in the second Félix Potin album of *Célébrités Contemporaines* sports some kind of facial hair). Carrel reminded Pozzi of "one of those little Italian priests I used to run into in Rome or Venice."

But there was nothing Catholic about what Pozzi saw in Carrel's laboratory: a dog with a bandaged neck, its carotid arteries removed and preserved in cold storage for subsequent grafts; two dogs, each with one forefoot grafted on from a third dog; another pair of dogs, one with a kidney grafted from the other. There was a dog whose left kidney had been removed and kept in Locke's solution for an hour, then grafted back into it again, before its right kidney was permanently removed; astonishingly, the dog not only survived on its one retransplanted kidney, but had given birth to eleven puppies. Carrel showed Pozzi his procedure for sectioning, clamping and suturing a carotid artery; the suturing done with Chinese silk thread and exceptionally fine needles; once the clamps were removed, the blood circulated normally.

Pozzi had never seen anything like this—or even heard about it—in all his travels. And just as he had been spurred to improve surgical

COLLECTION FÉLIX POTIN

SADI CARNOT

3ᵉ COLLECTION FÉLIX POTIN

CARREL ALEXIS
MÉDECIN

practices by what he had witnessed in the Franco-Prussian War, so Carrel had been inspired in his work by a later public event: the assassination in June 1894 of the French President Sadi Carnot. At a public banquet in Lyon, Carnot was stabbed by an Italian anarchist and bled to death the following day. This was inevitable: there was no way of repairing a slashed blood vessel. So Carrel began experimenting: he used thin rods of soluble caramel to hold the artery in place while suturing with the finest of embroidery stitches. It worked with dogs—and should do so with humans.

Carrel was wholly immersed in the science, and quite unconcerned about publication. Pozzi, who immediately grasped the future human application of the work, offered to write it up for him. Within a fortnight of his return to Paris, he is addressing the Academy of Medicine on "New Experiments by Dr. Alexis Carrel in the Suturing of Blood Vessels, the Transplantation of Organs and the Grafting of Limbs." His presentation was received with polite indifference, but published in *La Presse médicale*. Pozzi, now sixty-two, was aware that his generation had made their discoveries, and that the future belonged to those half his age. Selflessly, and without hesitation, Pozzi became Carrel's *porte-parole*.

Carrel may have looked like a little Italian priest, but it's unlikely that the Vatican would have approved of his experiments; or, for that matter, most readers of *La Libre Parole*. Nor was Pozzi just a bystander and reporter on these new developments: he conducted some of his own experiments. He and Carrel saw only science, and the future relief of human misery, in their research and speculations. Others—like the Catholic novelist Léon Bloy—saw it differently. In his journal for May 1913 (the year after Carrel was awarded the Nobel Prize), Bloy records that Pozzi has managed to keep a fragment of chicken heart alive for fourteen months. But it is the theological, rather than the moral or scientific consequences, which perturb him. "Death will be conquered," he predicts, "and human beings rendered eternal. But what will happen on the day God decides to call unto Him all those souls from which our spiritual faculties are derived? Those bodies will continue their movements *without any real life* and the world will be peopled by automata."

How to Treat Your Literary (and Social) Inferiors

1) Paul Léautaud's journal records a story told him by his friend the novelist Georges Duhamel. In 1906 Duhamel was one of the founders of a utopian group of artists and writers called L'Abbaye de Créteil. To help support the community, they set up a publishing house, and approached various well-known figures. Montesquiou graciously allowed them to issue one of his collections: "But he made us start all over again so many times, for one reason or another, until by the end of it we were well out of pocket." Then he came to visit the group, and spotted an ancient piece of tapestry which, though very beautiful, was

damaged. "Oh, you've got that, here? Give it to me—I'll get it repaired for you." He took it away, and they never saw it again.

2) Léon Bloy, cranky and ever-impoverished, recalls in his journal his attempt to sell Montesquiou fifty letters from Barbey d'Aurevilly. When the Count didn't reply to his initial suggestion, Bloy wrote him a second letter—this time in Latin, thinking it might help. It did, in the sense of warranting a reply: No. But Bloy had other plans too: he was an illuminator of manuscripts, and offered to spend a year decorating one of Montesquiou's books. At some point he even managed to get into the Count's house. Montesquiou declined to receive him, but Bloy saw enough to judge that the place was "furnished and laid out as if waiting to be photographed for the series 'Great Writers at Home.'" Stubbornly Montesquiou failed to see virtue in any of Bloy's plans, and eventually cut off contact in a letter from Switzerland. Bloy noted bitterly that the Count had failed to put enough postage on the letter, and that he had to pay fifty centimes in order to retrieve his rebuff.

In 1910 Pozzi went on the longest journey of his life, travelling for two months as a government representative in Argentina and Brazil, inspecting hospitals, polyclinics and institutions of all kinds. He was greatly impressed. Reprising his principle that "chauvinism is one of the forms of ignorance," he notes that the newest hospitals in Buenos Aires are fitted out with equipment from "French, German, Swiss and American" sources. "This judicious eclecticism is striking, and fully characteristic of the intelligent patriotism of this young nation. In their ambition to arrive at the first rank, they take the best from wherever it is to be found, not allowing a narrow nationalism to prevent them seeing what is best taken from abroad."

It might just have been chance—rather than a glancing reference to his "marital maenads"—that when Pozzi reported to the Academy of Medicine on his return to Paris, he highlighted a serotherapeutic institute outside São Paulo, where he saw venom being extracted from snakes, and a mental asylum near Buenos Aires. At the Butantan Institute he watched with fascination a fight between a "good" snake—one that is neither venomous in itself nor susceptible to the bites of other snakes—and a "bad" snake. Not just bad, but one of the baddest, the jararaca. The good snake won the battle by, essentially, eating the bad snake.

In Argentina, he visited the Open Door asylum—based on the original Scottish project of that name—and saw how a combination of gentle nursing and hard work rendered almost all of the inmates as docile and contented as was possible. There were no straitjackets or restraints; if patients became distressed, they were put to bed until they recovered. Occupations included agriculture, brickmaking, carpentry and forgework; the inmates made bread, brooms and shoes. This was not only therapeutic but also made the hospital economically viable. Pozzi was greatly impressed by the asylum's director, Dr. Cabred, who told him: "The raving lunatic should exist only on the stage or in a novel. It is violence committed against them that makes them rave." Pozzi concluded his report to the Academy with the words: "Dear friends, if ever I become mad, please take me straight to my great friend Cabred, at Open Door."

Aged fifteen, Catherine Pozzi noted in her diary the following exchange:

"I am in pain."
    "Where does it hurt? Your head? Your stomach?"
    (Moral pain does not exist for my parents.)

"I have a spiritual pain." That was all that I could say. I couldn't myself explain this acute, sudden pain which was shaking me to my core.

Catherine did not have a monopoly of family pain, even if she did claim a superior variety. Separation brought calm to neither parents nor children. Catherine's adult life was tormented, angry and unsatisfied; she, much more than Sarah Bernhardt, was "not made for happiness." And just as her mother had long heard gossipy voices behind her back pointing her out as the much-wronged wife of the famous lothario, so Catherine, moving in Parisian intellectual society, was to be noddingly identified as "Valéry's woman." She separated from her husband; she translated Stefan George, published poetry and corresponded with Rilke. Politically, she slipped back into the monarchism of her maternal line; in 1915, she joined Action Française. She had always denounced parliamentary democracy, and saw the return of royalty as the only bulwark against French Bolshevism, whose inner menace she viewed as greater than the outer German threat.

For the rest of her life she feuded with her brother Jean, usually over money, possessions, inheritance and access to La Graulet. Jean himself, perhaps discouraged by his parents' example, didn't marry until he was fifty and they were both dead. Catherine, in one of her very last diary entries, welcomed and dismissed Georgette Calouta as "Jean's little Levantine budgerigar-wife, a model of perfidious chatter and conjugal adoration."

Catherine's spirituality was not the sort that came with tolerance and forgiveness attached. When Thérèse died, in 1932, she wrote:

She was always escaping me, like some rebellious little girl. She was, in her own profound way, a stubborn little girl. So much sweetness, so much running around, a presence radiating harmony . . . and a stubborn little girl. A goddess resembling a young, stormfree Juno . . . and a stubborn little girl. The faultless way she carried herself, in her calm, slightly heavy way . . . and a stubborn little girl who wanted to see her pet dog again, and wanted to see Paris . . .

All three children escaped their parents in different ways: Catherine departed into a spiritual and intellectual superiority; Jean departed physically, into a diplomatic career; Jacques departed into psychological bewilderment. He was the late child, the "miracle child," and his fate was the cruellest and saddest. He is another "Pozzi mute," whom others speak for and about. At the age of nine or ten he was diagnosed as "mentally retarded" and sent away to an English school to be "tamed," which you would hardly expect to work. Though he served in the war, by the time he was twenty-five, he was working as a delivery boy. Catherine described him in pitiless terms:

> The younger brother is ugly, absurd, fat-bottomed, impotent, pederastic, angry, friendly when the whim takes him, banal and repugnant. And then what? Am I going to give him immortality? Jacques is a brute, and has been one since childhood, and that's all there is to say.

Around this time he became increasingly unstable and psychotic. He suffered from hallucinations, and could be violent, occasionally to Catherine. His paranoia grew to the point where he had to be hospitalised.

And here is the punitive irony: French mental asylums were much less advanced and much less gentle than the Open Door hospital

Pozzi had inspected outside Buenos Aires. They were closed places where restraint was everyday. Jacques was interned at Vanves, then at Saint-Germain, then at the Château de Suresnes (where Victor Hugo's daughter Adèle ended her days). After Thérèse's death, Catherine became his legal guardian. In 1933 she is shocked by a doctor's contempt when Jacques claims he is in communication with Martians; she takes her brother's side in this—"It is the doctor who is stupid." The following year she describes him as having "been abandoned for a year to his apathetic and greedy doctors, without visits, without presents." Finally, he is allowed to receive "clothes, scents, chocolates, the presents he likes. As a result, his violence recedes." (We remember Dr. Cabred arguing that it was institutional cruelty and restraint that caused a violent response in patients.) Eventually, Catherine had Jacques moved to Switzerland, to a clinic run by a woman, Dr. Repond, where he was able to live in "semi-liberty." That is our last news of him; he is thought to have died in the 1950s.

On 13 June 1911, Dr. Aimé Guinard, head surgeon at the Hôtel-Dieu in Paris, was crossing the hospital courtyard when he was shot four times, in the groin and the back. The assailant, Louis-Jaciento-Candido Herrero, a thirty-eight-year-old tailor from Barcelona, had previously been a patient of Dr. Guinard's. In accounting for his actions, Herrero explained that he had initially gone to the hospital suffering from a fistula, and had asked for ignipuncture. Dr. Guinard, however, ignoring his patient's request, insisted on operating immediately. Since when, Herrero stated, he had been crippled and unable to work. He had gone to see Dr. Guinard and complained of his surgical butchery, but Guinard had laughed in his face. That was when he had decided to act.

The surgeons who operated on Guinard reported that there were multiple gunshot wounds to the abdomen. A medial laparotomy was performed; six perforations of the small intestine were sutured; also, a ligature of the upper right colic artery.

The hospital stated that Dr. Guinard's operation on Herrero had gone perfectly, and that the patient was completely cured. His actions could therefore only be regarded as those of an unbalanced person.

Herrero himself asked to be examined by "a conscientious doctor," who would easily be able to ascertain that he had been "pointlessly martyred and mutilated."

Dr. Aimé Guinard died on 17 June. Four days later, there was a grand funeral in the courtyard of the Hôtel-Dieu, where he had been shot.

Naturally, Pozzi was there.

As with the American Revolution, the French Revolution had established the citizen's right to bear arms (also the right to keep five kilos of gunpowder at home). And as with America, what began as a necessary means of defending the republic against external aggression and the return of monarchical oppression morphed into a ubiquitous civil right. A right which remained intact despite unforeseen developments in weaponry.

In August 1911, two months after Aimé Guinard's murder, a jury at the second session of the Seine assizes handed the president of the court a formal address to be passed to the Minister of Justice. It called for much stricter gun control: "Carrying a revolver has now become as normal for men, women and young people as carrying a purse or a bunch of keys. Further, the act of habitually carrying a revolver, which is easy to conceal and easy to use, diminishes the notion of respect for human life." The jury asked for a strict control on the sale and carrying of guns; also, on the resale of weapons found at the scene of a crime.

This petition was part of a wider movement at the time in favour of gun control. But all the elements familiar to us today slowed things down: an active gun lobby, a parliamentary process extended to the point of inertia, an inconclusive debate about open carry, and so on. It was not until December 1916 that it was all rolled into a law ready to be presented to the Chamber of Deputies. By which time mass, rather than individual, slaughter was of greater concern; and there was no problem with open carry in the trenches.

Sarah Bernhardt once said: "Legend remains victorious, in spite of history." Montesquiou had seen this process at work after his distinguished ancestor had been fictionalised by Alexandre Dumas *père*. One day, he opened *Le Figaro* to see the headline: "D'Artagnan, the Principal Hero of The Three Musketeers—Did He Really Exist?" The Count reflected: "Is it possible that legend has gnawed away at history to this extent?"

It certainly was—and more so in his own case, in which fiction munched away at biography. All through his life, he had to compete with parallel, invented versions of himself: from Huysmans (1884), Jean Lorrain (1901), Edmond Rostand in his play *Chantecler* (1910), and finally Proust (from 1913). When, near the end of his life, Montesquiou sat down to write his autobiography, he found himself tugged by the genre's usual conflicting impulses: to tell the truth yet be entertaining; to correct the record without seeming petty or rancorous; to hold natural vanity in check while also making clear how special your life has been . . . But, underlying the three volumes of *Les Pas effacés*—published in 1923, two years after his death—was a much more primal urge and obligation: to rehabilitate his own authenticity.

It was not an easy task. He knew what was out there. When he sat in the audience for the dress rehearsal of *Chantecler*, Rostand's burlesque fable starring an anthropomorphised bestiary of farm and forest, he heard those sitting near him openly identify him as the

Peacock. This was not difficult. When the Peacock enters, the Guinea Fowl clucks, "Adored master, come towards these sunflowers! Peacock, sunflowers—I think it so Burne-Jones." The scene is a parody of a literary soirée, with the Peacock boasting that he is "the prince of the unexpected adjective" and "a Ruskin, but more refined." And there is a mocking parody of the Count's highflown wordplay:

Petronius-priest and Maecenas-Messiah,
Words I volatilise, being volatile:
Words which, o gemmate judge, midst my enamels,
This taste betokens of which I am guardian.

In part, as Montesquiou acknowledged, this was reasonable payback for the numerous gibes and caricatures of Rostand and his entourage in articles he'd written. But at least Rostand had known him well at one point, and studied what he was now satirising. Whereas the shadow of Des Esseintes had fallen across him for a quarter of a century, and Huysmans had met him only once, years after the publication of *A Rebours*, and not a word had been exchanged. Many of the Count's writer friends had declared publicly that there was no true connection between the fictional character and the real person; but there was no shrugging the association off. In *Les Pas effacés*, Montesquiou wonders if it was all somehow the fault of his own "aggressive character." He also suggests that he shouldn't be regarded as the "model" for Des Esseintes, but rather as the character's "author." This feels a risky line to take.

And then there was Proust. In 1913, twenty years after their first meeting, Proust published *Swann's Way*. In the meantime, he had copied the Count's mannerisms, hoovered up his stories of aristocratic life, supplied him with Léon Delafosse, flattered him, dined him, quarrelled with him, flattered him again. He once wrote an article with the hilarious title "On the Simplicity of Monsieur Montesquiou," which unsurprisingly no newspaper wanted to print. When *Within a Budding Grove* came out in 1919, Montesquiou, displaying this famed simplicity, cut the pages using a Persian dagger with a jade handle, and slowly discovered the fourth and final shadow self which would accompany him to the grave and beyond.

The other two members of our "strange trio" also feature fleetingly in *A la Recherche*. Edmond de Polignac appears twice under his own name: renting the Prince of X's castle for the Bayreuth Festival, and lounging in the foreground of Tissot's *Le Cercle de la rue Royale*. Pozzi is said to be distantly refracted in the figure of Dr.—later Professor—Cottard, though is visible less as himself than through Mme Cottard, who is keen on wifely duty while being constantly betrayed by her husband. But the principal public identification was that of Montesquiou with Baron Charlus.

The Count didn't immediately spot the linkage. Charlus begins as a pious married (then widowed) heterosexual with a reputation for (heterosexual) escapades, physically distinct from Montesquiou (much heftier), though also a dandy and an aesthete; gradually, he is revealed to be homosexual, ever more shamelessly and scandalously so. This is not exactly the path the Count himself trod. On the other hand, here is one of Charlus's remarks: "In these days everyone is a Prince Something-or-other; one really must have a title that will distinguish one: I shall call myself Prince when I wish to travel incognito." This was—word for word—what Montesquiou had said when a cousin of his was made a Prince in Bavaria. And if he recognised this, so would others. As they did Charlus's manner of speaking, his timbre of voice, his arrogance, his social behaviour, his need for a disciple . . . and here was a former disciple exploiting and distorting his former master. The

Count, who liked to repeat to and of himself, "I am good and have a beautiful soul," was being transformed into a monster of turpitude.

Initially, Proust maintained that Charlus was based on the decadent Baron Doäzan, who many years previously had lost out on the services of Gabriel Yturri. But Montesquiou saw through this, as did the rest of Parisian society. Anna de Noailles, supposedly the only person in the city intelligent enough to suspect that "the Father" in *Agnès* was Pozzi, had no difficulty in declaring that "Charlus is Count Robert." She also did a fine imitation of Montesquiou's voice, and liked to declaim Charlus's tirades to her dinner guests, with such authenticity that those arriving late were convinced, as they climbed the stairs, that it was the Count himself holding forth.

So Montesquiou "was" Charlus in the public literary mind, just as he had been—and would continue to be—Des Esseintes. Proust lexicons list half a dozen other Parisian doctors besides Pozzi on whom Proust drew for Cottard; and similarly half a dozen other social hierarchs on whom he drew for Charlus (including Jean Lorrain—which would have annoyed the Count). There can be a trainspotter side to this aspect of Proust-reading. It ought to be the case that the greater the novelist, the more powerful the characters he or she creates, the more real and vivid they stand in our imagination and memory, the less we ought to be interested in the paler figures who once trod the earth and from whom these enduring characters might in some way have sprung. But "ought" works no more in literature than it does in history.

Any practising novelist will be familiar with the jocular-yet-serious response when someone newly met discovers what you do. "I'd better watch what I say, then, hadn't I?"; or, sometimes, "I've got a great story for you." You (well, I) will tend to answer, "It doesn't work like that," because it doesn't. There is nothing more useless than someone else's already highly worked-up anecdote—"varnished for eternity," as Léon Daudet said of Montesquiou; nor does a novelist "study" a real-life person with any deliberate intent to copy and paste them into a novel. The whole process is usually much more passive, sponge-like and haphazard than that. The reader's motive—wanting to understand the process of literary creation—is of course legitimate, but also ultimately futile, since even the most self-conscious novelist often cannot properly explain what it is he or she does, and how it comes about.

Montesquiou felt ambivalent about *A la Recherche*, only half of which he lived to read. "I am ill in bed," he wrote to one friend. "Ill from the publication of three volumes which have knocked me down." Proust had betrayed their friendship. The Count even consulted a clairvoyant about the novelist. The "spirit communication" he paid for assured him that the estrangement was caused "not because of infatuation but incomprehension"; further, that "There is dimness," but that "There will be return."

And there was. In 1919 Proust won the Prix Goncourt and officially became a great man. When the second volume of *Cities of the Plain* came out, Montesquiou filled a notebook with comments. He was also intelligent (and literary) enough to see beyond his own representation into the novel's fullest scope. He wrote to Proust:

> For the first time somebody dares, you dare to take as a straight subject—in a way that an idyll by Longus or a novel by Benjamin Constant treats of love—the vice of Tiberius or of the shepherd Corydon. That was your intention, now we shall see the consequences of it . . . Will you be enrolled in the batallion of the Flauberts and the Baudelaires, passing through infamy to reach glory?

There were, the Count realised, worse fates to attend one after death than to be taken for a major character in a masterpiece. At his last public appearance, in December 1920, he observed ruefully, "I ought to start calling myself Montesproust." And after all, he had never wanted to be *liked*.

In the meantime, he set himself one final task in *Les Pas effacés*. The best way to prove that he was "not"—or not just—Des Esseintes or Monsieur de Phocas or Chantecler or Baron Charlus was to prove that he *was*, above and beyond these shadows, Robert de Montesquiou, poet, prose-poet, novelist and now memoirist. The problem here was twofold. First, most of his work had been published in small, private editions, exquisitely printed and bound, and very expensive to buy: hence, widely unknown and unread. And secondly, given his "aristocratic pleasure of displeasing," the Count scorned the average novel reader, poetry reader and theatregoer. These were the people who lightly mistook him for those fictional simulacra—and whose foolish prejudices he now needed to overturn.

Which involved the vulgar necessity of trying to prove that his work was more important than was generally assumed. The Count is the Professor of Beauty, a member of a self-selecting elect, a definer and dictator of taste in a narrow world. Yet now, all of a sudden, here he is like Coriolanus down in the marketplace, trying to get the unwashed to vote for him. It is an awkward performance, though not without its comedy. Look at this review by X! he boasts. Read what Y wrote about me! he pleads. See this letter I got in return for sending a dedicated copy of my latest poems to Z! I'm important, I'm a contender! Honestly!

It is this insecurity, gurgling away beneath the arrogance, which humanises Montesquiou, if anything will. For instance, he reveres Degas, but realises (correctly) that Degas doesn't have a high opinion—perhaps no opinion at all—of his work. And so he registers the quaint complaint that Degas, though a "great artist" in the fullest sense of the term, did make him "rather cross" at one time by obstinately declining to acknowledge that there was a distinction between humble "art critics" and a higher category called "interpreters of art"—"among whose number, I, for my own modest part, include myself." It is hardly a matter over which the world has been dolefully shaking its head during the subsequent century or so. During which time *Les Pas effacés* might have sold a few hundred copies: more than the Count's other works, but hardly enough to put a dent in the *idées reçues* of Proustians and Huysmaniacs.

Around and aside from this unusual purpose of proving himself to be himself, Montesquiou the autobiographer is true to Montesquiou the living man: snobbish, vain, name-dropping, generous to some, unforgiving to more. Those he writes about are by now mostly dead, so he knows his final judgements will not reach them. Even so, he decides to offer Jean Lorrain a little aristocratic forgiveness. Of course, for one who imagined himself a dandy, Lorrain had terrible clothes—"not so much inelegant as pretentious and provincial." Still, "he was not a bad boy, he was even good, with some of the bourgeois virtues—obviously not all of them, but some."

Edmond de Polignac, on the other hand, remains stringently unpardoned. Montesquiou recalls that trip to London thirty-five years previously. "I took along with me an old travelling companion, by whom I thought myself loved (and who proved, subsequently, that I was thoroughly mistaken)"; but also, more happily, "*mon cher grand Pozzi.*" Polignac's very name is erased from the roll call of memory, while Pozzi is never mentioned without being "*notre grand Pozzi,*" "*notre cher et illustre Pozzi,*" and suchlike. Indeed, it becomes clear from one of the most touching and unaffected passages, that while the

Count might admire others for their artistic brilliance, noble birth, wit, elegance and so on (while still holding himself their equal or superior), Pozzi is not just someone he admires, but for whom he feels that most unfamiliar of emotions, envy:

> My dear and late-lamented Pozzi used to assure me that on waking, he could scarcely contain the exhilaration he felt at the many alluring things the day held in store for him . . . As the sun rose, this man of rare good sense and rare good taste . . . saw the prospect of operations to perform, and his hospital to decorate, so that illness might be made beautiful, and suffering almost happy; of noble poems to read, and others to write; of antiques to acquire, of suffering to alleviate and friends to delight; and as, during the day, he was filled with knowledge and purpose, so, in the evening, he was filled with grace and charm . . . All this, and many other things beside, added up to a daily uniqueness which is, alas, now lost to us.

Montesquiou envied Pozzi his daily cheerfulness, his direct approach to life and his usefulness; but also the way his willpower controlled his temperament. He liked to quote Pozzi's remark: "I could become old, if I wanted to." But Pozzi never did want to.

Gaston Calmette, editorial director of *Le Figaro*, was a friend of Pozzi's. More famously, he was a friend of Marcel Proust's. He published a number of articles by Proust, and in 1913 received the dedication of *Swann's Way*: "To Monsieur Gaston Calmette, as evidence of my profound and affectionate gratitude." What Proust added in handwriting to Calmette's personal copy, however, reeked of authorial insecurity:

"I have often felt that you did not really like what I wrote. If you ever have time to read a little bit of this work, especially the second part, I believe you will finally get to know me."

In January 1914, *Le Figaro* began a campaign against Joseph Caillaux, a former leftist prime minister who was currently Minister of Finance. First, they weakened his position by publishing compromising financial documents. Next, they planned to bring him down by attacking his private life. They threatened to publish intimate letters written by him to his wife at a time when their liaison was still secret—for the simple reason that he was married to someone else. As was she.

Many judged that, even by the standards of Parisian journalism, this was a bit low. At six in the evening of 16 March 1914, Henriette Caillaux, "a calm fortyish blonde with blue eyes," as the newspapers liked to put it, went to the offices of *Le Figaro*, presented her card, and asked to see Calmette. The novelist Paul Bourget, who was just leaving the editor's office, advised against admitting her: such an impromptu call seemed to him strange. "I cannot refuse to receive a woman," Calmette told him. Bourget left, and Henriette Caillaux was shown in. "You know why I have come?" she asked. "Not at all, Madame," he replied. Whereupon she took a revolver from her black otter-skin muff and fired six bullets at the editorial director. Three of them struck him: one in the chest, one in the upper thigh, and one in the pelvic cavity. Henriette Caillaux then waited calmly for the police to arrive, though declined to be transported to their headquarters in a vulgar van; instead, she insisted that her chauffeur drive her there. Calmette died nearly six hours later, close to midnight, just as the surgeon's knife cut the skin for a laparotomy.

The French and British judicial systems reflect, sometimes to the point of parody, their different national characteristics. The British

never allowed the notion of a *crime passionnel* into their law—perhaps because they believed that only hot-blooded foreigners could behave in such an emotionally unhinged way. And even if they had, killing a journalist whose newspaper was targeting your political husband might seem to be overstretching the adjective *passionnel*. In France they knew—or knew themselves—better. From the start, it was clear that the murder was premeditated rather than spontaneous: as the evidence revealed, Mme Caillaux was familiar with hunting rifles but not revolvers. So at three o'clock in the afternoon of 16 March, she had gone to Gastine-Renette and bought a .32 Browning automatic pistol, plus the ammunition to go with it. Then she was taken to the rifle range in the gun shop's basement and shown how to use it. A few hours later, she went to *Le Figaro* and killed Calmette.

The trial began on 20 July 1914, two weeks before war broke out, and occupied more space on the front pages than the doomy political developments. Mme Caillaux's lawyer, Maître Labori—who had defended both Zola and, at his second trial, Dreyfus—ran two parallel defences. On the one hand, the extraordinary circumstances of the case (the size and public nature of the potential scandal, the importance of the participants, and, centrally, the very nature of womanhood) made the deed a crime of passion. But if not, then, on the other hand, it wasn't Henriette Caillaux who had actually killed Calmette: the surgeons who operated on him, despite all being distinguished, had made a botch of their job. Much evidence was given on the delay between the patient's arrival at the clinic and the time of the operation: five hours or so. Calmette barely had a pulse when first examined, and the surgeons therefore decided to wait until he was stronger. It was the ongoing argument at surgical congress after surgical congress. Pozzi, the famous advocate of the earliest possible intervention in such circumstances, had gone to the clinic where his friend was lying, but had not been consulted by his colleagues there. Now, he was consulted by the court; and with his aid, Maître Labori argued that it was not his client, but rather medical dilatoriness, that had killed Calmette. Whichever defence the jury actually prioritised, they found Henriette Caillaux innocent.

By early 1915, Sarah Bernhardt's right leg—injured first by falling on the deck of a ship, aggravated later by jumping from the battlements at the end of *La Tosca* only to discover that no mattress had been placed to break her fall—required amputation. Pozzi had been involved in earlier parts of the treatment, encasing her whole leg in plaster at one stage; but when it came to the operation, despite her pleas to "*mon docteur Dieu*," he declined to take charge. Bernhardt was by now living in a villa on the Arcachon Basin, twenty-five kilometres west of Bordeaux. She had moved there after being warned that she was on a list of French hostages to be seized as soon as the Germans entered Paris (she may have been told so, but historians have discovered no such list). The leg was amputated above the knee by Jean Denucé, one of Pozzi's former interns, with Pozzi advising from Paris: for instance, he suggested a discreet Wassermann test in case the knee was syphilitic. The operation took a quarter of an hour, no more than six grams of blood was lost, and Bernhardt woke up while still on the table.

Three weeks later, she was released from hospital to her villa at Andernos-les-Bains. Pozzi immediately took the overnight train from Paris to spend a few hours with her. He returned via Bordeaux, where he dined with Denucé—though only after they had inspected the amputated leg.

At which point P. T. Barnum, entrepreneur, circus owner, "the Shakespeare of advertising," "the Prince of Humbugs," briefly enters the story. In 1882, during Wilde's tour of America, it was whispered that Barnum had offered Wilde a considerable sum to parade about, a lily in one hand and a sunflower in the other, in front of Jumbo, the elephant Barnum had recently bought from the London zoo. This was an exaggeration—indeed, the invention of a rival British lecturer—though it was true that Barnum had been in the front row at Wilde's second New York appearance.

As for Sarah Bernhardt, a recent biography of her repeats the story that "Barnum apparently cabled her, offering 10,000 dollars for her amputated leg." This seems deeply implausible, given that Bernhardt had her leg amputated twenty-four years after P. T. Barnum's death. A rival version is that the manager of a department of the Pan-American Exhibition in San Francisco offered 100,000 dollars to a charity of her choice if they could display her leg. Bernhardt supposedly cabled back, "Which leg?"

But what did become of Bernhardt's leg? For a long time it formed part of a cabinet of curiosities in the anatomy laboratory of the faculty of medicine in Bordeaux (along with a Siamese-twin foetus, a heart pierced by a knife, and the rope with which a man had hanged himself). In 1977, the laboratory moved, a triage of specimens took place, and a number of lesser items were incinerated. By 2008, what purported to be Bernhardt's leg—a right leg, amputated above the knee, long and thin—seems to have turned into a left leg, amputated above the knee, with a foot the size of an orthopaedic boot and a missing big toe. An investigation by *L'Express* magazine turned up a retired professor who well remembered the actress's leg, and insisted that the current one was an imposter. The lab assistant charged with getting rid of unwanted specimens back in 1977 was described as "a bit of a rogue, a wrestler, a chap who didn't always see very well." If he had incinerated the wrong leg by mistake, he was in any case—as often in such stories—by now usefully dead. And according to experts, it would now be "too complicated" to do a DNA test.

When Montesquiou died in Menton in 1921, he left everything bar a few specific legacies to Yturri's successor, Henri Pinard, his dull, faithful and much-tyrannised secretary for the last fifteen years. Among the many items noted, disposed of and catalogued for auction, there is no mention of the bullet that killed Pushkin. Indeed, there is no mention of it in Jullian's biography of the Count. Or in the biographies and diaries of those who knew him. It is, I realise, single-source: I have come across it only in Léon Daudet's *Fantômes et vivants*, his first volume of memoirs, published in March 1914. During a few scornful pages about Montesquiou, Daudet is especially contemptuous of his manic acquisitiveness ("intellectual and decorative shopping"), and the pomposity with which he would explain his sacred knickknacks to the tiring visitor. He would emote over each new treasure, at first exultant, then growing calmer, and finally confiding, *"C'est bien bô!"* ("How byootiful!").

Daudet, like Jean Lorrain, was a rich source of anecdote and scandal.

As one later editor of his memoirs put it: "He didn't hesitate to ruin reputations and certainly inflicted deeper and more lasting injuries

3ᵉ COLLECTION FÉLIX POTIN

DAUDET LÉON
HOMME POLITIQUE

with his pen than ever he did with his sword." On one occasion, a bystander rebuked Daudet for telling lies. "Of course I do," replied Daudet. "If I never lied, I would be a mere railway timetable." So I look again at his list of the Count's curiosa: "A hair from Michelet's beard, an old cigarette once smoked by George Sand, one of Lamartine's dried tears, Mme de Montespan's bathtub, Marshall Bugeaud's cap, the bullet which killed Pushkin, a danc-ing slipper belonging to [Teresa] Guiccioli, a bottle of absinthe in which Musset had once drowned himself, one of Mme de Renal's day-stockings signed by Stendhal . . ."—and suddenly the list reads more and more like a sly and mocking fantasy on Daudet's part. Perhaps it always did. And if we pedantically approach the story from the opposite end, there is no evidence at all that Pushkin's doctors (including a military surgeon who had served in the Napoleonic Wars) ever removed, or attempted to remove, the bullet that killed him.

But if one of Montesquiou's supposed possessions disappears before our eyes, another one now reappears. His tortoise—dismissed, or diminished to a mere shell, by Huysmans' and Montesquiou's biogra-phers, and not actually witnessed alive by anyone—comes swaggering and glinting back into existence. In, of all obvious but much underread places, Montesquiou's own memoirs. Acknowledging that some of the household details Mallarmé passed on to Huysmans were correct, he continues:

And especially there was the gilded tortoise, which did so much for the novel's fame, that magnificent and misfortunate amphibian whose truth I do not in the least deny (indeed, I devoted a verse to it myself in my collection *Hortensias*) . . . My victim didn't have a name, so Huysmans gave it one. The elements essential to its decoration no doubt filtering through its shell, the beast did not long survive this excessive embellishment, which became its metallic and gemmate tomb.

You lose a leg and a bullet, but gain a tortoise: there are more uncertainties in nonfiction than in fiction.

In August 1916, Dr. Pierre Maubrac was appointed director of the Auxiliary Hospital installed at the Lycée Michelet in the Parisian suburb of Vanves. He was disturbed by what he found. The hospital was not just functioning poorly, but with a complete disregard for proper hierarchy. As far as he could see, it was being run by Sergeant Octave Tasso, a thirty-two-year-old from Corsica. The sergeant was widely liked and admired, but was operating way above his pay grade. Maubrac therefore sidelined him. When the sergeant protested, he was confined to barracks for a fortnight. Tasso exercised his right of appeal; but before his case could be heard, he began to suspect—or perhaps it was leaked to him—that his sentence would be "increased severely." So at ten on the morning of 28 August, he went to the director's office, and asked if this was indeed to be the case. Maubrac declined to comment, and told the sergeant to carry on with his duties. "Right, that's enough then, let's get it over with," Tasso was reported as saying, as he took out his revolver. He shot Maubrac in the left side, the heart, and the left temple. In the confusion, the sergeant escaped, and a chase ensued. Finally, at nine in the evening, he was spotted. On the point of capture, he shot himself in the head.

Tasso's actions were deemed the result of "madness." Furthermore, he was known to be "an inveterate morphinomaniac." That's what was said, anyway.

Giving evidence in the Calmette trial, Pozzi made reference to the Poulmier case of 1898, an event which had many structural similarities. A politician was being attacked on both professional and personal grounds by a newspaper, *La Lanterne*. The politician's wife, Mme Poulmier, responded to the provocation by taking a loaded revolver along to the newspaper office. Her attack, however, was less well targeted than that of Mme Caillaux: the man she shot—six times in the abdomen—was an innocent sub-editor called Ollivier, who had nothing to do with editorial policy.

Ollivier was taken to the Bichat Hospital where, in the absence of the head of surgery, a fourth-year intern called Antonin Gosset, aided by an equally young colleague, operated immediately, repaired ten perforations of the intestine—and the victim survived. However impressive this was and remains, in most such cases, certainly the ones cited in this book—which are the standard as well as the most newsworthy ones of the time—when someone was shot in the gut, they died. Tourette was very lucky just to take a bullet to the back of the neck. But guns were so powerful, and so easy to manipulate, that even an incompetent assassin—or, to put it more precisely, a hitherto untrained one like Mme Caillaux—could buy a revolver at three o'clock, be shown how to load and fire it, and then go out at six o'clock and put three bullets into Gaston Calmette.

Medicine was at its progressive, inventive best, and Pozzi, having written more than forty papers on the treatment of gunshot and other war wounds, was a leading expert. But guns had become ever more murderously effective while the human body retained all its original vulnerability. This must have been something that often crossed Pozzi's mind.

Whistler's emblem was the butterfly, as short-lived as it is decorative. In human terms, the dandy is always likely—indeed, perhaps constructed—to crash and burn. And since it takes money to become a dandy, and financial carelessness partly makes a dandy what he is, it is often cash that leads to crash. Beau Brummell fled England in 1816 to escape a debtors' prison, and spent the last twenty-four years of his life in France, without ever learning the language. In due course, he discovered the inside of a French debtors' prison as well, before dying, shabby, syphilitic and insane, in the Caen lunatic asylum.

It was a warning from the primal dandy. Wilde also crashed and burned, though in a more complicated way; so did Jean Lorrain. And there are times when a spectacular combustion might have made a better end. Robert de Montesquiou, when war broke out in 1914, briefly imagined himself being shot by Uhlans on the steps of his final, much-loved house, the Palais Rose, before they proceeded to burn his collection; but it would have meant a long (and eventually fruitless) wait. Instead, he lived on until 1921. He had made a success of being a dandy for a very long time; of attracting followers, of being a cynosure, of being talked about. He had a long relationship with Yturri, which was an imbalanced success. But he came to realise that few took him seriously as a writer—even the slot of top aristocrat-poet had been taken from him by Comtesse Anna de Noailles.

Of course, being an aristocrat continued to work: there will always be those impressed by a Count. But he had outlived himself as a dandy. He had christened himself "the sovereign of transitory things," and was doubtless aware that sovereigns too are transitory. An old dandy is invariably a bit pathetic, his grasp on taste diminished, his wit reduced to malice, his group of faithful friends thinned by death and betrayal. The world had indeed moved on; and Montesquiou was lucid and unself-pitying enough to acknowledge it:

> It is a strange feeling—and more strange than painful—to real-ize suddenly, brusquely, without any warning, almost without having seen it coming, that *one's life is over*. You are still there, in a state of greater or lesser dilapidation, and still holding on, with your faculties intact but now ill-suited to the taste of the day; you have fallen into disuse, and have become a stranger to the very contemporary civilisation you once led, yet whose cur-rent manifestations do not wound or shock you as much as they appear empty and futile. An impenetrable barrier now separates you from such artistic concepts as Picasso, or Czechoslovakian aesthetics, or *Art nègre*, and these are not good ways to feel fashionable.

But it would not be like the Count to go gently into that good night; a philosophical valetudinarianism was not his style. Among the lega-cies he left was one typically malicious and misogynistic sign-off. The daughter-in-law of a certain Mme Armand de Caillavet had been long under the mistaken impression that the Count was in love with her, and she wrote to him constantly. In his will the Count left her a casket. His solicitor brought it over. The woman assembled her close friends to witness the moment. She lifted the lid of the casket. It contained all the letters she had sent to Montesquiou. They were unopened.

Baudelaire said that dandyism was "an ill-defined institution, as strange as the duel." Both institutions were effectively terminated by the First World War. Of the two, the duel was going much the stronger. One of the reasons for its survival long, long after it had fallen into desuetude in England, was that—this being France—there was a supportive theory behind it. The duel might have been locally about what Maupassant called that "clown," honour; but whatever the proximate cause (like the slimness of Sarah Bernhardt when playing Hamlet), it had become invested with a grander purpose: to morally reinvigorate the nation after the catastrophic defeat of 1870.

3ᵉ COLLECTION FÉLIX POTIN

PÉGUY
HOMME DE LETTRES

Duelling was not just the highest form of sport, it also required the highest form of manliness. Further, as Charles Péguy, the nationalist poet, propounded, its ethic was as vital as its practice. This stiffening of the soul would help the French overcome the ruthless, amoral, honour-free Prussians when the next time came, as it inevitably would.

One of the last literary duels before the outbreak of war was fought between Pozzi's great friend Paul Hervieu and Pozzi's great enemy Léon Daudet. Pozzi himself, however, was not the cause; nor was he present at the Parc des Princes in June 1914. The two combatants had first met "around Alphonse Daudet's desk": Hervieu was, if not exactly a protégé, one of his favoured young writers. Léon, who was ten years younger than Hervieu, initially admired him as well; but then, over the years, saw him gravitate towards "the Jewish milieu" and "official republican circles"; he despised Hervieu's pursuit of worldly advancement, his eagerness for an Academician's sword and cloak.

Their breaking point, as for many, was the Dreyfus Affair, in which Hervieu was on the side of what Daudet called "the Antifrance" (like the Antichrist)—"no doubt because he saw his own advantage in that choice." Thereafter, it was a matter of a friendship being merely a stage on the way to a quarrel that would inevitably give rise to a duel.

The actual grounds are confusing—or rather, multiple; also, long-burning. Here is the first of Daudet's versions. He was at a soirée chez Anna de Noailles, at the time when the state was "persecuting church-goers." Hervieu, "in order to pay court to a radical deputy who was present," started attacking the "obscurantism" of the Dominicans and the Jesuits "rather as Homais would have done." A dozen years then pass before Daudet formally quarrels with Hervieu "after he had taken the side, against me, of the Israelite dramatist Bernstein." The subject of the dispute is not mentioned, so was presumably irrelevant. When they meet at the Parc des Princes on a beautiful June morning, what passes through Daudet's head, as he aims his pistol at Hervieu, is: "He thinks my quarrel with him is about Bernstein. But it's really about his anti-clerical tirade in the avenue Henri-Martin."

However, Daudet also gives a quite separate explanation of the casus belli. With the European war (longed-for by Daudet and other Revengists) at last approaching, Hervieu had given a speech to the Students Association announcing himself in favour of "Universal Peace" and "world happiness." Not just a careerist and bootlicker, but a coward, traitor and defeatist as well! Daudet, who could find an enemy in an empty room, was incandescent: "His growing servility disgusted me, and I told him so in crude terms." Hervieu sent his seconds round, and they fought, exchanging two shots each without effect. This time, Daudet claims that, as he was taking aim, he was thinking "that it would be very distasteful to me, morally speaking, either to wound him, or to be wounded by him."

Daudet goes on to recall other duels he fought around the same time, against the "charming" lawyer and journalist Georges Clarétie, and against the "Israelite dramatist" Bernstein. He grows sentimental, remembering Bernstein as "a violent and loyal opponent." He goes on: "One of the great advantages of the duel is to wipe away any rancour between the combatants and, by means of a trifling wound, draw the venom out of social life, which is so easily poisoned." This seems naive as well as hypocritical, given that Daudet regularly injected venom into social life through his journalistic and political activities. Nor does the "rancour" between him and his recent opponent seem to have been wiped away very effectively, since he now describes Hervieu as "the perfect example of a writer whom the Academy, the salons and official life have annihilated." What Maupassant thirty-three years previously had termed "the Mentality of the Boulevards"—"quarrelsome, flippant, whirling and emptily sonorous"—seems much closer to reality than Péguy's chivalric, character-building ethic of honour. In any case, neither Hervieu, then fifty-seven, nor Daudet, forty-seven, were likely to be heading for the trenches in two months' time. Nor does any of this deluded business seem to have increased the chances of the French beating the Germans in the upcoming bout.

Things We Cannot Know

—What Hervieu was thinking as he aimed, or half aimed, at Daudet.

—What Mme Loth said.

—What Thérèse said.

—Whether Jacques Pozzi's psychological condition was the result of being a late child.

—How reliable the intense focus of Catherine's diary is: When the middle range is missing, how far do you trust the extremes?

—Whether anyone, anywhere in the world, ever, could have made her happy?

—What exactly Pozzi meant when he said that he had "to take vigorous, almost violent action" with Thérèse on their honeymoon, to break her free from family ties. But before we understand too quickly, we must set this against Thérèse's firm statement, after Pozzi's death, that at the beginning of the marriage "We were happy."

—Who was trying to kill whom in a duel, and who was just pretending? Hervieu and Daudet fired two shots each: Does this imply more serious intent?

—What exactly made Thérèse "coldly" consider a separation so early into the marriage? Did she suddenly—or slowly—realise she didn't love her husband? Was there a proximate cause for this: Did she see him flirting with other women? Or suspect him of more than flirting? And did she hold back from insisting upon a separation then because of her mother's advice?

—There was a year between the births of Catherine and Jean Pozzi, then twelve more until the birth of Jacques. Was his existence the result of a sudden thaw, or did the Pozzis have intermittent sexual relations (her wifely Catholic duty, after all) during that period? We have the evidence of Catherine, who remembers being in her parents' bed, with one of them on either side of her, at the age of eleven. We can date this to 1894, and presumably their bed-sharing was habitual, otherwise Catherine would have noted it. Her younger brother Jacques was born in 1896. Just as we tend to diminish, even dismiss, occasional *froideurs* in happy, successful marriages, so we often overlook—or fail to imagine—the occasional, or more than occasional *tendresses* in unhappy, or formal, or social marriages.

—Do gynaecologists make better lovers? It sounds like a bumper sticker, I agree. Are they more knowledgeable and sensitive because of their daytime profession; or does it make them (and their partners) more self-conscious? Of course, it's absurd to generalise. But we should note that Pozzi, in his writing and lecturing, is always insistent on the patient's comfort and personal ease, and on sparing her any embarrassment. And that when Jean Lorrain snarkily reports on "the Pozzi method of suturing, which leaves not the slightest trace that might repel either a husband or a lover," this is not an inconsiderable matter. For the woman herself, that is.

—When I described this book to a female friend, she exclaimed immediately, "Oh, women and their gynaecologists, everyone knows about *that*." To what extent is this a factor?

—What would have happened if Oscar Wilde had taken advice, and the next boat train, rather than wait to be arrested? He might have enjoyed a cheerful French exile, like so many other scamps and scoundrels before him. He would not have been broken in health; but neither would he have written "The Ballad of Reading Gaol."

—Are there, in this period, any French descriptions of Englishwomen which allow them to be pretty, graceful and well dressed? Or of Englishmen which allow them to be modest, warm-hearted and genial? It was the composer Erik Satie who is credited with the witticism "An Englishman is a Norman who has gone to the bad." The future Edward VII is said to have approved and repeated this quip.

—Charles Meigs thought that doctors should only conduct manual examinations of female patients as a very last resort, for fear it provoke "a lax moral sense in the patient." This sounds like a grotesque projection of puritan America; but it was also a male anxiety well alive in Catholic France. There was a line of sexual advice given to men (by other men) which went: it is dangerous for a wife to experience sexual pleasure, because once she has discovered that sex can be pleasurable, she is much more likely to run off and commit adultery. As a certain

J. P. Dartigues put it: "With the habit of pleasure in a marriage, [women] slide imperceptibly into adultery." Commentators and advice hounds encouraged husbands to have only the most uninspired and uninspiring sex with their wives. Nightgowns were sold which exposed only the hands and feet, yet had a Mormon-style slit in the front so that children could be created with as little flesh-on-flesh as possible. As Edward Berenson, in his study of the Caillaux trial, observes: "One's wife was not to be an object of sexual desire, since to desire her was to degrade her." We sense the authentic whiff of male terror at the idea of female sexuality.

So it became normal for men of a certain social rank to believe that a wife was for dowry, children and social status, while a mistress (or prostitute) was for pleasure. And given that they were allowed so little pleasure themselves, there must have been many wives who were happy to be free of their husbands' cold, dutiful sperm-donating, and even some happy to accept the devious male argument that men, poor things, were the weaker sex, and women the stronger as well as the more virtuous. Some husbands probably behaved better to their wives when feeling guilty, or relieved (or even permitted). Not all husbands were beasts, not all wives martyrs.

Robert de Montesquiou, in his memoirs, describes meeting at the salon of a Baroness a man who subsequently became an eminent professor. The two of them were friends for thirty years, and the professor, from near and far, watched over the Count's health. This makes him sound remarkably like Pozzi, but it proves not to be him. "I often dined at his house, in the lifetime of his charming wife, whom he loved so much, and grieved for so much, despite his many adventures, some of them notorious." Montesquiou reflects on this seeming emotional contradiction:

It is, and I am not afraid to affirm it publicly, a false idea to consider a man's adultery to be an absolute negation of conjugal love; they are two separate things, which do not exclude one another; one would not ask of one's wife, and one would not accept from her, what one would allow, require or ask of a mistress: thus there is a place for both in the life of a man, and the use he makes of both should not make us question his sincerity.

So: procreative sub-sub-vanilla sex at home, but playing (and sometimes paying) away from home for hotter, dirtier, more exciting sex. It is emblematically patriarchal; it is called having your cake and eating it. And we might not accept the Count as the best explicator of heterosexual conjugality. But at the same time, we should believe that the anonymous and long-dead professor did indeed love his wife, and truly grieved for her, because if we don't we are simplifying things to make it easier for us to condemn them.

So where, in all this, do we find Samuel and Thérèse Pozzi? We cannot know what went on between the sheets in those first weeks, months, year or two of marriage when they were happy. Or indeed, if this is where we should look to understand what went wrong. When they screamed at one another in front of the servants and children decades into the marriage, was it all or only about sex? Money is a great divider as well; so is religion; so too is a mother-in-law to whom one is no longer speaking. Do we want to arraign Pozzi on that favourite British charge of hypocrisy? Yet he seems to have been (fairly) open about his motives and (fairly) discreet about his deeds; that is hardly hypocrisy.

—We cannot know everyone he went to bed with. Clearly, Sarah Bernhardt and Emma Fischoff. Other names: Mme Straus (the widow of Bizet), Judith Gautier (daughter of Théophile), the actresses Réjane and Eve Lavallière, Jeanne Jacquemin . . . How interesting are they as lovers, when so little texture to the relationship is discoverable at this stage? Add or invent an extra few dozen, few score, few hundred, *mille e tre* . . . does that tell us anything more?

—Other things we cannot know: whether Benjamin Pozzy preferred his son to be an atheist rather than a Catholic.

—If Gaston Calmette's life could indeed have been saved by immediate intervention.

—What specifically caused Thérèse to insist on a legal separation in 1909.

—Whether, if Fashoda had not been experienced as a moment of national humiliation in the mind of the infant Charles de Gaulle, Britain would have been allowed to join the European project much earlier, would have become fully committed and embedded, and would not have voted to leave in 2016.

All these matters could, of course, be solved in a novel.

When war breaks out, Thérèse Pozzi leaves Paris, taking her mother, her grandson Claude and seven of the eight servants. Catherine herself stays, alone in the apartment with Edouard's manservant and a Siamese cat. It is not just the Germans who are proving a nuisance. "Colette has taken a shine to me and is being annoying," she writes in her journal as Liège is bombarded and Zeppelins fly over Paris. "Her husband makes advances to me. But these threesomes, to which Georgie [Raoul-Duval] failed to convert me, tempt me less than ever. However, I remain equivocal and friendly."

Equivocal: perhaps, if she hadn't believed that a woman was "an inchoate mass of possibility waiting to be moulded by a man's hand," she might have been happier with a woman. She was always at ease with lesbian company. Here she is in 1920 listening to music with "the ten noblest Sapphos of our time," including "the old [Princesse de] Polignac and Clermont-Boum-Boum" (the nickname of Elisabeth de Clermont-Tonnerre). She is wearing her "exquisite" Callot dress, "and I had become pretty again—what an astonishing discovery." Not that her eye or brain softened. Her last diary entry on Polignac, from 1927, reads: "The Princess is extremely American, and resembles a soldier whose ambition is to be a *maître d'hotel.*"

In August 1914, Pozzi starts taking his daughter to the Broca to acquire some basic medical instruction. "I stock up on surgical knowledge in a general kind of way, as one stocks up on provisions." The society ladies who play at being nurses alongside her revolt her with their frivolity. She watches her first laparotomy, leading to a total hysterectomy for a case of cancerous fibroma. "I was brave, but at the moment the human body fills me with horror. Horror of the flesh which can endure all that, horror of this instrument of love, within which putrefaction brews." If those society women were too frivolous to make proper nurses, Catherine was too high-minded and too sensitive for her own good, and for that of the patients. A few days later, her father, without asking, signed her up as a nurse at the Val-de-Grâce. "Will I have the strength? The hospital is already exhausting me. When I get home I fall into bed and manage to sleep for two hours. I am thin and pale and ugly, a large strand of vermicelli with big eyes." Five days later, she left for La Graulet.

Robert de Montesquiou, also not central to the war effort, decided not to wait for the Uhlans, and instead prudently departed for Trouville. There he met Isadora Duncan, who apparently expressed the desire to bear his child. This being a non-starter—there might have been a lot of vomiting—he retired for the duration of the war to the family chateau of D'Artagnan in the Béarn, where he was much hated by his neighbours. There were two reasons for this. The first was his "unsavoury reputation"; the second, because in years past he had once bought up all their "unfashionable" old furniture and had it shipped to Paris, where he sold it for a considerable profit.

Pozzi, now in a lieutenant-colonel's uniform, stays in Paris. The Val-de-Grâce opens a new annexe in rue Lhomond, in a former Jesuit convent close to the Broca. Pozzi is in charge of a "division" of one hundred beds (out of six hundred); he is also responsible for seventy-five beds at the Broca (fifty for military wounded, twenty-five for syphilitics), twenty in the rue Noisiel at the other end of Paris, plus the private patients who still come to him at the avenue d'Iéna.

1915. The war continues. The Italians enter on the Allied side. Advancing Alpini capture from the Austrians the hill fort of Pozzi Alti. July marks the thirtieth anniversary of that London shopping trip. Médecin-Principal Pozzi is deeply involved in the theory and practice of war wounds. But he also finds time to operate on a private patient who has written to him from Boulogne-sur-Mer. Pozzi is now sixty-eight, and it would be understandable if he restricted himself to his military duties. But no, he agrees to see a certain Maurice Machu, a clerk in the indirect taxation branch of the Boulogne revenue office. Unsurprisingly, Machu is far from rich: he sends Pozzi a signed document that, in exchange for surgery to be performed on Sunday 18 July, he will pay the sum of 500 francs over the next two years.

The operation is for varicose veins of the scrotum, a condition which is congenital rather than acquired, and which is treated by tightening the skin of the testicles by partial resection. The only danger in the condition or its treatment is psychological rather than surgical. Why did Pozzi agree to see this minor civil servant from the

Pozzi in uniform

north, so different from his distinguished Parisian clientele? We cannot know. We might guess: perhaps the notion that, in the middle of mass European carnage, a man might worry about his scrotum, appealed to his sense of the absurd. Or perhaps it was simpler: here, at least, is something I can fix.

In October Pozzi's old friend Paul Hervieu—who had wanted to put the word "love" into the marriage contract—dies in his sleep, unexpectedly, at the age of fifty-seven; he did not himself marry. In December Maurice Machu sends Pozzi a bank draft for 125 francs and a report on his current condition. His state of health is only marginally improved. The varicosity in his scrotum, if less marked than at the time of the operation, is still visible under palpation, though not when the testicles are at rest. The feeling of heaviness in the testicles is less than before the operation, but Machu considers it prudent to continue to wear the supporting bandage. Erections are very rare, two or three a month, always in the morning, immediately after urination. He has had a single nocturnal emission about two months previously. His supporting bandage remains dry, whereas before the operation it was constantly wet and sometimes had reddish-brown stains. Mental work has become easier. The prickling sensations in his eyes have more or less gone away. In sum, there is no reason to despair, since the surgeon has said that it might take a year to make a full recovery. Please find attached a bank draft for 125 francs. And Monsieur Machu sends Monsieur le Professeur Pozzi his best wishes for 1916.

The war continues. Or rather, the wars, the trivial ones and the deadly one. Léon Daudet publishes his second and third volumes of memoir, in which he denounces Pozzi for vanity, charlatanry and incompetence. He is (apparently) nicknamed "*Chelami*" because of the unctuous way he calls everyone "Cher ami"; he is pretentious, cooing, and fabulously ignorant, but surrounded by "Pozziphiles" for whom he is an "incomparable treasure, an unprecedented genius, a demi-god." But of course, adds Daudet sardonically, "I wouldn't want to contradict those honourable South Americans, for whom Pozzi is a sage of incalculable importance." Montesquiou reminds his friend that one of the consolations of old age is that it frees you from the infantile fear of ridicule.

The war continues. Sarah Bernhardt departs on a ten-city tour of Britain, from Portsmouth to Edinburgh. This is to be followed by a fourteen-month tour of America. Pozzi goes to the cinema and sees on screen, in Sacha Guitry's *Ceux de chez nous*, many of his friends and patients: Sarah Bernhardt, Anatole France, Rostand, Rodin . . . also Monet, Renoir, and the only known footage of Degas, walking along the boulevard de Clichy. One of Emma Fischoff's sons is killed at Verdun. Maurice Machu sends a postal order for 125 francs, and his best wishes for 1917.

The war continues. Pozzi is profiled in the *New York Herald Tribune*, which describes him as "the most eminent surgeon in France." The journalist comments on some of his possessions: his coins and medals, his tapestries, his fifteenth-century marble St. Sebastian, a Renoir, a Carrière, plus "Sargent's masterpiece," his portrait of a princely figure of thirty-five, his hair and beard dark, and the hands "more delicately painted than I have ever seen before in a picture." The journalist describes what Pozzi is wearing as "a scarlet toga."

Léon Daudet publishes a fourth volume of memoirs, which contains further denunciations, ending with:

They say he is a good technician. For myself, I wouldn't even trust him to cut my hair, especially if there was a mirror in the room, for fear he might slash my throat while admiring his own reflection.

Pozzi continues adding to his collection, even in wartime, buying from "Spink, Medallists to His Majesty the King" in London and receiving from Tunis a Cyrenian coin on approval. Sarah Bernhardt falls ill with a kidney infection; Pozzi is transatlantically consulted; Sarah sends a card of thanks to "Docteur Dieu." Montesquiou publishes a poem in honour of Emma Fischoff's son; she writes that he is her "ideal poet and divine consoler." There is no evidence that Maurice Machu sends a postal order for 125 francs, let alone his best wishes for 1918.

The war continues. Both Pozzi's sons are now in uniform, the elder, Jean, serving with British troops as an interpreter. Thérèse Pozzi is in Montpellier, staying with her cousin and near-homonym, Thérèse Pauzat; Catherine has joined her there. In April, Pozzi is in Monte Carlo with Emma. "Given these uncertain times," he puts his affairs in order, drawing up a new will in front of her. In May, Gordon Bennett Jr., "the Commodore," on whose steam yacht (with milking cows) Pozzi had crossed the Atlantic, is buried in Passy; his tomb is unornamented except for a carved stone owl.

On Thursday 13 June 1918, Pozzi is driven to the military hospital in the rue Ulm. He visits the wounded and their families in the morning, operates in the afternoon until six o'clock, and then does paperwork. He is driven home, where two patients await him; the second of these is Maurice Machu. He is shown into a temporary consulting room. Pozzi advises him that he is suffering from a nervous complaint, and will recommend him to another specialist. According to which newspaper you read, Machu says either, "No, that's not what I want," or "No, no, I've had enough, I want to get it over with." But both quotes are spurious, as there were no witnesses. What is unambiguous is that Machu takes out his Browning revolver and shoots Pozzi three times: in the arm, the chest and the gut (or, alternatively, in the arm, the stomach and the back). A fourth bullet hits the curtains, though whether these are still the ones made from Liberty fabric we cannot know. Then Machu shoots himself in the head.

Pozzi, still conscious, is taken to the military hospital in the rue de Presburg, on the corner of the Champs-Elysées. He consults with the surgeon, Dr. Martel. They agree that the operation should be immediate; Pozzi specifies the anaesthetic he desires—enough to nullify the pain, but not enough to put him out. And so he is present at, and fully aware of, the last laparotomy he will attend in his life. If there are good—or less bad—deaths, then can there be a better one than this, with one surgeon collaborating fraternally with another, in an attempt to save the first one's life? The incision is made, and examination of the intestine shows ten (or eleven) perforations. All ten (or eight of the ten—or eleven) are swiftly sutured, a process which turns out to be a final homage to the patient's professional life and skill. But the question in such cases always remains: Where did the bullet go after travelling through the intestine? The answer comes swiftly. Pozzi vomits violently, the gut is forced out of the surgeon's hands, and blood begins to pour: the bullet has severed the left iliac vein. Pozzi quickly loses consciousness and dies.

When I first read of Pozzi's life, authorities ancient and modern, French and English, said that he was "assassinated by a madman." They didn't say "by one of his own patients." That letter of December 1915 is both very clear and also confusing. Machu is a fussy patient (though what man would not be, when his scrotum is being operated on?). It is evident that he had been sexually inactive, indeed impotent, for some time. Also, that he has been worrying about his general state of health, including ocular disturbances and his capacity for mental work. Pozzi has said that it might take a year to make a full recovery. From scrotal varicosity? Did he judge Machu close to nervous collapse? Did he perhaps promise more—or assume that once Machu stopped worrying about his scrotum, the rest of him would recover as well? Or was Pozzi, with his famously sympathetic bedside manner, merely giving some general reassurance to his patient, which Machu then misinterpreted?

It would hardly be surprising if a surgeon who spent all week dealing with hundreds of war wounded, many of whom could have been saved with better medical and military care, might at some level consider a tax collector's scrotum to be of lesser importance.

But it was not of lesser importance to Machu. In his pocket a note was found, detailing his complaints against Pozzi, "whom he planned to kill as a warning to doctors who do not respect the wishes of their patients." A Don Juan shot dead by a man who blamed him for not curing his impotence: What sort of a morality tale is that? In fiction, it would seem cutely snug. Nonfiction is where we have to allow things to happen—because they did—which are glib and implausible and moralistic. Also found on Machu's body were letters to the newspapers, and one to the commissioner of police, enclosing ten francs "to pay for the transporting of my body."

The next day, in Montpellier, Thérèse and Catherine learn what has happened only when the newspapers are delivered. In Paris, Jean Pozzi examines his father's desk, and finds open on it the commonplace book of Leconte de Lisle, one of his father's first patrons; the pages are smeared with blood. In London, *The Times* picks up the story from the Exchange Telegraph Company. Strangely placed under LATEST WAR NEWS, it reports FAMOUS SURGEON SHOT. The next day, there is a longer story by their own correspondent, headed A PARIS DOCTOR MURDERED. It describes Pozzi as "at one time leader of women's surgery in France, and [who] has done an immense amount for the development of medical science in his country." In Paris, *Le Figaro* calls him "a sincere lover of both science and art, a kind of beautiful work of art in himself, and a magnificent specimen of our race."

On Saturday 15 June, two days after the murder, Catherine writes in her diary:

Father, admirable, astonishing Father, you have now become a triumphant fairy prince in the world of legend, you whose mere name opened doors, you before whom the provincial, the outsider, the genius, the woman, the wise man and the artist were either pupil or conquest, you were a sun who annexed souls from Buenos Aires to New York, and from Beirut to Edinburgh, and you succeeded in the struggle—watched by me as baby, child, adult, and dying woman—which it seems to me that only I understood; you have bent hideous fate to your will a thousand times, and then a thousand times more. There is nothing around you which does not turn into clarity of thought and coherence, nothing within you which does not emerge as supple grace, a smile, goodness, beauty, success, happiness. You used to laugh when saying, "*Penser, panser*" [thinking, bandaging]. You healed people, didn't you? You didn't believe in God and yet everywhere you dispensed his power . . . I kneel before you, my Father and my acknowledged master.

(She was not, however, dying.)

Two days later, she wrote to Mme Bulteau, salon-tender and woman of letters who was her father's friend (and perhaps more) for nearly twenty years: "We were but a single being." The next day, she elaborated to her husband Edouard Bourdet: "He was my complementary being, like a kind of triumphant Catherine. He was all happiness and success, whereas I am all suffering; he was like a different translation of myself, one filled with joy." If Bourdet had any doubts why his marriage had failed, reading these words might have cleared them up.

Mme Bulteau, for her part, sent Catherine one of those bittersweet messages which the griefstruck sometimes receive. Catherine had always complained of her father's coldness towards her. Mme Bulteau tells her that this *idée fixe* was misplaced. In her last conversation with Pozzi, "He displayed an irritation with you that was very similar to that of a rejected lover. It was neither indifference nor detachment. It was the absolute opposite of that. He talked about you with a profound tension."

On Tuesday 18 June, the funeral service took place in the Protestant Temple of the Redemption in the avenue de la Grande Armée. High Parisian society bade him farewell, while low Parisian rumour did the same with the suggestion that he had deliberately rendered Machu impotent so that he could sleep with Mme Machu. The day after Pozzi's death, Thérèse (who, like Catherine, had stayed in Montpellier—both were unwell) wrote to their elder son:

Jean, this is an atrocious misfortune. I no longer loved him but I am nonetheless torn apart . . . I try to forget all the dreadful years and remember only the beginning, when we were happy.

In a subsequent letter, she wrote:

He was so afraid of death, and his final agony—all alone—especially without her—must have been atrocious. As for me, who still loved him so deeply, I feel that I shall always suffer; his presence, even when far away, was indispensable to me. To hear someone speak of him, to read his name, to see him sometimes—I didn't ask for more as I knew him to be perfectly happy . . .

Her admirable generosity continued:

Pozzi's cortège passes the Arc de Triomphe

Have you heard anything about Mme F? She must be in despair after twenty years of such complete happiness with him. Madame Gautier told Cath[erine] that it was a true adoration that Mme F had for your poor daddy. And he so loved to be loved!

Emma Fischoff wrote to Jean Pozzi. She said that after his father had made his will in Monte Carlo, he told her that he had left his friends material gifts, "But to you, I leave my heart." However, there were fifty or so items of hers, plus letters and diaries, stored at the avenue d'Iéna,

Thérèse Pozzi in old age

and for whose return she would be grateful. She attached a list. In reply, Jean sent her a drawing, but explained diplomatically that since his father had not made specific mention of the fifty items in his will, they would have to be submitted to his legatees for a decision. It is not known what happened when they were.

After brief inhumation in Paris, Pozzi was reburied in the Protestant cemetery of Bergerac in August 1918. Separated in death, as in life, by religion, his wife and daughter were later consigned to the Catholic cemetery in 1932 and 1934. The city named a hospital and a principal street after him: the Centre Hospitalier Samuel Pozzi and the rue du Professeur Pozzi are still there. A year on from his death, in June and July 1919, the dispersal of his collection took place in Hall 8 of the Hôtel des Ventes in rue Drouot. There were to be seven sales, comprising 1,221 lots. His antiquities and tapestries, his Greek coins and Pisano medals, his Persian miniatures, his Tiepolo ceiling (85,000 francs), his Bellottos and Guardis and Ziems of Venice, his Turner study for *Childe Harold's Pilgrimage* (3,100 francs), his four Corots and two Delacroix (a lion and a tiger), his Greek vases and Egyptian bas-reliefs, his Venetian cabinet, his Meissonnier and his Millet, his Claude and his Ruisdael and his Gericault, and his Sargent portrait of *Madame Gautreau Drinking a Toast* (4,200 or 14,200 francs)—all went under the hammer.

All his treasures but one. At the last minute, *Dr. Pozzi at Home* was withdrawn from sale by the family. In its early days it had been shown—to very little public or critical notice, let alone enthusiasm—in London, Brussels, Paris and Venice. Then, for many years, it lived, mainly shrouded by a cloth, in the place Vendôme and avenue d'Iéna. After Thérèse Pozzi's death, it went to her son Jean, who held it until his death in 1967. *Dr. Pozzi at Home* finally re-emerged into public display in 1990, at the Armand Hammer Foundation in Los Angeles. It is how we think of him today; and this is not wrong.

Author's Note

"Chauvinism is one of the forms of ignorance." I was writing this book during the last year or so before Britain's deluded, masochistic departure from the European Union. And Dr. Pozzi's maxim came frequently to mind as the English political elite, unable to imagine themselves into the minds of Europeans (or unwilling to do so, or too stupid to do so), repeatedly behaved as if what they themselves wanted, and what was going to happen, were likely to be the same thing. The English (rather than the British) have often prided themselves too smugly on being insular, on being incurious about "the other," preferring the easy joke and the idle slander. So the sitting foreign secretary, during the Conservative Party Conference of 2018, straightforwardly compared the European Union to the Soviet Union. The Baltic States, like others who had spent decades under Soviet occupation, were unimpressed by this. But then the previous foreign secretary, during the Brexit campaign, had compared the EU's ambitions for Europe to Hitler's. Barbey d'Aurevilly's line is also relevant here: "England, the victim of its own history, having taken a step towards the future, has now gone back to squatting in its past."

There are many reasons for being dismayed at current English (not British—English) attitudes to Europe. I am the son of language teachers, both of whom would have been saddened at the decline in the study and teaching of modern languages in the time since their deaths. "Oh, they all speak English nowadays" is an often heard complacency. But as any teacher or student of languages knows, to understand a foreign language is to understand those who speak it; and, further, to understand the way they look at and understand your country. It loosens up the imagination. So we are now understanding others less well, while they continue to understand us better. Another miserable piece of self-isolation.

Still, I decline to be pessimistic. Time spent in the distant, decadent, hectic, violent, narcissistic and neurotic Belle Epoque has left me cheerful. Mainly because of the figure of Samuel Jean Pozzi. Whose ancestors migrated from Italy to France. Whose father married an Englishwoman *en secondes noces*. Whose half brother married an Englishwoman in Liverpool. Who had his suits and curtains made from material sent from London. Who first visited our islands in 1876 to seek out Joseph Lister and learn the procedures of Listerism. Who translated Darwin. Who got off the boat train in London in 1885, for a few days of intellectual and decorative shopping. Who was rational, scientific, progressive, international and constantly inquisitive; who greeted each new day with enthusiasm and curiosity; who filled his life with medicine, art, books, travel, society, politics and as much sex as possible (though all we cannot know). He was, thankfully, not without faults. But I would, nonetheless, put him forward as a kind of hero.

—JB, London, May 2019

Acknowledgements

I should like to thank: Jean-Pierre Aoustin, Surya Bowyer, Alexandre Burin, Dr. Philip Cavendish, David Chapman, Dr. James Connolly, Professor Caroline de Costa, Vanessa Guignery, Professor Lesley Higgins, Kathryn Johnson, Elaine Kilmurray, Brendan King, Hermione Lee, Francesca Miller, Professor Brian Nelson, Roger Nichols, Camille Ondet, Richard Ormond, Sumaya Partner, Graham Robb, Professor Richard Sonn, Teresa Vernon, Stephen Walsh and Dr. Olivier Walusinski. This is the last book of mine that Dan Franklin will publish, and I should like to thank him for a quarter of a century of genial and calming professionalism.

Illustration Credits

Brotman, Contemporary Art Council, Council of American Art, Jane and David R. Davis, Decorative Arts and Paintings Council, Robert B. Dootson, Mr. and Mrs. Barney A. Ebsworth, P. Raaze Garrison, Lyn and Gerald Grinstein, Helen and Max Gurvich, Marshall Hatch, John and Ann Hauberg, Richard and Betty Hedreen, Marty Ann and Henry James, Mrs. Janet W. Ketcham, Allan and Mary Kollar, Greg Kucera and Larry Yocom, Rufus and Pat Lumry, Byron R. Meyer, Ruth J. Nutt, Scotty Ray, Gladys and Sam Rubinstein, Mr. and Mrs. Allen Vance Salsbury, Herman and Faye Sarkowsky, Mr. and Mrs. Douglas Scheumann, Seattle Art Museum Supporters, Jon and Mary Shirley, Joan and Harry Stonecipher, Dean and Mary Thornton, William and Ruth True, Volunteers Association, Ms. Susan Winokur and Mr. Paul Leach, The Virginia Wright Fund, Charlie and Barbara Wright, Howard Wright and Kate Janeway, Merrill Wright, and Mrs. T. Evans Wyckoff. Photo: Elizabeth Mann / Seattle Art Museum, USA; **p. 153** *The Sedelmayer Family* (detail), Franz Rumpler. Photo: Narodni Galerie, Czech Republic / Bridgeman Images; **p. 172** Catherine Pozzi at eighteen. Alamy Stock Photo; **p. 206** Catherine Pozzi, in Parisian fashion, among her fellow students. Used by kind permission of the Principal and Fellows of St. Hugh's College, Oxford; **p. 209** *Louis-François Bertin*, Jean-Auguste-Dominique Ingres. Photo: Louvre, France / Bridgeman Images; **p. 216** Pozzi by Léon Bonnat. Photo: The National Gallery, UK; **p. 255** Pozzi in uniform. Photo: Roger-Viollet / Shutterstock; **p. 263** Pozzi's cortège passes the Arc de Triomphe. Photo: Roger-Viollet / TopFoto.

All other images courtesy of the author.

A Note About the Author

Julian Barnes is the author of twenty-three previous books, for which he has received the Man Booker Prize, the Somerset Maugham Award, the Geoffrey Faber Memorial Prize, the David Cohen Prize for Literature, and the E. M. Forster Award from the American Academy of Arts and Letters; the French Prix Médicis and Prix Femina; and the Austrian State Prize for European Literature. In 2017 he was awarded the Légion d'Honneur. His work has been translated into more than forty languages. He lives in London.

A Note on the Type

This book was set in Adobe Garamond. Designed for the Adobe Corporation by Robert Slimbach, the fonts are based on types first cut by Claude Garamond (ca. 1480–1561).

Composed by North Market Street Graphics
Lancaster, Pennsylvania

Printed and bound by Mohn Media
Gütersloh, Germany

Designed by Michael Collica

2ᵉ COLLECTION FELIX POTIN

POZZI
MÉDECIN

2ᵉ COLLECTION FELIX POTIN

COMTE DE MONTESQUIOU
HOMME DE LETTRES

3ᵉ COLLECTION FÉLIX POTIN

COLETTE
FEMME DE LETTRES

2ᵉ COLLECTION FELIX POTIN

HUYSMANS
HOMME DE LETTRES

COLLECTION FELIX POTIN

ALICE
PRINCESSE DE MONACO

2ᵉ COLLECTION FELIX POTIN

LEON DAUDET
HOMME DE LETTRES

2ᵉ COLLECTION FÉLIX POTIN

LISTER
MÉDECIN